AMERICAN
PROVIDENCE
★ A Nation with a Mission ★

AMERICAN
PROVIDENCE

★ A Nation with a Mission ★

Stephen H. Webb

continuum
NEW YORK • LONDON

The Continuum International Publishing Group, 15 East 26th Street, New York, NY 10010

The Continuum International Publishing Group Ltd, The Tower Building, 11 York Road, London SE1 7NX

Cover design: Corey Kent

Library of Congress Cataloging-in-Publication Data

Webb, Stephen H., 1961–
  American providence : a nation with a mission / Stephen H. Webb.
    p. cm.
  Includes index.
  ISBN 0-8264-1623-3 (hardcover)
  1. Christianity and politics—United States. 2. Christianity and international affairs. 3. Providence and government of God. I. Title.

  BR517.W43 2004
  261.8'7'0973—dc22
                              2004011555

Printed in the United States of America

04 05 06 07 08 09   10 9 8 7 6 5 4 3 2 1

For Jon, J. D, and Mark, fellow rebels in our small corner
of the American Academy—and Aron, too

"But we speak God's wisdom, secret and hidden, which God
decreed before the ages for our glory."
—*1 Corinthians 2:7*

Contents

—ɷ—

Acknowledgments

—ᴍ—

I am happy to say that all of the friends who read this manuscript permitted me to use their names. They carry a great responsibility for the content of these pages, because any controversial claims I make are the result of their failure to argue me out of them. Nonetheless, I appreciate how hard they tried. Moreover, the rhetorical, theological, and historical errors they did save me from are too numerous to count. I am amazed by their wisdom and their knowledge, and I hope that I have done justice to their comments, questions, and reservations. They are Jon Baer, Mark Brouwer, Rusty Reno, and Aron Aji. Wes Avram first started me thinking about this topic, and though I ended up in a different place than he imagined, I am grateful for his encouragement and friendship. I must also thank Lynn Robinson, who probably has no idea what an important role he played in the inception of this book. Conversations with Lynn several years ago helped me to see a way forward with my struggles over politics and theology. He said the right thing at the right time—in fact, he modeled for me a way of thinking politically that I had not been able to figure out on my own—and for that I am very grateful. Richard John Neuhaus, in a visit to Wabash College, moved me deeply by his wise counsel and generous encouragement. I will be thinking about his words for years to come. Rusty Reno invited me to give part of chapter 6 as a lecture at Creighton University, and I am overwhelmed by his hospitality and generosity. The responses from his students and colleagues were challenging and insightful, and the pressure of putting my thoughts into a form fit for a public lecture helped me keep going just when I was close enough to the end to feel like giving up. Debbie Polley was as efficient as she was cheerful in helping me to obtain so many interlibrary loans. Diane Timmerman also kept me in check with her occasional queries about just what it was I was writing. I tried to make sure to say nothing that she would find offensive. I also' must thank my parents-in-law, Mary and Dave Timmerman, for going overboard with grandparenting so that I could finish this book on schedule. I hope my children, Charis, Barek, and Asher, will understand, when they read this book, why I wrote it so much with them in mind. Tanner Kinkead, one of the brightest students I have known at Wabash, read the first two chapters without hesitating to circle my awkward phrases and poor word choices. I guess I am glad that he was confident enough to leave more marks on my manuscript than I leave on his papers. He would have read more of the book, he told me, if I would have gotten it to him sooner. He and his classmates put up with a slightly out-of-control teacher while I rushed to finish this book. I would like to think that I was teaching better than usual, but I am willing to consider the possibility that I was not. Finally, several of my students and former students at Wabash College have prodded me to be more open and honest about my politics and have helped shape my political theology by being as smart as they are outspoken. They know who they are.

July 4, 2004
Brownsburg, Indiana

Introduction
Unapologetic Providentialism

—⚅—

The relationship between America and Christianity has rarely been so hotly contested as it is today. September 11, 2001, and the subsequent war against terrorism have had an almost schismatic impact on the church. American Christians have been forced to ask some really hard questions about the relationship of faith and politics. Some churches have taken to displaying the flag in the sanctuary, while other congregations ask God's forgiveness for American arrogance and aggression. We remain one nation, but whether we are "under God" is a subject of much debate. Many theologians have been very harsh on the Bush administration. Liberals worry about the consequences of American imperialism for economically challenged countries, and pacifists denounce the use of the American military to promote and protect the new world order. Even Christians who support America's effort to export democracy to the Middle East and beyond have expressed uncertainty about whether our good intentions can be turned into effective foreign policy. Conservative Christians once dismissed internationalism as an infringement on national autonomy, while liberals celebrated the peaceful potential of one harmonious world. Now new responses are needed to the growing juggernaut of global capitalism.

While there were signs in recent years of better communication between religious liberals and conservatives, the war on terrorism and the second Gulf War have opened old wounds and further divided America's Christians. Supporters and critics of the regime change in Iraq talk past each other or do not talk to each other at all. Those who think that our policy on terrorism is a terrible mistake find it hard to understand why anyone would

1

believe differently, while those who support the deployment of the military overseas have been known to doubt the patriotism of President Bush's critics. The lack of a consensus on foreign policy is particularly disheartening for American Christians who want the church to take a stand on issues of national importance. What can church leaders say about Iraq when opposing passions run so hot? Moreover, what should church leaders say when one of the main criticisms of the Bush administration is that the president has used talk about God and faith to bolster the nation's commitment to the war on terrorism? Some would suggest that it is time to separate theology and politics by making it very clear that Christianity is about peace and not war. The likelihood that peace can be achieved without war, however, seems as remote as the possibility that America can be conceived apart from religion.

On a practical level, religion runs so deep in every current of American life that dredging the channels of America foreign policy for the religious debris left by the war on terrorism is a task that only the most diligent of secularists would attempt. On a theoretical level, then, we need more than ever a reasonable theological assessment of the role that America, along with its particular brand of Christianity, plays on the world stage. America is so determined (postmodernists would say overdetermined) by the conviction that we have a special destiny in world history that only a careful account of the doctrine of providence can shine a clear light on the course that lies ahead. Given the indisputable dominance of America in world affairs—what we might call the Great Fact of our day—it is pernicious to deny any providential meaning to America's shaping of the globe.

Any interpretation of America's self-understanding as a world power must deal with another indisputable fact: the role that Christianity has played in American history. More specifically, no sharp line can be drawn between American motivations in the international arena and the Calvinistic drama, brought to our shores by the Puritans, of a nation conceived as a vehicle of God's will. As Archbishop Francis George of Chicago lamented at a meeting of the Synod for America, a gathering of bishops and other Catholic Church leaders from all of the Americas, even Catholics in the United States are "culturally Calvinist."[1] America cannot be analyzed apart from the way providential theology has shaped its understanding of foreign affairs, just as globalism cannot be grasped without confronting the singularity of American power. Nevertheless, scholars and journalists alike commonly wrestle with America's superpower status while ignoring the role of providence in American history, as if this doctrine were a bit of theological fashion that belonged to the age of bowlers and bodices.

To associate providential rhetoric solely with Evangelical Christians and the religiously conservative wing of the Republican Party would be tempting, but this would significantly underestimate the power of what I am calling

"American providence." Although surveys do show that Evangelicals differ significantly from non-Evangelicals when it comes to international affairs, the same surveys show that Evangelicals and mainline Christians converge on a wide variety of issues.[2] The very term "evangelical" has changed from the name of a somewhat isolated brand of sectarian Christianity to a style of worship that is embraced by all kinds of Christians. Moreover, before the Vietnam War, providentialism was embraced by both political parties. One hundred years ago, in the buildup to World War I, progressive Christian leaders eagerly anticipated a new world order, worked for the union of church and state, unabashedly promoted democracy abroad, and financed countless Christian missionaries in order to, in the words of Shailer Matthews, one of the leaders of the Social Gospel movement, "revolutionize and reorganize civilization in the name of Christ."[3] These same progressive Christians trumpeted World War I—the "war to end all wars"—as a means to the realization of the kingdom of God, while conservative and fundamentalist Christians were accused of being unpatriotic for their suspicions of internationalism. Likewise, after World War II Democrats enthusiastically led the way in building a Cold War consensus around the idea that America was specially chosen by God to combat communism. Rather than frame the debate about providentialism in terms of liberals and conservatives, then, it would be better simply to talk about providentialists and antiprovidentialists.

Even given these qualifications, however, the case can still be made that providence serves as one way of slicing the political pie. Though providence does not cleanly divide the left from the right, it can serve as one indicator of where people can be located on the political spectrum. Many of those even slightly to the left of the political center, for example, often find embarrassing the idea that God is using America to achieve something special in the world. Sophisticated people just do not talk that way. The cultural elite dismiss the doctrine of providence as the illusory product of fundamentalist fantasies. Providence is caricatured as a theological version of hide-and-seek. (Is God working here or over there? Surely if you look really hard you can find him!)

There is some truth to this caricature. When history is treated like a secret message, theology becomes little more than cryptology. For some popular fundamentalist authors, providence enables the believer to decipher divine communication that is unintelligible to those not in the know. The whole point of playing the "countdown to Armageddon" game is to figure out the proper decoding system. Nevertheless, this caricature badly distorts the traditional understanding of providence that has guided countless lives. Christians do not search for Jesus Christ as if he were a hidden God, lurking behind historical events. It is more true to say that all history points to Jesus than that Jesus points to the end of history. Christians are interested in the direction the world is going because they try to discern the direction that God is leading them. Of all Christian doctrines, providence involves the exercise of a skill that can be easily overused or misapplied, but it can also be allowed to atrophy through fear of making mistakes or simple neglect.

The art of reading history providentially is acquired not by abstract study but by active participation in the various ways the church reenacts the Bible's dramatic account of the unfolding of revelation. The biblical narrative, which like all good stories is seething with drama, is a trustworthy account of what God has done, is doing, and will continue to do in the future. The premise of the Bible is that God's actions reveal God's nature. Far from being just another character who is depicted according to anthropomorphic projections, the God of the Bible is the one agent who is fully and truly free. That is, God does not act according to a law external to and constraining of the divine nature. God's nature is eternal, subjected to nothing and restrained by nobody, yet God creates, sustains, and enters into the world as he pleases. God has style, and providence is what God's style looks like.

Biblical patterns of providence cannot be reduced to simple formulae along the lines of, "God helps those who help themselves" or "God always rewards the righteous and curses the wicked." Neither of these statements, or the naive sentiments they express, can be found in the Bible. There are providential maxims that derive from the Bible, like, "Your kingdom come," and "All things work together for good for those who love God, who are called according to his purpose" (Matt. 6:10; Rom. 8:28, respectively). These statements, however, are hardly designed to be mechanically applied to specific events. That God's kingdom is coming gives us the courage to hope. That God has a purpose for us gives us the strength to carry on. If we left providence at that, however, there would be no need to inquire into the specifics of a Christian reading of current events. The Bible offers practical providential advice, but it often takes the form of correcting human presumptions about the ways of God. Crucial in this regard is the reminder that "the Lord disciplines those whom he loves" (Heb. 12:6), as well as the wisdom that "The human mind may devise many plans, but it is the purpose of the LORD that will be established" (Prov. 19:21). Providence is humbling as well as encouraging.

Accepting the future, whatever it brings, can be a way of declaring allegiance to God's rule, but providence is not fate. If it were, the most that could be said about the future would be that God's ways are inscrutable. While God's will is not revealed in rules that permit us to decode the hidden meaning of every historical event, God's will is given to us in a narrative that teaches us to read history according to a broad but concrete plan. This narrative is of a peculiar kind, in that it absorbs all other narratives into itself. The Bible is the story of stories, told with the finality of truth, yet it is also unfinished, pointing toward events yet to come. The Bible, in fact, is one of a kind. Scripture has many twists and turns but has one abiding center in the divine person of Jesus Christ. Christians can attend to the perplexities of history without undue anxiety because they are confident about how it will all end.

When the disciples asked Jesus for signs of the end of the age, he gave them warnings instead, as if he wanted to restrain their natural curiosity (Matt. 24:3–14). It takes little effort to imagine false prophets and rumors of wars, which are common in every age. Jesus appears to be soothing his disciples' anxiety by telling them not to look for clear signs pointing to the end. He also wanted to prepare them to find their way in suffering, not success. He asked them to trust in the future, but providence is not blind. Jesus was explicit about what needed to be done to bring history to a close. The "good news of the kingdom will be proclaimed throughout the world as a testimony to all the nations; and then the end will come" (Matt. 24:14). Jesus commands his followers not to stand back from history but to change it. Christianity was animated from the very beginning by a universal impulse. Only when the whole world is filled with God's Word will the biblical story of history come to its rightful conclusion. Given this command, the most pressing task of a theology of providence today clearly is to interpret the connection between globalism and Christianity, especially as America mediates that connection.

Even if America were not a great empire, I would have to view the world through the lens of American history. By its very nature, the doctrine of providence cannot be developed apart from a profound recognition of the social location of all theology. I am an American, and it would be arrogant for me to try to think about providence from any other perspective. Richard John Neuhaus, in a prophetic book written in 1975, sounded the alarm on the eclipse of providentialism in America and prepared the way for its revival, though few were listening. He wrote *Time toward Home* in the aftermath of Vietnam, when doubts about American virtues were becoming dogmatic. Many people had come to the conclusion that America was more like Babylon than Israel. Neuhaus disagreed with this position, but he acknowledged the fact that these critics of America were taking history seriously. Indeed, the analogy with Babylon is a prime example of providential rhetoric; the doctrine of providence states that the more God blesses a nation, the more God demands from it. Neuhaus did not recommend that the Babylonian analogy be replaced with the analogy of America as a new Israel. As patriotic as Neuhaus is, he has always insisted that there is only one Israel, and that God has not made an identical covenant with America. Nevertheless, if we are redeemed through history, then nationality is not irrelevant to God's purposes. Neuhaus goes so far as to say that, "When I meet God, I expect to meet him as an American," and that when we are redeemed, "part of the American experience [will be] redeemed."[4]

This is not mere patriotic prattle. Neuhaus is pointing out the fact that, when it comes to providence, Christians cannot be apolitical. I do not mean that Christians must necessarily be loyal to a political party. Christians should not feel compelled to take one of the two sides that are offered to them in every political debate. Christians should try to be on God's side, which means that Christians take unpopular positions on many issues or refrain from some debates altogether. In trying to conform to the political order of the coming kingdom of God, Christians often give their allegiance to earthly parties and platforms only in a qualified manner. Nonetheless, Christians cannot step outside of the political altogether. God is involved in history, and Christians must be also. Not taking a position on a political issue might be the theologically correct thing to do in a given situation, but even withdrawing from politics is a political act that requires wisdom and discernment. Christians must take the risk of deciding where the Spirit is blowing and tack their sails accordingly.

Providence asks Christians to get off the sidelines and into the game of history. It does not ask Christians to be uncritical in their expressions of national loyalty. *American Providence* is intentionally not entitled *Providential America*, because keeping the focus on providence as the constant and America as the variable is important. I do not mean to say that America is uniquely providential, nor that the doctrine of providence should be reconsidered only in the light of American history. Nevertheless, I do mean to take the risk of reflecting on what God might be doing through America today. God's providence is, no doubt, universal, but all theology is concrete. Providence is, in the words of Joe R. Jones, the "grammar of a long and meaningful middle."[5] God continues to preserve, govern, and sustain the world between the initial creation and its consummation. Thinking providentially is a matter of learning to listen to God's symphonic movement through history in the political, economic, social, and cultural melodies by which our short lives are measured.

The Psalms declare that "God is king over the nations" (Ps. 47:8), but many Christians today no longer read the history of nations providentially. Part of the problem is that providence is often collapsed into the doctrine of creation, so that God's action in history is made to look like the natural laws that regulate the material universe. The scope of providence can be no more narrow than the range of creation. The universal range of God's concern for creation, however, does not mean that the category "universal" best specifies the means and manner by which God pursues the goal of bringing history to a final consummation. Somehow, the idea that providence is universal frequently becomes confused with the idea that God acts in history in a uniform way. To assume that God works uniformly, along the model of modern notions of scientific law, is to suggest that God acts impersonally. God's involvement in history is not partial, but neither is it impartial. The Bible is more than colorful heightening of an essentially neutral and thus gray force in the world.

Given that the purpose of creation is to glorify God, the doctrine of creation could be considered a subset of the doctrine of providence. More carefully put, *creatio ex nihilo* (creation out of nothing) and *creatio continua* (the continuing creation of providence, which brings new things into being rather than just preserving what already is) must be understood together, not separately. *Creatio ex nihilo* alone results in deism, where God begins the world but then steps aside, while *creatio continua* alone leads to pantheism, where God is involved in the world but is not sovereign, majestic, and transcendent. God not only creates the world and guides history, but God also creates new historical forms in order to bring creation to its end.

What is truly significant about the relationship of providence and creation is the idea that the goal toward which God moves history is mediated by the things of creation. What God creates, in other words, God preserves, sustains, and guides to its proper end. How God acts in history cannot be unrelated to the ways in which humans organize themselves to achieve their own ends. This approach suggests that God works in history not only through individuals but also through nation-states, if for no other reason than we are all political creatures, enacting our identities in families, communities, and nations. God is marching history toward the divine kingdom, but that does not mean that God is bypassing the kingdoms of this world in the process of achieving that end. The very notion of a divine kingdom suggests some kind of heavenly realm that transforms and thus is in fundamental continuity with the all-too-human political organizations of this world. And the very fact that God has determined to take time to establish the divine kingdom—history is the product of God's patience—suggests that the nations of the world play different roles in the coming of the kingdom. The destiny of all nations is the same—to worship God—but the missions of the nations vary according to how God decides to use them.

The suggestion that God works through the nations to achieve the divine plan is clear from the Bible, given that how God has chosen to bring the peoples of the world together is dependent on one particular nation, Israel. I want to add to that the observation that we cannot read providence from the pages of the Bible as if the current events recorded in the newspapers did not matter. God speaks to us through the words of the Bible, but what God is saying to us today, no matter how hard it is for us to hear his Word, is not unrelated to what the headlines scream. While Israel is the key to history, another nation has undeniably moved to the front pages of current affairs and will stay there for the foreseeable future. Some critics on the political left think that America is the return of Rome, an arrogant empire that can achieve little good in the world. I show throughout this book that these critics, no matter their secular intent, rely on the language of providence even as they seek to undermine any sense of a special mission for America. Those on the religious right may be tempted to use providence to baptize every American action on the international scene. Regardless, that America is doing more than any other nation to spread the kinds of political structures that can best prepare the globe for God's ultimate work of establishing the final kingdom is not theologically insignificant.

Antiprovidential Christians have long abandoned to their more conservative brothers and sisters the onerous duty of reading the signs that God posts along the way that lead to the end of history. Mainline churches have paid a great price for letting this theological skill lapse. One result has been the attenuation of the liberal theological imagination. Providence can only be understood within the ultimate horizon of eschatology. History, for Christians, makes sense only if Christians have the courage to imagine how God will bring about the end. Another result of an attenuated theological imagination is that mainline churches have largely given up the debate on whether America is a Christian nation, leaving secularists and fundamentalists to take polemical positions on that topic. I argue that American Christianity is not an oxymoron. That is, the depth and degree of the Christian commitments of the American founders is open to debate, but the fact that Christian commitments shaped much of American history and that a particular kind of Christianity is the product of these commitments is surely beyond debate. To be more specific, I want to honor the faith not of the founders but of the many men and women who prayed this country into being and who guided it along such a path that God is still using it to this day.

What liberal theologians have worried about is the problem of theodicy, which concerns the question of how a good and absolutely powerful God can permit evil in the world.[6] Discussions about providence by liberal theologians almost always gravitate toward the problem of theodicy, perhaps because the twentieth century was so full, in equal parts, of utopian views of history *and* record-setting levels of suffering and murder. Those who believe in human progress would naturally be puzzled by this contradictory state of affairs. What is odd is how seldom the collusion between utopianism and terror is recognized as a result of the perversion of the doctrine of providence. Providence is both the most hopeful and the most realistic of Christian doctrines, because it expects the transformation of the entire universe while trusting in God, not man. Instead of repairing the doctrine of providence, which has been so badly abused in the modern world, theologians more often have dedicated themselves to the task of showing how God is *not* in charge of the world, as if God needs to be excused from the mess we have made of it and we need to be given greater leeway to make amends for our mistakes.

In fact, one of the great projects of modern theology has been the problem of figuring out how to defend human freedom by limiting the power of God, as if unbounded conceptions of human freedom have not done enough harm in the world without the aid of theological justification. Like alchemists of old, theologians combine freedom, contingency, nature, and God into various mixtures, trying to get the proportions just right so that the resulting recipe is acceptable to modern tastes. I take a more traditional approach. Providence does not conflict with freedom, because God does not compete with humans. A concord—or to use an older theological term, a *concursus*—obtains between humans and the divine because God's governance of the world is a primary causation that operates in human freedom without obliterating it. Providence should be a consolation for rather than a victim of the problem of evil, just as providence should lead us to a deeper understanding of history while protecting the freedom of God.

Providence is not a doctrine that can be approached halfway. Any revival of it must be done on both a theoretical and a practical level. To revive the doctrine of providence for all Christians today, one would need to show how it is necessary, not just neglected. I hope to demonstrate the necessity of providence for three interrelated issues. First, I argue that political theology as such requires the doctrine of providence. Second, I argue that American history cannot be understood apart from this doctrine. Third, I insist that any theological analysis of nationalism, globalism, and the future of the church requires a strong grasp of providence. These three issues are interrelated because any analysis of the transnational destiny of the church must include reflection on how God is using the most powerful nation in the world.

A providential reading of world history must account for America's miraculous rise to world power, and it must give an interpretation of God's blessings for America as well as America's responsibilities for those blessings. Such a reading must do this without displacing Israel from the center of God's design for history. Americans have been sometimes too quick and too sloppy in their use of the language of chosenness. In a comprehensive work on American exceptionalism, Russell B. Nye observes that "No nation in modern history has been quite so consistently dominated as the United States by the belief that it has a particular mission in the world, and a unique contribution to make to it."[7] Nye borrows a phrase from Abraham Lincoln for his title—*This Almost Chosen People*—in order to signal his critical distance from the tradition of America as a New Israel. Lincoln was tortured by reflection on the transcendental meaning of the American experiment. Nye puts the emphasis on "almost," but Lincoln never lost sight of the "chosen."

The statement from which Nye's title comes is worth quoting in full: "I shall be most happy indeed if I shall be an humble instrument in the hands of the Almighty, and of this, his almost chosen people."[8] On theological grounds alone, no nation can replace the central role of Israel for the doctrine of providence, but God also chooses other nations in order to accomplish the task God gave to Israel.

In many ways, this book represents an alternative to Stanley Hauerwas's popular and influential argument in *Resident Aliens* that America and Christianity should have nothing to do with each other.[9] Christians might live in America, Hauerwas observes, but they should live here as aliens whose loyalties lie elsewhere. American Christians, in fact, inevitably need to betray the ideals of their country, because their higher loyalties do not coincide with the realm of democratic politics. I argue that Christians are true residents in America—more like resident advisors than resident aliens—precisely because America has a Christian history. Of course, just because America is the product of Christian ideals does not mean that Christians should never challenge American leaders. On the contrary, because Christians can claim America as their own, they can be vociferous in their criticisms of its excessive ways. If Christians are aliens in America, on the other hand, then what could they possibly contribute to debates about foreign and domestic policy? Precisely because Christianity and America are joined so deeply together, Christians need to be careful about what they can and do contribute to the American political order. Christians are not only residents in America, with all the rights and obligations that entails, but also advisors to the makers of the American dream. They have the obligation to advise precisely because so much of the American dream comes from and continues to overlap with the Christian dream of the kingdom of God. That obligation to advise does not end when Christians find themselves in tension and even open conflict with the American government. Christians are not stateless, even as they long for the proper end of all states under the dominion of the divine ruler.

American Christians have a significant measure of responsibility not only for America but also for the fate of democracy worldwide. Modern democracy is, to a large extent, a product of Christian ideals and values, so that Christians of any nationality have a stake in America's attempt to support the growth of democracy abroad. Samuel P. Huntington, an internationally respected political scientist, has documented the close association between Christianity and democracy. He observes how democracy and Christianity both expanded in South Korea at the same time, which is far from being a mere coincidence. He quotes one South Korean that Christianity "made a difference, because it promotes the idea of equality and respect for some authority independent of the state."[10] Americans who have worked so hard to spread Christianity around the globe can hardly be expected to ignore the ways in which Christianity stirs the desire for freedom and provides a foundation for faith in democratic forms of government.

Americans are often accused of being antiintellectual, but the average American Christian has done a better job of intuiting the risk and the power of the doctrine of providence than most professional theologians. I have come to my own understanding of providence only by trusting in the basic wisdom that has guided most Americans on this subject. Most Americans believe that God acts in history, and they believe that one of those acts is the choosing of their nation for a special mission in the world. That mission, however, is not to fill the American coffers at the expense of others. Instead, the mission has to do with the spread of political freedom and the Christian faith, two goals that are inextricably interconnected, as critics of the American Empire themselves keep insisting. These claims have come to seem like common sense to me, but even as I write them I realize how arrogant they are likely to strike many of my readers, if they have made it this far.

So I must immediately and clearly rebuff a typical misunderstanding. American providence does not mean that God has not chosen other nations for special missions, and it does not mean that God approves of everything America does. It does mean, however, that American Christians understand that the doctrine of providence stands or falls on the belief in a personal God. If God acts personally in the world, then God's relationship to historical agents cannot be subsumed into an impersonal pattern or rule. The Bible, not metaphysics, provides the clues to what God is doing and where God is going in contemporary events.

That God has chosen America for a special mission in the world is as common a claim for ordinary American Christians as it is controversial for professional theologians and other intellectual elites. This conflict between providentialists and anti-providentialists has come to a crucial point in the presidency of George W. Bush. Bush's life story is well known.[11] Although he went to some of the nation's best private schools, he lacked direction and ambition as a young man. His parents raised him in the church, but he did not have a personal relationship with Jesus Christ until he was an adult. He lived in the shadow of his father, trusting that God would give him direction and purpose. One might think that he found more than enough purpose when he was elected president, but Bush still seemed indecisive and unsteady at the start of his term. He even seemed ambivalent about the power of his office.

All of that changed with 9/11. Here was a man who had an inkling that God was calling him toward some special destiny, but even with success as a businessman and a politician, his leadership skills were largely untapped. Now his time had come. He clearly felt destined to lead the nation in this time of crisis, just as he believed that America is destined to lead the world

toward greater freedom and prosperity. The terrorist strike set free his
tongue. He spoke of the moral design of the world, the conflict of good and
evil, and the strength that is demanded by adversity. We have suffered
"because we are freedom's home and defender. And the commitment of our
fathers," he continued, "is now the calling of our time."[12] In his third State of
the Union message to Congress and the nation, he was unashamed to adopt
the language of a special mission: "America is a nation with a mission—and
that mission comes from our most basic beliefs."[13] And at the end of the initial combat operations in Iraq, President Bush congratulated the military
with the words, "Wherever you go, you carry a message of hope." He then
explained what he meant by quoting from the prophet Isaiah: "To the cap-
tives, 'Come out,' and to those in darkness, 'Be free.'"[14] Critics accuse the
president of bringing a sectarian and triumphalistic form of Evangelicalism
to the White House.[15] They are wrong.

Presidents often rely on the language of providence in times of military
crisis, but George W. Bush speaks the rhetoric of providence with both personal passion and a natural ease. What is fascinating is that he understands
that America's mission to the world must be one that is ultimately beneficial
for everyone. The president emphasized the universal good that should be
the aim of America's role in the world in his third State of the Union address:
"We also hear doubts that democracy is a realistic goal for the greater Middle
East, where freedom is rare. Yet it is mistaken, and condescending, to assume
that whole cultures and great religions are incompatible with liberty and
self-government. I believe that God has planted in every heart the desire to
live in freedom."[16] Whether every culture and religion have equally contributed to the social and political foundations that are necessary for the full
exercise of freedom is debatable, of course, but the president's meaning is
clear: God has planted the seeds of freedom, and the mission of America is
to nourish those seeds as best as she can.

Several of my friends warned me not to write this book, because, they
thought, the topic alone could damage my reputation. I make no apologies,
but I ask the reader to continue to the very end of the book, just as those who
believe in providence know that the interpretations we make of history, no
matter how full of the Spirit, are but a fragmented glimpse of what will be
revealed at the end of history. I was heartened, as I wrote these pages, to find
that even a staunch critic of American political policy like Robert N. Bellah
has admitted that "America is the center of a new kind of empire, but it is the
only empire there is. Americans are, like it or not, citizens of that empire and
responsible for the whole world." Bellah goes on to say that everyone in the
world has two nationalities now, the nation of their birth and, whether they
like it or not, their participation in the American way of life. Then Bellah

makes an extraordinary remark: "Chosen it seems we are, if not by God then by geopolitics."[17] Bellah is careful to point out that being chosen does not legitimate triumphalism, and I agree. My concern in this book is to explore how the geopolitical does not lie outside of God's plan. God works through nature and through individuals, but God also works through the great movements of entire peoples that are the world's nations. Christians do not, or at least should not, believe in luck, nor should they believe that the geopolitical, anymore than the astrological, controls our destiny. The geopolitical is not our destiny; God is. Nevertheless, the road on which humanity must travel into the future leads through America, so it is incumbent upon every theologian to try to read the signs God has posted along the way.

—ᘯᘯᘯ—

I begin this book—appropriately, I think—with something concrete. Chapter 1 examines a case study in the use of providential rhetoric in contemporary politics in order to show just how rusty the skills in talking about American providence have become. Chapter 1 makes the case for a rhetorical gap between those who are reviving providential language in the wake of 9/11 and those who are deaf to its religious appeal.

Chapter 2 demonstrates the depths to which American history is indebted to the doctrine of providence. Of course, just because Americans used providential rhetoric in the past does not mean that we should use it today. I argue, however, that America is a nation whose very being is providential. The American experiment, because of its fragile nature, requires a providential reading of history. Especially after 9/11, American Christians must choose whether the providential understanding of America makes sense or not. The alternative to providential America is pluralistic America, but the case can be made that even our commitment to pluralism depends on the concept of providence. That is, we think we are uniquely pluralistic and thus chosen by God (or the forces of history) to model pluralism for the rest of the world. It is questionable, then, whether pluralism can be a satisfactory substitute for providential conceptions of the American experiment.

If America is so indebted to a providential interpretation of history, then why is such language also so controversial? Chapter 3 answers that question by examining the issue of preferentiality. Worries about preference lead many American Christians to accept general providence—that is, God's uniform and regular guidance of natural and human affairs—while neglecting special providence, which is traditionally defined as God's miraculous interventions into nature and history. Something about democracy, especially, mitigates confidence in special providence. Americans tend to want their

God to be as democratic as they are, and thus we hesitate to embrace a God who acts on the basis of preferential treatment. A preferential God is embraced by liberation theologians, who are influenced by the radical politics of Karl Marx, but Liberation theology is guided more by flawed economic theories than biblical patterns of history or political realities. God does choose sides in history, but God works through nations—beginning with Israel—rather than the abstract idea of a particular economic class.

The one theologian who has been most critical of American providence is Stanley Hauerwas. Even he, as I show in chapter 4, resorts to the very doctrine of providence in order to dismiss America's special role in global history. Providence has two sides—the one involving God's blessing, the other involving divine judgment. Hauerwas emphasizes the judgment side to the extent that America seems like a nation specially chosen to serve as a vehicle of God's wrath. Even the most vociferous critics of America demonstrate just how much they still operate within the orbit of this doctrine.

In chapter 5, I broaden the discussion by presenting an overview of various theoretical problems involved in the doctrine of providence as well as my own reading of this doctrine. Most pointedly, I reject the idea that general providence should circumscribe how we understand special providence. I argue that all providence is special, in the sense that providence is personal and particular. Providence is another way of expressing confidence that the action of God in history is the story of God's authorization of Jesus Christ to be the ruler of history.

I offer my own reading of the providential use of America in chapter 6. This book stands or falls on the usefulness of such a reading of the current geopolitical situation. "Globalism" is a word that has entered the theological vocabulary, and rightly so. Christ's reign is cosmic, and our planet is destined toward the unity that is to be found among the three persons of the Trinity. Globalism embodies many trends and forces and can be defined in a variety of ways that make it look good or bad. Nonetheless, the idea that the world is becoming unified—and the role America is playing in the spread of democracy and the opening of markets in that unification—cannot be shoved aside in any discussion of God's ultimate designs for humankind. Reading globalism providentially is a risk, but one that cannot be avoided, least of all in a book dedicated to the idea that God works through nations to establish the political freedom that is a foretaste of the politics of the kingdom yet to come.

My argument in chapter 6 is fourfold. First, I point out the compatibilities between the aims of globalization and the aims of Christianity. Second, I show how Christianity can keep the excesses of globalization in check by moving it toward the end anticipated by providentialist theology. Third, I examine Islam as the major impediment to this twin process of globalization and Christianization. Fourth, I demonstrate how pluralism is the reigning ideology of the cultural elite in America and thus the primary alternative to a providential interpretation of American history. Christianity can be compatible with pluralism. Indeed, the case can be made that Christianity—which severed the traditional ties that bound religion to family and tribe—is the source of the Western idea of pluralism. In its current, cosmopolitan form, however, pluralism tends to relativize truth, divinize the earth, and rationalize every human desire. Whether America has become an exporter of pluralism to the extent that it will increasingly become an importer of Christianity remains a crucial and open question.

Finally, in chapter 7 I examine the controversial work of German political theorist Carl Schmitt. One way to dismiss this book would be to see it as a paean to American democracy. In fact, one can acknowledge the connection between Christianity, freedom, and American democracy without overlooking the limits of democracy and the peculiarity of its American form. Christians especially have a strong sense of the limits of democracy, given that it will not be the political order of the kingdom of God. In thinking about the nature and limits of democracy, I have found no more profound political theologian than Carl Schmitt. His work is crucial for an understanding of why Christians should be proud of the American experiment and why they should defend it without turning it into a premature version of heaven on earth.

NOTES

1. Quoted in Richard John Neuhaus, *Appointment in Rome: The Church in America Awakening* (New York: Crossroad, 1999), 45.

2. George Gallup Jr. and David Poling, in *The People's Religion: American Faith in the 1990s* (New York: Macmillan, 1989), found that Evangelicals supported Israel and criticized the Soviet Union at significantly higher rates than non-Evangelicals. D. G. Hart has recently argued that Evangelicalism is a concept that has little explanatory power (*Deconstructing Evangelicalism: Conservative Protestantism in the Age of Billy Graham* [Grand Rapids: Baker Academic, 2004]).

3. Quoted in Richard M. Gamble, *The War for Righteousness* (Wilmington, DE: ISI Books, 2003), 71.

4. Richard John Neuhaus, *Time toward Home: The American Experience as Revelation* (New York: Crossroad, 1975), 64, 56.

5. Joe R. Jones, *A Grammar of Christian Faith: Systematic Explorations in Christian Life and Doctrine*, vol. 1 (Lanham, MD: Rowman & Littlefield Publishers, 2002), 259.

6. For an insightful reflection on the limits of using providence as a means of doing theodicy, see Nadine Pence Frantz, "Re-Imagining God's Providence," in *Brethren Life and Thought* 44, no. 3 (Summer 1999): 7–21.

7. Russel B. Nye, *This Almost Chosen People* (East Lansing, MI: Michigan State University Press, 1966), 164.

8. From a speech to the New Jersey Senate, February 21, 1861, in *The Collected Works of Abraham Lincoln*, ed. Roy P. Basler, 8 vols. (New Brunswick, NJ: Rutgers University Press, 1953), 4:236.

9. Stanley Hauerwas and William H. Willimon, *Resident Aliens* (Nashville: Abingdon Press, 1989).

10. Samuel P. Huntington, *The Third Wave: Democratization in the Late Twentieth Century* (Norman: University of Oklahoma Press, 1991), 74. For his analysis of the "patriotism gap" between the elite and the average American, see Huntington, "Dead Souls: The Denationalization of the American Elite," *The National Interest* (Spring 2004): 5–18.

11. For a good analysis of President Bush's evolving sense of purpose, see Stephen Mansfield, *The Faith of George W. Bush* (New York: Penguin, 2003).

12. President's remarks at National Day of Prayer and Remembrance, the National Cathedral, Washington D.C., September 14, 2001.

13. From the transcript of the address in *New York Times*, January 21, 2004.

14. George W. Bush, speech to the nation, "America Is Grateful for a Job Well Done," *Washington Post*, May 2, 2003.

15. For this criticism, see Claes G. Ryn, *America the Virtuous: The Crisis of Democracy and the Quest for Empire* (New Brunswick, NJ: Transactions Publishers, 2003), 7, 138.

16. *New York Times*, January 21, 2004.

17. Foreword to Richard T. Hughes, *Myths America Lives By* (Chicago: University of Chicago Press, 2003), xii. For Bellah's own explanation of his remarks, see his letter to the editor in *Christian Century*, March 9, 2004, 49.

CHAPTER ONE

One General and Two Americas:
A Case Study in Providential Rhetoric

Technological advances have rendered the first rule of rhetoric—know your audience—if not null and void then at least practically impossible to follow. In the age of high-speed communication, it is easy to eavesdrop on slow-moving traffic, so that no matter how carefully you stay within your lane, you can never keep from being tailgated. More simply put, words spoken to one audience can be picked up by another that hears them in a way the speaker never intended. Consider the case of Lieutenant General William G. Boykin, who was a victim of audience whiplash when the media abruptly snapped his words about the war on terrorism out of their original context and sped them throughout the network of communications.

Boykin is a highly decorated officer. He is also a devout Evangelical Christian. He is, in fact, a modern-day descendant of the tradition of American providence, but to many in the media he is like a ghost from the distant past who has come back to haunt us. Boykin attends many meetings where he reports on his various duties as deputy undersecretary of defense for intelligence gathering, a post that the Pentagon created to guide America's efforts to find the most high-profile terrorists. He also speaks frequently before church groups, which in itself appears as a conflict of duty to many zealous guardians of the strict separation between church and state. When the media broadcast the message he was delivering, behind closed doors, to church groups, editorial writers across the country accused him of violating ethical codes of professional conduct. Even worse, some liberal pundits acted like they had intercepted secret correspondence that revealed him betraying the military mission of his country.[1] Unlike Benedict Arnold, however, Boykin did not switch sides for money. He did, however, raise the question of for which side he was ultimately fighting.

What he did, to be more specific, was to use religious language to frame the war against terrorism. In particular, he suggested that America's true enemy is Satan, that President Bush has been appointed by God, and that Islamic extremists hate America because we are a Christian nation. What especially galled the *Washington Post* is that Boykin told a recently captured terrorist, who had boasted that Allah would protect him, that the terrorist had underestimated "our God."[2] If Boykin had said that the terrorist had underestimated our "national will" or "our American ingenuity," his language would have been on safer ground. The general's statements, in fact, were not objectionable from a conservative theological perspective, but his timing was all wrong. Boykin had the temerity to challenge the tenets of religious pluralism just at that moment when those tenets were most being used to clear America of any ulterior motive for going to war against Iraq. Religious pluralism is so deeply ingrained in America that historical judgments about Islam—say, a socioeconomic analysis of the root causes of its being left behind by the forces of modernization—are acceptable in a way that theological judgments are not. Theological rhetoric that does manage to enter the mainstream media is always tolerant and inclusive; the media is a business that cannot afford to offend anyone, except those who transgress the rules of tolerance and inclusivity. Boykin accidentally violated one of the cardinal tenets of civility in a liberal society, which is that statements about specific religious beliefs, in contrast to vague spiritual sentiment, should be kept out of the public realm of politics, which includes the military.

Many in the media were worried that such comments might make it seem that the fight against terrorism is a battle between Christian America and Middle Eastern Islam. Boykin was not the only one, however, who suspected that more was going on in the Middle East than a search for weapons of mass destruction. Some critics of the war dismissed it as a thinly veiled grab for oil. These criticisms were widely published and discussed. Boykin represents a position that received significantly less attention, namely, that the war *against* terrorism is also a struggle *for* something, and that what we are fighting for has something to do with our most important beliefs.

Boykin's words were an act of insubordination, although he was never told by a superior officer not to speak in churches. His insubordination went much deeper than that, although the media was never very clear about the precise reason his conduct was so questionable. It is not adequate to say, as many in the media did, that he can be accused of violating the separation of church and state. Even a soldier has the freedom of religious speech. Boykin did not just mix religion and politics, which are mixed up all the time. Blending these two categories of discourse is perfectly acceptable as long as religion is only a minor ingredient added to any argument meant for public consumption. Boykin mixed a much headier brew. By speaking about America in terms of a special, divinely appointed mission, he committed the liberal equivalent of blasphemy.

A providential interpretation of American history has not totally disappeared from contemporary political rhetoric, but such an interpretation has been relegated to the private realm of conservative churches and their publications, which rarely enter the mainstream media. Extremist Muslims use their ideas about God to defend their use of the sword, but reasonable Americans do not. This statement does not mean that America is not in some significant way a Christian nation. What keeps most Americans from publicly proclaiming that God is on our side in times of crisis is, in fact, a secular version of Christian morality that privatizes religious faith. Religion is tolerated as long as it does not interfere with serious national affairs. In other words, if it were not for liberal Christianity, America would be more dramatically divided between a secular and religious constituency, and providential language would be more commonly heard from religious quarters. The great accomplishment of liberal Christianity is to fuse faith and flag in a civic religion that trumps religious passion with the common sense of civility. Church and state are united by a truce that allows the nation to show all outsiders a friendly face.

Civil religion has declined in America since the 1960s, but it is still important, especially in time of war. America's civil religion rejects the idea of a holy war, but religion still shapes the way many Americans think about warfare. Because civil religion values tolerance and pluralism as the highest expressions of the American experiment, gloating and arrogance are excluded from American warfare. Civil religion prescribes a small dose of Christian compassion and humility in order to make war more palatable to the American people. We can rest assured that our faith in God is superior to radical Muslims because our mixture of theology and war is so much weaker than theirs. Secularists who deny that Christianity plays any constructive role in American politics miss the extent to which the limitation put on the mixing of religious and political language is itself a product of religious faith—in this case the faith of religious liberals who believe that religion works best when kept separate from matters of national interest.

The irony is that Boykin *was* upholding the order of liberal society by offering his theological interpretation of the war against terrorism in church and not in staff meetings. The national anxiety about what kind of war we were fighting, however, needed little disturbance in order to burst through its First Amendment seams. Partisan politics had given birth to a widespread nervousness about President Bush's close ties to the religious right. And for many Americans, reeling from the destruction of 9/11, an even deeper current of nervousness existed about a nefarious enemy with its own religious connections, in this case to a world religion that has frequently played an exotic and threatening role in Western history. President Bush was doing his utmost best to emphasize that the war against terrorism was not a religious war, but critics on the left had their suspicions, while those on the right talked about a clash of cultures that seemed almost apocalyptic in its global scope. It was a most inappropriate time to raise the question of whether God takes side in international conflicts and, if so, whose side God is on.

Boykin was guilty of bad timing, but his political theology was nothing new. The doctrine of providence, albeit in various forms and rarely without contentious debate, has been at the very heart of American history, especially when it comes to thinking about America's role in the world. Political scientists, even after the incredible yet steady emergence of America as the world's lone superpower, often argue that democracies cannot shape a consistent and farsighted foreign policy. American foreign policy is thus usually stereotyped as an uneven oscillation between idealism and isolationism. Prince Otto Bismarck was so frustrated by how far America had risen to power in his time that he attributed our success to dumb luck—the special providence that watches over drunks, fools, and the United States.[3] Americans, who have a share in the Calvinist heritage, know better than that. In its plainest sense, the doctrine of providence states not only that God works through all of nature and all of history to reveal God's glory, but also that God chooses specific individuals and particular nations to accomplish the divine plan. The American Revolution largely cut off the new nation from its European roots. A common observation is that it took the Civil War to make the states united. Whatever sense of unity the states had before that came from a shared expectation of a bountiful future rather than a common burden of an unshakable past.

Because the outright rejection or drastic modification of providential rhetoric has been so recent, mapping this development in any precise way is difficult, but the further back you go in history, the clearer it becomes just how habitual and ordinary are claims about an American providence. For example, it is hard to imagine anyone taking issue with Ethan Allen, the Yankee colonel who led the expedition that earned the first colonial victory of the Revolutionary War. When Allen, who was named—like his brothers Heman, Heber, Levi, Zimri, and Ira—for a biblical warrior, was asked by what authority he was taking Fort Ticonderoga, he plainly proclaimed, "In the name of the Great Jehova and the Continental Congress." Some historians have argued that the Allen story is apocryphal. He was, after all, a notorious freethinker. He was also a loudmouth and a braggart, so he quite possibly said these words merely to spite the British. Perhaps he just said them tongue-in-cheek, to make his fellow soldiers laugh. The important point is not how he said them or even whether he said them, but whether they drew any adverse attention when reported in the press. They did not.

The American revolutionaries believed that God was on their side, and even today most Americans would probably have little argument with that proposition. The question is not whether God has stopped taking sides in wars. Presumably, God is still working through human events, including wars, to achieve God's purposes. The question instead is whether we have lost the cultural coherence—and the resulting confidence in America's purposes—that make the question of God's providential role in American history meaningful and feasible.

We lack the skill of reading history providentially because we lack the religious and moral imagination to see a relationship between America and God's purposes. Those skills were in great supply during the Revolution, but the groundwork for their erosion was prepared before that, during the Enlightenment. The leading thinkers of the Enlightenment wanted to talk about universal principles and natural religion rather than the specific claims of Christianity. Enlightenment rationality has in many ways diminished Christian faith to a minimal set of modest beliefs, but surely the doctrine that has had the least success in surviving the age of suspicion is the doctrine of providence. Even for those people who believe that the orderliness of nature is evidence for the existence of God, history is so disorderly that it does not seem to offer such consolation. More to the point, the orderliness of nature flatters the modern mind that there are no limits to scientific progress, whereas a belief in the orderliness of history has just the opposite effect. The idea that God is truly in charge of history threatens the modern myth that humans are in control of their own destiny and are able to shape the future through their struggles to understand the past and act in the present. R. R. Reno's definition of modernity superbly captures the eclipse of providence: "We are modern insofar as we will not suffer that which we have received."[4] To gloss this fine statement, we could say that modernity understands the past as a burden that the present has already escaped rather than a debt that, through the process of a grateful repayment, becomes one's destiny.

No modern theologian has reflected more deeply on the matrix of freedom, nature, and history than Reinhold Niebuhr. Controversies over Darwin's theory of evolution can mislead us into thinking that God's governance of nature is more problematic than God's authority over history, but Niebuhr argues that the reverse is true. "In modern culture the idea of progress was substituted for the idea of providence a full century before the concept of evolution was substituted for the idea of creation. The historic development of human institutions and the emergence of novelty in historic time was more obvious and therefore more quickly discerned than the fact that the forms of nature were also subject to temporal mutation."[5] The belief in God's ordering of nature is compatible with the belief in progress, but the belief in God's lordship over history lacks such coherence. Modern people did not first emancipate themselves from nature and then from history. Indeed, and this Niebuhr also understood, the mastery of nature actually led to a reversal of the modern confidence in the human ability to shape history. It is a great irony that the more we know about nature, the less we think we are free. As Niebuhr puts it, "modern forms of determinism have annulled human freedom more completely than Christian ideas of Providence."[6] Modern people began by rebelling against the doctrine of providence because it restricted human freedom and ended by embracing a naturalism that left human freedom more problematic than ever before.

Providence smacks of a tyrannical God who tries to smash our wills and restrict our freedom. Its dismantling goes hand-in-hand with the inflation of the value of human freedom and the subsequent fear that God will compete with or even obliterate our freedom. Modern theology replaces the traditional portrait of God as omniscient and omnipotent with a revisionist account of an open, limited, vulnerable, and changing deity. William C. Placher has called this "the domestication of transcendence."[7] We find it comforting to imagine God as more like us, rather than trying to think about how we can become more like God. Much attention has been given to the adequacy of modern versions of the doctrine of God, but the passing of providence has produced little comment and even less protest. This approach is shortsighted, because faith in God's ultimate and unbending control over the course of history is nothing but a corollary to traditional ideas about God's multifaceted perfection. The best way to attend to the inadequacies of revisionist accounts of classical theism is to examine the thinness of revisionist discussions of providence.

Peter C. Hodgson's theology, heavily influenced by process philosophy, is a good example of how difficult modern theologians find it to reconstruct a doctrine of providence after deconstructing the doctrine of God. In *God in History: Shapes of Freedom*, Hodgson recognizes that if speaking of God in the modern world is possible, then theologians need to explain how God and history intersect. For Hodgson, history is a fragile and complex process of actualizing human freedom. God can be said to be at work in history when we recognize events and patterns that lead to a wider arena for the exercise of human freedom. He criticizes what he calls the classical model of providence for using royal metaphors about God's governance over worldly affairs. He draws on process theology to sketch a theology of providence that is noninterventionist, nonmiraculous, and nonlinear. The upshot is that God does not direct history. Instead, God and history are "co-constitutive" categories.[8] History is in God as much as God is in history. It is not so much that we cooperate with God's will, but that God can work through history only by cooperating with us. God is limited to the role of persuasion. Much like the parents of fully grown adult children, God can cajole, advise, and even condemn, but the rest is up to us. Indeed, for Hodgson, we can only know God is at work in the work of our own hands. Where we see the results of our own struggle for freedom, we can certify God's presence.

Hodgson is reacting to the way that providence, of all Christian doctrines, most violates our modern sense of fairness. Providence suggests that, on the level of nations as well as individuals, God plays favorites. Christian providence makes no sense, therefore, aside from the history of Israel. The history of Israel is unique, but it is also a template that must be used with care as Christians try to understand how that particular history resonates throughout all of history. Bad political theory, in fact, begins with misreadings of Israel, as demonstrated by the way that Christian supersessionism— the idea that the church has altogether abrogated Israel's chosenness—can lead to an idolatrous nationalism. Hodgson is particularly worried that throughout much of Western history providence provided the steady drumbeat behind the triumphal march of God in the twin processes of Christianity solidifying its hold on Europe while Europe sunk its hooks into the rest of the world. For Hodgson, this proves how easy it is to slide from a theocentric recognition of God's freedom to work out the divine plan as God chooses to a Eurocentric rationalization of human greed and power. It is just as plausible to argue that Eurocentrism results from a one-sided reading of Israel that sees the movement from tribalism to kingship as the prelude to the further movement from nationalism to imperialism. The case of Eurocentrism shows how any providential interpretation of history must be grounded in the very particular history that is recounted in the Old Testament.

After the twentieth century, the bloodiest in the history of humankind, theologians like Hodgson can be excused for casting providence to the margins of Christian faith. After all, providence has its roots in the history of Israel, the chosen people of God, and making sense of what God was trying to do through the Jewish people in the Holocaust strikes many people as an example of the most egregious kind of theological speculation.[9] The idea of being chosen by God entails special benefits as well as responsibilities, and thus brings into focus how God both blesses and judges the people through whom God works. This dialectic of blessing and judgment is clear in the Old Testament, but the Holocaust appears to render it useless, because it is utterly mysterious how punishment on this unimaginable level could serve any reasonable purpose of a good God. The Nazis were a pagan movement, but they also adopted, distorted, and intensified the kind of Christian supersessionism that sees the Jewish people as essentially displaced from their role in world history. It is almost as if the Nazis were in competition with Israel, trying to become a new chosen people by usurping God's blessings from the

Jews, which left the truly chosen people with nothing but judgment. In their perverse parody of providence, the Nazis set themselves up as a vengeful pagan deity who turns upside down the Christian doctrine of election by blessing the murderous and destroying the meek and mild. Perhaps the Nazis had the intuition that the world was big enough for only one chosen people. If so, they were right, which is the reason that their demonic empire came to such a terrible end.

Nonetheless, for Christians to mention the Holocaust as an excuse for disbelieving in providence, while many Jewish thinkers stay the course, is too easy. Christianity, which has had so many historical successes, affords the luxury of doubting providence in the abstract in a way that Judaism, which has had so many historical tragedies, does not. Judaism has an intimate awareness of how the good tends to bring out an evil response. Thus Hayyim Kanfo relies on the same passages from the Prophets that support Protestant premillennialism to show that evil will be strengthened preceding the arrival of the Messiah. Orthodox Jews killed in the Holocaust were an unblemished sacrifice on the path God has chosen for Israel and its mission to bring every nation into obedience to God.[10]

The Holocaust was a turning point in the history of the idea of providence because it made election seem like a curse rather than a blessing. The truth is, however, that the doctrine of providence was in trouble well before the twentieth century. It hardly needs to be pointed out that nation-states can do terrible things in the name of God. Arguably, some form of the doctrine of providence is foundational for the formation and rise of nation-states in the West, because the conviction that an ethnic group (or a set of such groups) should express itself through a unique configuration of political power requires the belief that it has a special destiny to play on the world's stage. The Nazi ideology, for example, was dependent on the idea of a favored people (*Lieblingsvolk*), though it was often unclear by whom they were favored. Increasingly, Hitler took the place of God by functioning as the one who cast his blessings on the German *volk*. Germany needed more room, Hitler argued, because all German-speaking people deserved to be incorporated into the German state. In its secularized form, providential understandings of national histories can be stretched out of any specifically Christian shape, even to the point of becoming explicitly anti-Christian. As a result, national expansion and military power are justified regardless of the moral cost. Poor providential theology frequently drives out good providential theology. It does not follow that providence should be jettisoned altogether. If some form of providence is an unavoidable element in the rhetorical construction of national identities in the West, then clarity about what the doctrine actually means is all the more important.

One of the main points I argue throughout this book is that the dialectic between blessing and judgment needs to be carefully held together for providence to make good theological sense. That this dialectic has broken down in our society should be obvious by the way some Pentecostal churches preach a gospel of prosperity that comes dangerously close to equating faith with material success while some mainline theologians see nothing but judgment on the horizon for American greed and power. When blessing and judgment become separated, the preaching of providence can sound like special pleading on the one hand or sour grapes on the other.

Boykin offended both the naysayers against God and the naysayers against America. The intensity of the reactions to Boykin's comments can serve as an index to how far many Americans have come from thinking about their nation in positive providential terms. Boykin was a victim of a kind of time trap, because the language he used had once been an integral part of American theology and American politics as well. One comment from the 1950s stands out in its striking similarity to one of Boykin's remarks. Secretary of State John Foster Dulles was the son of a Presbyterian minister, and when he talked about foreign affairs, he spoke in fluent Calvinism. In a special issue of *Life* magazine devoted to Christianity, he opined, "It seems clear that Communism is Satan in action, to be resisted by all means at all times."[11] Dulles was stating if not the obvious, then at least the unobjectionable. Most Americans still believed in good and evil in the fifties, and the government conducted America's foreign policy accordingly. When President George W. Bush nearly fifty years later momentarily slipped into the language of a crusade in framing the war on terrorism, he quickly backed away. His political instincts (or his political advisors) told him he could not say what he had been brought up believing and, no doubt, believed still.

The decline of providential rhetoric in America did not begin until the 1960s—Langdon Gilkey called providence the "forgotten stepchild" of contemporary theology in 1963—although that observation needs to be nuanced.[12] Rather than rejecting providence, intellectuals in the sixties tended to stand it on its head. God now was thought to have turned his back on America. Blessing had become curse. Americans needed to repent of the idealism that had led to Vietnam. Ironically, this call for repentance was yet another example of the power of providential thinking, which shows just how deeply this theological trope is ingrained in the American mind. As America lost confidence in its mission abroad, it lost confidence at home as well. President Lyndon Johnson imagined America in providential terms as a Great Society that could eliminate poverty and racism in a few short years, but America's sense of a domestic mission could not survive apart from the fate of America's sense of a special mission overseas.

The sixties were in many respects just another religious revival.[13] The Great Awakening this time, however, involved flaunting the growing generation gap in an orgiastic embrace of excessive forms of behavior fueled by utopian political theory. When young people began chanting, "Hell no, we won't go," they were doing more than expressing their dissatisfaction with the prosecution of the war in Vietnam. Vietnam is often portrayed as having brought the Manichaean certainties of the Cold War to an end, but it is more accurate to say that it transferred those certainties from a military fight against the slayers of freedom abroad to a spiritual struggle against the restrainers of freedom at home. The gurus of the 1960s promised unlimited freedom at little cost. Spiritual technologies designed to develop one's personality to the fullest, rather than moral discipline, were supposed to save the nation's soul. What Americans began doubting was not whether they were on a salvific mission, but whether they could save any nation other than their own.

Vietnam was traumatic in part because it demonstrated that the triumph of virtue is not inevitable, and thus God does not always decide to pursue the divine good through our good intentions. Providence met theodicy, and theodicy won: Whatever God was doing in history, it was not identical with American foreign policy. The era of postcolonialism struck at the heart of American self-understanding by calling into question the nature of our intentions. The emergence of new nations across Asia and Africa made it seem as if the American mission to spread the good news of democracy and freedom was paternalistic at best and exploitative at worst. Such self-doubt, however, could not last for long, because Americans require a mission in order to realize their sense of unity and purpose. The backlash against moral cynicism and national uncertainty began with Ronald Reagan and his revival of Cold War rhetoric. Reagan wanted to finish the business, which had been given up by many, of defeating the Soviet Union. Reagan knew how to evoke the old sense of good vs. evil—he rightly called Russia "the evil empire"— without explicitly naming God as our secret weapon. It would take a few more years before somebody had the audacity to do that.

And thus we return to General Boykin, who was the ultimate name-dropper—by dropping the name of the ultimate—in his defense of the war on terrorism. What had changed? It was not just that America had become more confident in its use of the military since Vietnam. And it was not just that Iraq provided us with an opportunity to return to our self-image as a virtuous nation whose revolutionary origins makes us obligated to fight tyrants abroad for the sake of liberty everywhere. It was that some Americans, at least, had regained their confidence in theological terms—or, better put, had realized that their national confidence could only be justified if it was submitted to theological deliberation. This moral confidence is what the cynics could not understand and what drove them to keep searching for the "deeper" reasons—usually having to do with oil—for the second Gulf War. The battle over Boykin's remarks was so intense because he inserted something so very American into public debates about the war on terrorism. If what he said was really marginal and irrelevant to American history, it would hardly have received such passionate scrutiny.

NOTES

1. Nina Totenberg, a reporter for the National Public Radio, declared on the TV talk show *Inside Washington*, "Well, I hope he's not long for this world because you can imagine . . ." When pushed by other panelists if she was putting a hit on the general, she pleaded, "No, no, no, no, no, no! . . . In his job, in his job, in his job, please, please, in his job" (http://www.mediaresearch.org/realitycheck/2003/fax20031020.asp). Many editorial writers called for Boykin's resignation. The *International Herald Tribune* was appalled that "a high-ranking government official made remarks that espoused a single religious view," implying that multiple religious viewpoints would have been acceptable (http://www.iht.com/cgi-bin/generic.cgi?template= articleprint.tmplh&articleId=114735). Reaching deep for something to justify his firing, some editorialists argued that his lack of judgment in wearing a uniform in church demonstrates his lack of fitness for effectively accomplishing his military mission, although the connecting link in this argument was never spelled out. General Boykin made it clear that he was speaking his personal opinion, and not for the Pentagon as a whole. Martin E. Marty, the historian and apologist for mainline Protestantism, could not be bothered to take Boykin seriously in a mocking and condescending column, "A guy named Satan," *Christian Century* (November 15, 2003), 47. Marty especially takes issue with a picture Boykin showed some church groups of black slashes over the sky in Mogadishu. Boykin interpreted the slashes as evidence of a cosmic battle, but Marty wisecracks that if such slashes are really significant, then they should make it easier for Boykin to track down the terrorists. No newspapers, by the way, raised the question of the legality of a reporter secretly taping a church meeting for public broadcast.

2. *Washington Post*, October 19, 2003.

3. See Walter Russell Mead, *Special Providence: American Foreign Policy and How It Changed the World* (New York: Routledge, 2002), xv, 34. This is the wisest and most comprehensive of recent books on America's involvement in international affairs, and I have learned much from it. It is telling that political scientists are much more apt than theologians to recognize the enduring significance of providence for American history.

4. R. R. Reno, *The Ruins of the Church: Sustaining Faith in an Age of Diminished Christianity* (Grand Rapids: Brazos Press, 2002), 18.

5. Reinhold Niebuhr, *Faith and History* (New York: Charles Scribner's Sons, 1949), 36. Many people find it easier to think of God as determining the events of nature than those of the human realm, where freedom holds sway. After Darwin, it should be just the opposite: Darwin conceives of nature as ugly, violent, and viciously random. God is much more likely to be working to influence human decisions than to steer the course of a biological mechanism that renders individuals as the transient vehicles of the reproduction of their genes.

6. Ibid., 79.

7. William C. Placher, *The Domestication of Transcendence: How Modern Thinking about God Went Wrong* (Louisville, KY: Westminster John Knox Press, 1996). His discussion of providence in chap. 7 has greatly influenced me.

8. Peter C. Hodgson, *God in History: Shapes of Freedom* (Nashville: Abingdon Press, 1989), 44. Also see Hodgson's entry, "Providence," in *Handbook of Christian Theology: New and Enlarged*, ed. Donald W. Musser and Joseph L. Price (Nashville: Abingdon Press, 2003), 414–17.

9. Defending providence in spite of historical tragedy is nothing new. E. Frank Tupper has shown how the slaughter of the innocents in Bethlehem was the single greatest challenge to providence in the New Testament. This story also shows that providence always has a geography, and that all events must be read in the light of the Old Testament. See Tupper's "The Bethlehem Massacre—Christology against Providence?" *Review and Expositor* 88, no. 4 (Fall 1991): 399–418.

10. Hayyim Kanfo, "Manifestations of Divine Providence in the Gloom of the Holocaust," in *I Will Be Sanctified: Religious Responses to the Holocaust*, ed. Rabbi Yehezkel Fogel, trans. Edward Levin (Jerusalem: Jason Aronson Inc., 1998), 15–23.

11. Dulles quoted in "Foreign Aid and Our Moral Credo," *Life*, April 22, 1957, 42.

12. Langdon Gilkey, "The Concept of Providence in Contemporary Theology," *Journal of Religion* 43 (July 1963): 171.

13. See James A. Morone, *Hellfire Nation: The Politics of Sin in American History* (New Haven, CT: Yale University Press, 2003), chap. 14.

CHAPTER TWO

Providence American Style:
A Short History of the Construction of the Idea of America

The Great Seal of the United States is a curious thing. A pyramid rises above an arid desert. Inscribed on the pyramid is the year 1776. Above the pyramid is an all-seeing eye, with a Latin inscription that means "God has favored our undertakings." Below lies a Latin phrase that means "a new order of the ages." Perhaps what is most notable about the seal is that the pyramid, which symbolizes America, is unfinished. It points toward heaven and is crowned by God's benevolent gaze, but the accomplishment it represents lies in the future.

The unfinished pyramid invites us to ask what America is and where it is going. Arguably, America is not a place. America's geography was barely known as its borders kept expanding throughout the nineteenth and even into the twentieth century. Nor is it a people in the sense of a shared ethnicity. If it is not a place or a people, then perhaps it is best thought of as an idea, something like a hypothesis, or a laboratory for the strongest mixture of faith and freedom.

Providence is how Americans test whether their formula works. While an orthodox theology of providence lies at or near the heart of much American history, Americans are also very adept at using the rhetoric of providence to serve their own purposes. Providence defines America as a nation—it is more accurate to say that America is a product of this doctrine than to say that Americans projected their history onto this theological theme—but Americans do not easily agree on what "providence" means. Providence provides a kind of grammar that allows us to talk to each other by opening the question of what America is in the first place. We are not a particular people, in terms of a shared set of rituals and beliefs, which makes us a people set apart from other nations, whether we like that status or not. The question is, What (or who) has set us apart, and for what purpose?

Some historians argue that nature, not history, provides the proper setting for American democracy. Catherine L. Albanese has developed one of the most rigorous arguments that it was the wilderness that Americans were forced to read, not history.[1] Europeans had long conquered the wild and thus had the luxury of downplaying nature in their theological accounts of God's providence. What was radically new in America was an open frontier that both beckoned and threatened. The wild environment was the one thing that early Americans could boast of when they wrote to their friends and relatives back home in the Old World. In Europe, God spoke through the grand architecture of ancient buildings as well as the beauty of traditional rituals, but in America, God had a less civilized tongue. Nature came to symbolize the divine in all of its dangers as well as its possibilities. Nature was gift and promise but also burden and task, the sacramental conveyance of God's grace and an object in need of investigation. Albanese draws a straight line from the Puritans and Jonathan Edwards to the Transcendentalists up to Annie Dillard, but that line was not something early Americans found in nature itself. Nature spoke to Americans because they saw themselves as a people set apart, on a mission, and thus not unlike the ancient Israelites in their quest for the promised land. Canaan itself was most strategically positioned, it was thought, for the purpose of God's covenant with Israel, just as America was in the best position for a new covenant. Americans have taken their measure from the wild expanse of nature, but only because nature is conceived as the setting for the drama of God's work in history.

Many countries have some kind of providential view of themselves, but America's providential theology came together at a propitious time. This unique confluence of a set of theological ideas could not have been synthesized at any other time in history. Historians break down the constituent parts of American providence in different ways. Anders Stephanson sorts these parts into four categories: election and covenant; choice and apostasy; prophecy, revelation, and the end of history; and territory, mission, and community. John F. Berens makes a list of five characteristics: the motif of America as a New Israel; the jeremiad tradition; the deification of America's founders; millennial expectations; and providential historiography. Richard T. Hughes prefers to talk about myths Americans live by, which he delineates as the myth of the Chosen People, the myth of Nature's Nation, the myth of the Christian Nation, the myth of the Millennial Nation, and the myth of the Innocent Nation. Russel B. Nye frames the national purpose in terms of serving as an example of peace and justice to the rest of the world, acting as an agent to achieve God's plan, and providing a haven for the oppressed of the world. Among political scientists, these characteristics are often simply grouped together under the rubric of "American Exceptionalism," a phrase that can obscure their religious origins.[2]

Other lists could be made and the influences on American providence should not be limited to Protestantism. Before the Calvinists came to America, messianic hope inspired the Spanish Empire to look to the New World for the fulfillment of history and the universal reign of God's kingdom.[3] Nevertheless, the Puritans who shaped American history inherited a very specific form of Protestant Reformation theology. Just as the impulse for freedom was igniting throughout Europe, God had made known a new continent, hidden for centuries from European sight. English separatists and Puritans could not help but see this new land as the last best chance for the purification of the church. The failure of the Puritans in England coincided with their opportunity in America. Under the influence of Calvin, the Puritans wanted to established a holy city in America. Calvinism was not stoic in its acceptance of fate but instead energized believers to become participants in God's plan. Calvinists, in fact, delighted in their minority status, because it allowed them to see themselves as persecuted for the sake of God. Providence, for them, was partisan.[4] The Puritans interpreted their journey as an escape from Egypt/England and an arrival in the promised land. The New World gave them the geographical distance necessary to mount a break from the Old.

Far from being a peculiar theological project, the Puritans could hardly have interpreted their experience in any category other than providence. God gave them a unique geopolitical history, which demanded a bold theological response. Since the rise of the papacy in its attempt to fill the vacuum left by the fall of the western half of the Roman Empire, the secular and the sacred had competed for the loyalty and obedience of Europe's masses. After the Protestant Reformation, nationalism grew unchecked by transnational religious loyalties, which frequently resulted in the restriction of the freedom of the church. In America, by contrast, revolution required a centralized form of government in order to ensure the freedom of the people. The American government was on the side of religion; the political had made it possible for the religious to come into its own. What had hitherto seemed impossible—that a strong government would nevertheless empower its citizens to worship as they please—had miraculously come to pass.

The Puritans interpreted their history providentially, which does not mean that their interpretation of their history is accurate. Part of the Puritan mythology passed down to subsequent generations was the idea of a Christian golden age, so that the story of America is the story of a decline from a purely religious past. Scholars today are likely to read American history in the opposite direction. As Charles L. Cohen writes, "If Christianity came to America in the first ships, it arrived as did the other passengers, seasick, scurvied, and emaciated."[5] Jon Butler has been at the forefront in arguing that America was not born Christian; instead, it was made that way.[6] The Puritans did not bring a full and true church to America, but they did bring a doctrine that allowed all Americans to see their story as one of ultimate success.

Americans were not the only ones to see themselves providentially. Andrew Burnaby, an English clergyman, visited the middle colonies in 1759–60 and offered this testimony to American dreams: "An idea strange as it is visionary, has entered into the minds of the generality of mankind, that empire is travelling westward; and every one is looking forward with eager and impatient expectation to that destined moment, when America is to give law to the rest of the world."[7] Burnaby could conceal neither his wonder nor his distaste for this species of national pride. What is evident from his observation is that long before Americans had any realistic basis on which to be confident about their national prospects, they drew an inordinate national confidence from God.

From the vantage point of the present, it is hard to conceive how the Puritans could have avoided being steeped in providence, but they are often blamed for this doctrine, as if they invented it out of spite for the Native Americans or love of moral grandstanding. True, the Puritans were hardly the harbingers of modern notions of religious freedom. They sought freedom for themselves but not others. They did not even really seek religious freedom; they sought to put themselves (and others!) under the watchful eye of God and thus promoted obedience to God's commands. Roger Williams rebelled from their notion of providence, arguing that God chose only one people, and that was long ago: "The State of the Land of Israel, the Kings and people thereof in Peace & War, is proved figurative and ceremonial, and no pattern nor precedent for any Kingdom or civil state in the world to follow."[8] The Puritans were right to reject Williams's restrictions on the reading of the Bible. Biblical history for the Puritans was ongoing, and they used figurative, typological, allegorical, and analogical interpretations of Israel in order to locate themselves in that history. Their reading of the Bible was so strong that their opponents had to borrow their theology in order to criticize them.[9] Williams sought to restore the purity of the primitive church and was driven by providential logic in founding the new colony of Rhode Island. He named the site for his new city after the providence that had safely brought him there. Williams thought God was doing wondrous work in establishing freedom in the New World; he just did not think it was limited to the people of New England.

Williams shows how hard it was to escape the Puritan narrative. As Hughes states, "The Puritans told a focused, compelling, and convincing story that no other immigrant group could match. Nevertheless it was a story with which many immigrant groups could identify."[10] Perhaps it was so persuasive because it was so biblical, at least as the Bible was interpreted by

John Calvin. The Puritans borrowed from Calvin their principal theological idea of covenant. Sometimes, they thought, God chooses a group of people to work God's will in the world. This was definitely true of Israel, but it also seemed to be true of themselves. God does not choose groups (or nations) on the basis of their moral goodness or political shrewdness. The reasons for God's decisions remain wrapped in mystery. Moreover, God does not choose nations based on their military power or natural resources. God gives nations what they need, and when God chooses a nation, God makes demands as well as distributes blessings. Indeed, to be chosen is to be commanded. Providence is a burden, even given the assumption of a divine grace that is abundant and free. The burden of providence has provided a strong check against any superficial American triumphalism. Probably no American leader felt the burden of providence more strongly than Abraham Lincoln, and no greater expression of this aspect of providence can be found than in Lincoln's second inaugural address, where he interpreted the Civil War as a judgment of God on the sins of both sides of the Mason-Dixon line. The deaths of Lincoln and Stonewall Jackson proved to both the North and the South that God's will in the Civil War was far more mysterious than anyone had anticipated.[11]

How did the New England theology of covenant end up guiding America through the Civil War? Berens argues that the key period in providential thinking in America came between 1740 and 1763. Before 1740, providence as a doctrine belonged to New England theologians. After 1740, thanks to those crucial years of revival known as the Great Awakening, it not only spread throughout the colonies but became the glue that held the colonies together. America was New Englandized. Catholics and Protestants alike embraced providential thinking. Not all settlers came to America for religious freedom, but that became the official story of America's origins. The lack of an ancient history with its accompanying myths forced Americans to scrutinize their recent past for evidence of an emerging story. That America is where freedom and faith meet became the master plot of American history. "Liberty was always the divine intent because it was necessary in order for men to live virtuous lives on this earth and ultimately attain salvation."[12] Victory in the French and Indian War cemented in the American mind the connection of providence and national purpose. The patriots killed in the Boston Massacre seemed like martyrs nourishing the cause of freedom with their spilled blood. As Berens makes clear, the doctrine of providence led to the establishment of "an American nationalism before the creation of the American nation itself."[13] Providence turned into patriotism as the cause of liberty became identified with the cause of God.

In the process of turning providence into patriotism, the founding fathers were depicted as biblical patriarchs. Typological readings of the Old

Testament had long been popular among Puritans, but allegory gained new significance by allowing Americans to see George Washington as a new Moses. Many Americans practically deified George Washington, referring to him as the "savior" of the country. He survived so many close calls with the enemy, and his character was so finely tuned to the task he had to accomplish that his life begged for a providential interpretation. Washington himself, something of a deist, could not think about his career in any other terms. He used the rhetoric of providence liberally. To take just one example, pulled almost at random, when he entered Boston after the successful siege, he declared that "the hand of Heaven is visible in this."[14]

What kept this idealization of America in check was the jeremiad tradition. Jeremiads were prophetic sermons preached on fast days in the late seventeenth century, showing how God's election typically brings God's displeasure. The term can be expanded to include any written or oral form of castigation, in which the people chosen by God are warned of dire consequences for not living up to the conditions of the covenant. God punishes those God loves. Indeed, punishment is one of the chief signs of having been chosen by God. God punishes because God is just, and God punishes national as well as individual sins. The point of God's punishment for the elect, however, is reform, not destruction.

The process of fusing providence and patriotism slowed down during the period of the constitutional debates, which was relatively free of theological speculation. It was a religious calm caught between revivalistic storms. Nevertheless, portraying the generation of the founders as a secular bunch is misleading. Secularism in the sense of a nation founded on principles completely void of any religious content was inconceivable. America was fulfilling its destiny by providing for the broadest possible expression of Christian faith; it was not a nation designed to marginalize that faith. Some, like John Adams, wanted a more explicit national affirmation of Christian orthodoxy, while others found in orthodox Christianity an affirmation of religious dissent. These differences came to a climax in the presidential campaign of 1800, where Thomas Jefferson's religious beliefs were carefully and passionately scrutinized. What guided many was the belief that true religion needed no official confirmation by the government. Thus it is misleading when Frank Lambert, an American religious historian, asserts that the founders gave Christianity no privileged place of authority and that they saw theological debates as the source of division and dissension.[15] Even the deists, who were not in the majority among the founding fathers, were, no matter how theologically misguided, Christians of deep faith. Michael Novak is right to stress the extent to which practically all Americans were immersed in the Old Testament. "The language of Judaism became the language of the American metaphysic—the unspoken background to a special American vision of nature, history, and the destiny of the human race."[16] The story of the Jews, more than the story of the early church as found in the New Testament, was crucial because Americans were confronted with the task of building a nation and needed a deeply political theology.

Whatever else they doubted, most eighteenth-century deists believed in providence. Enlightened philosophers believed that God acted in history; indeed, they believed that God acted just as they did, with circumspection and tact. This outlook was especially prominent in America, where deism was not as skeptical toward religion as in Europe. American deists believed that their country was the model of a fully rational nation precisely because God has brought the course of history for the first time to the point of revealing reason's decisive shape. Congress could add a line about providence to Jefferson's draft of the Declaration of Independence—"with a firm reliance on the protection of divine Providence"—because almost everyone believed that God was on their side. As Conrad Cherry has concluded in a study of this issue, "The American Founding Fathers were as vigorous in their pronouncements of America's providential destiny as any clergyman."[17] That the Constitution makes no explicit mention of providence is evidence only of the fact that God was thought to have settled the matter of America's survival. Now the American fathers could get down to the business of framing a government.

Even Benjamin Franklin, a prime example of a colonial deist, affirmed a strong faith in providence. Franklin was convinced that humans can know with certainty nothing about God beyond God's existence as the first cause of all things. Yet he was equally convinced that people could not do without the practical benefits of a fuller faith. For most people, he thought, confident action in the world requires confidence in God's own acts. In a talk he delivered to a science and philosophy club, he argued that God "sometimes interferes by his particular Providence and sets aside the Effects which would otherwise have been produced."[18] Franklin could not live comfortably with the idea that God is aloof and uninvolved in human affairs. That he placed providence on the foundation of practical theology, treating it almost as a useful fiction, does not detract from the importance he gave the doctrine. On the contrary, it shows just how inescapable this doctrine was during the Revolutionary period.

Henry F. May, in an important article on providence, issues a helpful taxonomy for sorting out the various kinds of deism that were popular at America's founding.[19] His list of types includes agnostic, troubled, and radical deism. None of the American representatives of these types of deism, he points out, rejected—no matter how much they doubted or reformulated—divine providence. Indeed, radical deists were as zealous in their passion for providence as any Calvinist. They hoped that the French Revolution would inaugurate a new age, in which God would take humanity by the hand with the French standing first in line on the way to liberty. In the early stages of the French Revolution, Calvinists shared this enthusiasm, but for different reasons. Calvinists hoped the revolutionaries would purify France of Catholicism, their old enemy, even if the revolutionaries included ungodly men who acted in despicable ways. Overall, deism stretched the doctrine of providence to its breaking point by minimizing the active role of a personal God in history, which is one reason that the more skeptical varieties of this theological movement were found to be unappealing and soon disappeared.

After the peak of deism in the eighteenth century, the doctrine of providence in America became more biblically based, although it absorbed much of the optimism and progressivism of the deists. The gloomy picture of providence provided by the Calvinists needed modification to fit the American spirit. For the Calvinists, God made use of historical events to restrain the sinful tendencies of the righteous. Their emphasis was on how God set necessary limits to our lives, not on the infinite possibilities that lie before us. After all, for most of human history, political news was usually bad news. When ordinary people became involved with the national government, it usually meant that sons were being sent to war or taxes were being collected. In America, providence could be joined with the hope for God's millennial reign because the successful American Revolution put God—and national politics—on the side of the people. Calvin recognized the role of the magistrate in restraining sin, but in America, the government restrained itself in order to let religion burst forth.

America reinvented Calvinism by connecting providence to an optimistic expectation of Christ's millennial reign on Earth. The Second Great Awakening erased any doubts about whether the Constitution was written to expedite the spread of Christianity. Confidence in the coming of the kingdom of God was so widespread that it would be futile to list the names of prominent theologians, writers, and politicians who held to some form of this view. Augustine had drawn a fine but straight line between the City of God and the City of Man, and Calvin, who was no fan of apocalypticism, traced this line in his own interpretation of predestination, but Americans smudged that line with abandon.

Portraits of the millennium, the thousand-year reign of Christ, varied. Premillennialists thought that the Second Coming would occur before the advent of a golden age on Earth, while postmillenialists, who were more prevalent during the nineteenth century, believed that human initiative could achieve a reign of peace that would precede the return of Christ. Millennialism is as old as the nation itself. Jonathan Edwards, in a 1742 treatise entitled "Some Thoughts Concerning the Present Revival of Religion in New England," thought that the dawn of the new age was right around the corner and that it would take place in America. Christ was born in the Old World, but, "as Providence observes a kind of equal distribution of things," Christ will be spiritually reborn in the New.[20] Edwards did not think that God is just in the business of blessing. Edwards thought the destruction of the Tower of Babel was a prime example of how God chastises the proud and wicked. "Christ's kingdom is established by bringing down every high thing to make way for it."[21] The city of Babylon and its tower were set up in opposition to God, and God had them destroyed to teach the people to build their cities on a true foundation.

However it was understood, most Christians did not confuse the coming millennium with the consummation of all time in heaven above. The triumph of the millennium had to be based on good politics and sound morals, in preparation for God's final triumph over the powers of evil. When good politics prevailed, the world would become united like one large family. American Christians were extremely practical in their view of this process. Ernest Lee Tuveson, in his book *Redeemer Nation*, observes that nineteenth-century theologians did not shy away from spelling out the preconditions for global unity, chief of which would be the triumph of a common language.[22] Millennialism was not simply an optimistic and self-congratulating theology. It taught Americans to stand on their guard in order to ensure the moral integrity necessary for the completion of their task. The spread of Christianity should lead to the reform of every aspect of society. Far from being a force of conservation, providence was the foundation for social change.

God's precise role in social improvement was the subject of a lively debate conducted in the late 1820s and 1830s. Alexander Campbell, one of the founders of the Disciples of Christ, and Robert Owen, an English reformer, debated each other in front of large and enthusiastic crowds in 1829. What they disagreed about was not the inevitability of progress but its means. Owen wanted a utopian return to humanity's lost perfection, Campbell a more gradual entry into a rational universal guided by divine grace. Campbell chastised Owen for underestimating the impediment of human weakness, but they shared more than enough common ground to carry out a series of entertaining and productive debates.

Nearly everyone in the nineteenth century could agree about the centrality of providence in America. Lyman Beecher, in the 1830s, stated, "When I first encountered this opinion [that the millennium would commence in America], I thought it chimerical; but all providential developments since, all the existing signs of the times, lend it corroboration."[23] Herman Melville, in his novel *White-Jacket* (1850), captured the mood of the nation well: "We Americans are the peculiar, chosen people—the Israel of our time; we bear the ark of the liberties of the world. . . . In our youth is our strength; in our inexperience, our wisdom. At a period when other nations have but lisped, our deep voice is heard afar. Long enough have we been skeptics with regard to ourselves, and doubted whether, indeed, the political Messiah had come. But he has come in *us*, if we would but give utterance to his promptings."[24] Melville has let his gift for hyperbole get the best of him, but his sentiments struck a chord.

Since Beecher's and Melville's time, fewer people have been so quick and so loud to sing America's praises. One reason many people have a visceral reaction to any talk of providence is that it is so often confused with "Manifest Destiny." Manifest Destiny, ironically, has its roots in deism, not Puritanism. Thomas Jefferson rejected Alexander Hamilton's argument concerning the need for a strong federal government to compete abroad, but he did not depart from the providential thinking of his time, deist that he was. Instead, he intuitively understood that America could expand westward while remaining a republic precisely because such expansion could remain agrarian—"those who labour in the earth are the chosen people of God"[25]— and under the supervision of a limited government. Jefferson's redaction of the New Testament—he published an edition in which he deleted all the miracle stories so that Jesus looked like a wise sage and not the Son of God— was consistent with his hopes for the new nation: Leave Europe and its traditions behind on a decidedly Western journey. Western expansion thus allowed Americans to distance themselves from their Old World roots while simultaneously fulfilling the mission that they inherited from England.

Jefferson did not coin the phrase; in fact, "Manifest Destiny" is one of those rare popular phrases that historians can trace to its first use. John O'Sullivan first used it in 1845. O'Sullivan meant it to resonate with the American tradition of providential theology, but American providence is broader and deeper than the jingo of Manifest Destiny. Manifest Destiny is one particular expression of American providence, but it is not typical of providential thought. The earliest exponents of American providence, for example, did not associate it with Manifest Destiny. They were happy to have the Atlantic seaboard colonies and viewed the deep and dark forests to the west as hideous and desolate. They also knew the history of Rome and drew the lesson that a vast territory could prove disastrous for a republic founded on virtue. Moreover, American destiny, for the Puritans, was held tightly in the hand of God. Destiny was revealed in the Bible, most particularly in the story of Israel; it was not made manifest by an abundance of land and a triumphal militarism. The ideologues of Western expansion took all the mystery out of providence. They also drained it of any notion of covenant. God's chosenness no longer was a burden but now was a call to arms.

Manifest Destiny is not simply the manifestation of what Americans always thought about their destiny. It is not the national theology of early America. It is only a particular form of American providence, and, from the standpoint of the most traditional strains of providential thinking, plainly heretical. In Paul C. Nagel's apt description, "For many Americans [during the 1830s and 1840s], providential agency was in the Union, creating around it a secular religion. The Union was Providence incarnate as American doctrine looked to future attainment."[26] Such heretical sentiments dissociated God's blessings from God's commands. American providence is prophetic, which means that it has a universal message. Providence is not for the benefit of America alone. Where Manifest Destiny went wrong was in associating America with a New Rome rather than a New Israel.

A wide variety of noxious isms can be laid at the threshold of Manifest Destiny, which is a term as wide open as the geographical expanse that inspired it. Racism and the lust for land were important factors in America's scramble westward, away from Europe and into the wild. A potential for a kind of racism in traditional accounts of providence became rampant in the doctrine of Manifest Destiny. Anglo-Saxons could equate providence and ethnicity, as demonstrated by their insistence that the purification of the church was really accomplished by Wycliffe, "the morning star of the Reformation."[27] As religion in America became more diverse throughout the nineteenth century, however, providence became more, not less, important as a force for unity. The doctrine of providence thus proved to be remarkably resilient. Roman Catholics embraced the notion of American providence in a bid to become a part of the American story, in spite of Protestant prejudice; others were not given this opportunity. The consequences for Native Americans and Mexicans were tragic. The impact on the doctrine of providence was also disastrous, as providence became conflated with progress. William Gilpin, an early governor of Colorado, wrote in 1873, "Progress is God." He made it clear that the "occupation of wild territory . . . proceeds with all the solemnity of a providential ordinance."[28] The hand of God was on the plow of progress that pushed America westward, intertwining Christianity and western expansion. The rubric that brought them together was *civilization*. To the pioneers, the land was as savage as the natives who had failed to tame it.

One of the tasks of providential America was to serve as a sanctuary for the world's deprived and persecuted, which means that providence was the foundation for American pluralism. Manifest Destiny demonstrates how easily this task could be perverted. Providential theology could stretch but it also could be twisted into racist forms. What was twisted could be untwisted and made right. Black Americans adapted providential theology to their own end, just as the Puritans did. In a brilliant essay on this topic, Sandy Dwayne Martin has argued that providence was at the heart of what he calls the black Christian consensus. Just as it helped Calvinists come to terms with their political struggles and minority status, providence helped African Americans find a pattern in their struggles against slavery. Providence made Africans

American, just as it made America American. As Martin explains, "It was in the colonies, not on the Mother continent, that the Yoruba, Ibo, Ashanti, and Fante would become true Africans, transcending their particular ethnic identities and discovering a collective self-identity as one race of people, something discovered much earlier by Europeans. This new collective racial consciousness of being first and foremost African required one Supreme Being who had a plan and a purpose that included this one group of people. That need was met in Christianity." Muslims accounted for, at most, a fourth of African slaves, but Islam did not grow among the slaves. The emphasis in Evangelical Christianity on a search for religious freedom resonated deeply with the slaves. They elaborated a Josephite theology, wherein they saw themselves as having been betrayed by their African brothers and sisters but, like Joseph, they were placed in the providential role of being able to spread the blessings of religion and culture to their continental kinspeople. Psalm 68:31 was a favorite passage: "Princes shall come out of Egypt; Ethiopia shall soon stretch out her hands unto God" (KJV). Black leaders saw providence at work in the Civil War, in the trials and tribulations of Jim Crow, and in the triumph of the civil rights movement. Yet black nationalists "de-Christianized the struggle and took away or obscured the sense of black providential mission."[29] Martin ends his essay suggesting that black liberation depends on the sense of mission, purpose, and solidarity that can only come from a strong doctrine of providence.

Given how easy it is to distort providential thought, we should avoid the temptation of thinking that average Americans living in the middle of the nineteenth century were not as wise as we are. Lewis O. Saum has written the most extensive study of the popular mood of pre-Civil War America, and he has uncovered a much deeper and more subtle providential theology than the public policy of Manifest Destiny would lead us to expect. On the level of the common man, "the providential emphasis is on the personal and the immediate, not on the optimistic and the future; on an unknown destiny, approached prayerfully and resignedly, not on a destiny rendered manifest and accompanied by assertive, guilt-relieving noises."[30] The speeches of this period, especially those given on July Fourth celebrations, betray all the arrogance and self-righteousness that has entered the standard account of Manifest Destiny. Documents from common folk—letters, journals, small-town-newspaper editorials—demonstrate a quite different providential strain. Providence might have brought the nation to a flourishing point, but most people had every reason to be circumspect and humble about God's future plans. "Man can appoint, but God can disappoint" was a common saying. While Americans today are all too ready to attribute their good fortune to their own hard work, their ancestors gave all the glory to God. American success meant greater responsibility. Indeed, economic growth throughout the nineteenth century forced Christians to ask why God provided such an outpouring of prosperity. Nineteenth-century Christians knew God was not nice! They affirmed God's jealousy and awaited God's punishments for their abuse of God's good gifts. Saum found many sources, for example, documenting how people expected God's punishment for the Mexican War. "However, not one source covered ascribed to God any active guidance or support in the undertaking, and some agonized over the country's defiance of God."[31] A favorite verse at the time was Hebrews 12:6: "Whom the Lord loveth he chasteneth" (KJV). Christians thought that the argument from divine favoritism was little short of blasphemy when it was disconnected from the foundation of a moral covenant with God.

For the typical Christian of the nineteenth century, providence meant not knowing more than knowing. There was a thin line separating resignation from despair. Providence demanded the acceptance of suffering and tragedy, but it did not offer any easy answers. Providence was a hard doctrine, which is why spiritualism became popular during the latter part of the nineteenth century. Spiritualism undermined providence by promising to publicize the secrets of the divine. Spiritualism offered direct contact with the beyond that went beyond the biblical boundaries of providence.

From the perspective of providence, the nineteenth century was the age of Methodism, although Mormonism could also be understood as the apotheosis of providential speculation.[32] The evolving role of providence in Methodist theology can serve as a model for the fate of this doctrine. Wesley himself believed in particular, not just general, providence, and his church followed his lead.[33] Methodists saw themselves as providentially chosen to reform the expanding continent. The ordinary means of clerical training could not meet the needs of the growing nation. Methodist circuit riders were as mobile as the country itself. Nevertheless, by the end of the nineteenth century, as Russell E. Richey points out, Methodism was a victim of its own successes.[34] The more Christian America became, the less driven were Methodists by the providential conviction of a special mission. Providential passion was hard to sustain.

After the Civil War, providence faced its greatest intellectual challenge in Darwin, just as it was being translated more and more into the secular notion of progress. Christians of a Calvinist background were better able than most to absorb the Darwinian thrust. They were already sensitized to God's patient and inscrutable ways.[35] In the long run, however, Darwin sucked all the air out of providence for many Christians. Consequently, the range of this doctrine was narrowed from the public and the historical to the private and the personal. On the face of it, the impact of Darwin on theology appears to have collapsed the doctrine of creation into the doctrine of providence. That is, Darwin persuaded many theologians to conceptualize the creation of living beings as occurring through biological processes of a long duration. Creation is no longer thought to be a once-and-for-all event—or something that occurs over six days—but rather a long and drawn-out process. Consequently, as Langdon Gilkey writes, "the action of God as creator becomes difficult to distinguish from the creative work of God as providential orderer."[36] What this statement leaves out is the way that the expected fallout of these two doctrines was actually reversed. Ironically, rather than creation being vacated in place of providence, providence was modified to look like creation. That is, God came to be seen as working in human history in the same basic way as God was understood to work in natural history, primarily because the laws governing nature's evolution were so much clearer than any pattern that could be discerned about historical change.

Darwin challenged the literal interpretation of scripture, but he also raised anew the problem of theodicy. The laws of evolution require struggle, suffering, and death for the advancement of species. If God works directly through these laws, then God plays a mean game of biological change.[37] How could God have invented such a cruel way for the propagation of life? Many theologians came to the conclusion that it is better to vacate God from the midst of nature's mighty battles rather than attribute the bloody struggle for genetic survival to the divine plan. One way to do this was to rely on the familiar distinction between the parts and the whole. Theologians after Darwin increasingly portrayed God as more involved on the level of the world as a whole than in its specific parts. God provides parameters for biological change, but the actualization of that change is left to the freedom of individual entities. God's hands were thus kept clean of nature's redness in tooth and claw.

Darwin also opened the door to fundamental revisions in how we think of God's nature. When the idea of a recent and rather sudden creation of the world was jettisoned by nineteenth-century science, some theologians were compelled to modify their understanding of God's relationship to time. Evolutionary theory, to the extent that it left room for God at all, favored a deft touch by the divine hand. If nature evolves slowly, then God too must work slowly and gradually through the processes of biological development. Some theologians began arguing that God does not stand outside of time, bringing all things into being with the sound of the divine voice. Instead, God crouches inside of time, moving at such a glacial pace that God is hardly seen, or heard, at all.

If God works so slowly through nature, what does that say about his relationship to history? Theological revisionists argued that the slow duration of natural change displaces or at least problematizes God's active intervention in historical events. We measure historical change by a different scale than we measure ecological change, but the two scales must be related. Human change takes place in and through our relationship to nature. If God is powerless over natural change, or at best works through nature only with the lightest of touches, then it seems reasonable to assume that God's involvement in human affairs must not be completely otherwise. It is hard to imagine God working with the same basic material (we are, after all, physical creatures and thus a part of nature) but at two different speeds and with two contrasting methods—slowly emerging from within nature to bring the evolutionary pot to a boil, so to speak, and holding sway over human affairs from above to ensure that when the pot boils over, things will go as God ordains. From a social scientific perspective, there are not two different laws regulating the physical changes in humans and all other material entities, so how can God's law be so divided?

In light of these conceptual challenges, as well as the eventual triumph of Darwinianism throughout much of American society, one might think that the doctrine of providence would have disappeared in the twentieth century, but this conclusion would be shortsighted. Some scholars have argued that providence did play a diminished role in America in the period after World War I. The Depression landed a serious blow on American providentialism, though the great majority of Americans did not lose their faith in either God or democracy. Franklin Roosevelt's fight to save democracy was aided by his liberal use of providential rhetoric to justify the expansion of government and America's commitment to freedom for all.[38] Following Roosevelt's lead, America saw a revival of providential rhetoric during World War II. In 1941, for example, Henry Luce, the founder of *Time* magazine, proclaimed the "American Century," yet the political left blasted him as a throwback to an earlier time, with his unabashed Calvinism. Luce's thinking about foreign affairs was hardly out of the mainstream. He believed that "the American capacity for successful cooperation [in the international arena] is directly related to our country's constitutional dependence on God."[39] By the 1960s, Korea and Vietnam had taken the purplish shine off providential rhetoric. American Senator J. William Fulbright reflected the sentiments of many when he said that the idea of an American Empire was incoherent because "we are not God's chosen savior of mankind but only one of mankind's more successful and fortunate branches, endowed by our Creator with about the same capacity for good and evil, no more or less, than the rest of humanity."[40] For many Americans, Fulbright's words were little more than common sense, and they should have brought the history of American providence to a close.

America, however, continued to expand and grow, and Americans have never been able to think about their role in the world without relying on some form of the doctrine of providence. Americans could interpret their rise to global prominence in terms of progress, but it has never been easy in

American political theology to disentangle progress from providence. Walter Russell Mead has written *Special Providence*, a fascinating study of American foreign policy. He divides American thought about international relations into four schools: Hamiltonians, with their reliance on a strong national government and support of big business; Wilsonians, who are inspired by the moral obligation of spreading American democratic influence abroad; Jeffersonians, who check the power of both Hamiltonians and Wilsonians with a more domestic agenda; and Jacksonians, who tie foreign involvement to American security and economic well-being. Although America is often accused of having no consistent foreign policy—or simply oscillating between selfish isolationism and arrogant idealism—Mead argues that the balance of these schools has led to a remarkably wise and careful shepherding of American interests. The one element that holds these schools together is a sense of America's special mission in the world.

Wilsonianism is usually associated with liberalism, but the war on terrorism has brought Wilsonianism back into American politics under the guidance of a Republican administration. The combination of Wilsonianism and Jacksonianism in the Bush administration causes much confusion and reaction among liberals. Surprisingly, Mead includes in his discussion of Wilsonian idealism the rise of the missionary movement in America. Missionary work abroad was a direct result of the providential thinking that created America in the first place, and it represents an impulse that beats deep in the heart of America's global aspirations. This impulse was at one time inseparable from Wilsonian idealism. Wilsonian idealism emerged from Evangelical, low-church traditions that wanted to take foreign policy, so to speak, into their own hands. Christian missionaries, as Mead points out, counterbalanced the Hamiltonian quest to build a world order suitable for commercial interests. The rise of American global influence and a truly global Christianity go hand-in-hand.

Historians often neglect mission work because they do not associate it with the story of American foreign policy. Missionaries make antiprovidentialists nervous, but as Mead points out, the work of missionaries is behind much of twentieth-century liberalism. "The modern ecumenical movement, like many of the pioneering figures of liberal theology, emerged from the missionary world. A dispassionate study of the American missionary record would probably conclude that the multicultural and relativistic thinking so characteristic of the United States today owes much of its social power to the unexpected consequences of American missions abroad." Missionaries translated the Bible into local languages. They also interpreted their task to include the development of medical and educational resources, preparing the way for agencies that work against child labor, female circumcision, and debt peonage. Missionaries often protected their congregations from the worst forms of Western imperialism. Mission boards, which Mead calls "the first multinational corporations in American history," laid the groundwork for global communication.[41] It is hard to imagine international civil society today without the groundwork of the missionaries. According to one survey that Mead quotes, roughly 50 percent of the foreign culture experts during World War II were missionary offspring.

Mead credits mission work for planting the seeds that eventually produced the fruit of American pluralism. Pluralism is one possible outcome of a providential interpretation of American history. America is uniquely placed to be the most pluralistic nation the world has ever seen, and that fact alone should result in many benefits for the rest of the world. The problem is that pluralism cannot nourish its own providential roots. A providential history of America can account for pluralism, but putting pluralism at the center of American history will inevitably marginalize the doctrine of providence. From a pluralistic perspective, providence is, at best, the closest America comes to the "noble lie" that Socrates proposes in the Republic. Socrates thought the citizens of the ideal city needed to believe that they were one large family, rooted in a common soil. Americans know that they do not share the ties of blood, and Americans have little patience for the social hierarchies that such traditions defend. Instead, Americans tell themselves that they are joined together not by the past but by the future, and not by blood and soil but by a transcendent moral purpose. For many Americans today, however, providence is nothing more than a lie, and hardly a noble lie at that. Nonetheless, providence is not so easily denied. Pluralism does not so much replace providence in America as it becomes a new form of providentialism. Without the premise that America is a nation set apart for a special purpose, the celebration of American pluralism would make little sense.

Pluralism is the single most significant alternative to a providential reading of American history, but how much of that history can it account for without relying on the very doctrine it is so eager to replace? A comparison of two textbooks on American history can help answer that question. One is *The American People: Creating a Nation and a Society*, written by six well-respected historians. This is one of the two or three most popular American history textbooks in colleges and universities across the nation. A student reading this book would never know the constructive and positive role Christian faith, let alone the doctrine of providence, played in American history. There is a section on Luther and Calvin as background for the earliest migrations to America, but Calvin is portrayed as a social control freak who directed society "down to the last detail." That portrait sets up the analysis of religion in the text: Religion is something Americans had to get away from, rather than something they were relying on to start their nation anew. Keeping with this theme, the Puritans are characterized according to their attempt to "banish diversity." Rather than grasping the truly universal nature of Puritan providentialism, the authors chastise their narrow-mindedness: "Their historic mission was too important, they believed, to allow the luxury of diversity of opinion in religious matters." The racism of Manifest Destiny is attributed to a "white culture" that was a legacy of Puritan utopianism. Even the section on perfectionism in the nineteenth century attributes the mobilization for reform to "increased participation in the political parties of Jacksonian America," rather than an increasingly enthusiastic and millennialistic interpretation of providence.[42] As the foreordained end of American history, pluralism is the unquestioned norm by which every historical judgment is to be made. The authors have thus managed to write a thoroughly providential history of America without once, as far as I can tell, mentioning that very word.

Professional Christian historians, under the pressure to prove their objectivity to their secular colleagues, generally hesitate to offer in their scholarly productions providential readings of the past.[43] Amateur historians, however, are able to take risks that university scholars cannot afford. Compare *The American People* to Peter Marshall and David Manuel's *The Light and the Glory*, and one might wonder if the same country is being discussed.[44] The latter is a popular history, written for a wide audience and frequently used by conservative Christians in homeschooling and in church groups. Marshall and Manuel place God's glory rather than multiculturalism at the end of history. Their position is not necessarily less biased than the authors of *The American People*, but at least their biases are more faithful to the actual beliefs of the people they study. Indeed, Marshall and Manuel are very honest about their strong reading of American history. *The Light and the Glory* is written in a novelistic form, with the premise that something has been forgotten and is need of recovery. Marshall and Manuel teach history as an object lesson in morality, though the same can be said of authors of *The American People*, who use history to promote a multicultural agenda.

Written in the aftermath of Watergate and its attendant cynicism about all things political, Marshall and Manuel want to restore America's self-confidence, and the only way they can conceive of doing this is by urging Americans to recall their Christian heritage. "Did God have a plan for America? Like all those who have discovered the reality of the living Christ, we knew that God had a plan for each individual's life—a plan which could, with spiritual effort, be discerned and followed. What if He dealt with whole nations in the same way?" This startling question pointed the authors back to America's providential origins. It is a fantastic thought: What if, as in the time of Israel, God still engages people corporately as well as individually? If so, then God's blueprint for the world has something significant to do with the founding of America.

The Light and the Glory and its sequels have a devoted following among those who are suspicious of the elitism of higher education. It is a book that promises to present the uncensored truth of America's history. The result is grassroots history at its best—an engrossing narrative with a populist edge—but that does not mean it is without its flaws. At times, it goes to the other extreme of *The American People*. The reader is led to think that every early settler was a Calvinist. The research, however, is meticulous, and the results are worth pondering. Surely in an era when history is increasingly concerned with the recovery of lost voices and restoring the point of view of those who have been defeated in the battle to control official scholarly versions of the past, academics might find something of value in a book of this type. Nonetheless, its approach to America remains anathema in history departments, where certain groups are privileged in terms of their need for justice and others, most notably conservative Christians, are disciplined for their allegedly oppressive ways.

Marshall and Manuel not only have written moving history. They also have written creative theology. Nonetheless, their theology would be as welcome among professional theologians just as little as their history is embraced by academic historians. The theoretical framework of their history is clear. First, God has called the people of the world to America for a specific purpose. America is to be representative of God's intentions for the whole world, a new Jerusalem and thus a model of the kingdom of God. Second, this call took the form of a covenant with God and with each other. The vertical relationship with God demands horizontal results in the way society is structured. God's call requires an answer of obedience. Third, providence teaches us humility and discipline. Marshall and Manuel point out that in the countless pages of diaries and personal papers that they studied, the first response to calamity was, "Where do we need to repent?" National pride is beside the point. "Inherent in God's call upon our forefathers to found a Christian nation was the necessity to live in a state of constant need and dependency upon His grace and forgiveness."[45] Americans once understood providence from the inside out, which makes it a shame that most historians cannot even grasp it from the outside in.

Is it possible to revive providential thinking today? In the light of 9/11, what choice do we have? Under the leadership of President Bush, the Republicans have begun a long and slow process of bringing the religious rhetoric of mission and purpose back to the center of American politics, but what about the Democrats? If providence resides in one political party only, then it will be used in a partisan way to paint liberals as un-American and to baptize every Republican wish as a divine mandate. Providence once united America; it would be a tragedy to see it tear the nation apart.

NOTES

1. Catherine L. Albanese, *Nature Religion in America: From the Algonkian Indians to the New Age* (Chicago: University of Chicago Press, 1980).

2. Anders Stephanson, *Manifest Destiny: American Expansion and the Empire of Right* (New York: Hill and Wang, 1995), 6; John F. Berens, *Providence and Patriotism in Early America, 1640–1815* (Charlottesville: University of Virginia Press, 1978); Richard T. Hughes, *Myths America Lives By* (Chicago: University of Chicago Press, 2003); Russel B. Nye, *This Almost Chosen People* (East Lansing, MI: Michigan State University Press, 1966). For a work of political science that provides an excellent theological background to the notion of exceptionalism, see Siobhan McEvoy-Levy, *American Exceptionalism and U.S. Foreign Policy: Public Diplomacy at the End of the Cold War* (New York: Palgrave, 2001), chap. 1.

3. See Jan Willem Schulte Nordholt, *The Myth of the West: America as the Last Empire*, trans. Herbert H. Rowen (Grand Rapids: Eerdmans, 1995).

4. The way providence leads to responsibility is nicely emphasized by Andrew Pettegree, "European Calvinism: History, Providence, and Martyrdom," in *The Church Retrospective*, ed. R. N. Swanson (Rochester, NY: Boydell Press, 1997), 227–52. I have also benefited from Richard Forrer, "The Puritan Religious Dilemma: The Ethical Dimensions of God's Sovereignty," *Journal of the American Academy of Religion* 44, no. 4 (December 1976): 613–28. Also see Philip Benedict, *Christ's Churches Purely Reformed: A Social History of Calvinism* (New Haven, CT: Yale University Press, 2002), and Perry Miller's classic treatment of this topic, *Errand into the Wilderness* (Cambridge, MA: Bellknap Press, 1956).

5. Charles L. Cohen, "The Colonization of British North America as an Episode in the History of Christianity," *Church History* 72, no. 3 (September 2003): 555.

6. Jon Butler, *Awash in a Sea of Faith: Christianizing the American People* (Cambridge, MA: Harvard University Press, 1990).

7. Ernest Lee Tuveson, *Redeemer Nation: The Idea of America's Millennial Role* (Chicago: University of Chicago Press, 1968), 101.

8. Roger Williams, *The Bloody Tenent of Persecution for the Cause of Conscience*, in *American Christianity: An Historical Interpretation with Representative Documents*, vol. 1, *1607–1820*, ed. H. Shelton Smith, Robert T. Handy, and Lefferts A. Loetscher (New York: Scribner's, 1960), 153.

9. Sacvan Bercovitch makes this point in *The Puritan Origins of the American Self* (New Haven, CT: Yale University Press, 1975), 82.

10. Hughes, *Myths America Lives By*, 33.

11. David B. Chesebrough, "God Has Made No Mistake: The Response of the Presbyterian Preachers in the North to the Assassination of Lincoln," *American Presbyterians* 71, no. 4 (Winter 1993): 223–32; Daniel W. Stowell, "Stonewall Jackson and the Providence of God," in *Religion and the American Civil War*, ed. Randall M. Miller, Harry Stout, and Charles Reagan Wilson (New York: Oxford University Press, 1998), 187–206.

12. Hughes, *Myths America Lives By*, 36.

13. Ibid., 72.

14. Ibid., 67.

15. Frank Lambert, *The Founding Fathers and the Place of Religion in America* (Princeton, NJ: Princeton University Press, 2003), 246–48.

16. Michael Novak, *On Two Wings: Humble Faith and Common Sense at the American Founding* (San Francisco: Encounter Books, 2002), 7.

17. Conrad Cherry, *God's New Israel: Religious Interpretations of American Destiny*, rev. ed. (Chapel Hill: University of North Carolina Press, 1998), 64.

18. Quoted in Robert C. Fuller, *Religious Revolutionaries: The Rebels Who Shaped American Religion* (New York: Palgrave Macmillan, 2004), 44–45.

19. Henry F. May, "The Decline of Providence?" in *Ideas, Faiths, and Feelings: Essays on American Intellectual and Religious History 1952–1982* (New York: Oxford University Press, 1983), 130–46. May was mistaken to say that "The central doctrine of liberal Christians was that Calvinism was wrong about the nature of Providence" (138). He should have substituted "predestination" for "providence."

20. From the selection reprinted in Cherry, *God's New Israel*, 55.

21. Jonathan Edwards, *A History of the Work of Redemption*, ed. John F. Wilson (New Haven, CT: Yale University Press, 1989), 154.

22. Tuveson, *Redeemer Nation*, 62–63.

23. Lyman Beecher, "A Plea for the West," in Cherry, *God's New Israel*, 123.

24. Herman Melville, *White-Jacket* (New York: New American Library, 1979), 153.

25. *Notes on the State of Virginia* (Philadelphia, 1825), 224, as cited in Tuveson, *Redeemer Nation*, 109.

26. Paul C. Nagel, *This Sacred Trust: American Nationality, 1798–1898* (New York: Oxford University Press, 1971), 53.

27. For a thorough examination of this issue, see Tuveson, *Redeemer Nation*, chap. 5.

28. William Gilpin, *Mission of the North American People: Geographical, Social, and Political* (Philadelphia, 1873), 99. Quoted in Roderick Nash, *Wilderness and the American Mind*, 3rd ed. (New Haven, CT: Yale University Press, 1982), 41.

29. Sandy Dwayne Martin, "Providence and the Black Christian Consensus," in *The Courage to Hope: From Black Suffering to Human Redemption*, ed. Quinton Hosford Dixie and Cornell West (Boston: Beacon Press, 1999), 42, 58.

30. Lewis O. Saum, *The Popular Mood of Pre-Civil War America* (Westport, CT: Greenwood Press, 1980), 6.

31. Ibid., 18.

32. See A. Bruce Lindgren, "Zion as a Doctrine of Providence," in *Restoration Studies I, Sesquicentennial Edition*, ed. Maurice L. Draper (Independence, MO: Herald Publishing House, 1980), 287–95.

33. "On Divine Providence," *The Works of John Wesley*, 14 vols. (Grand Rapids: Zondervan, n.d.), 322–23.

34. Russell E. Richey, "Methodism and Providence: A Study in Secularization," in *Protestant Evangelicalism: Britain, Ireland, Germany and America, c.1750–c.1950*, ed. Keith Robbins (Oxford: Basil Blackwell, 1990), 77.

35. James R. Moore, *The Post-Darwinian Controversies: A Study of the Protestant Struggle to Come to Terms with Darwin in Great Britain and America, 1870–1900* (Cambridge: Cambridge University Press, 1979).

36. Langdon Gilkey, *Nature, Reality, and the Sacred: The Nexus of Science and Religion* (Minneapolis: Fortress Press, 1993), 21. This collapse of creation into providence (or "preservation") was already the position of Friedrich Schleiermacher, as Gilkey notes. See Schleiermacher, *The Christian Faith*, ed. H. R. MackIntosh (Edinburgh: T & T Clark, 1986), 146. For Gilkey's discussion of the intricate relationship between the distinguishable but not separate levels of nature and history, see *Nature, Reality, and the Sacred*, 165–73. I have also found helpful an article by David N. Livingstone, "Evolution, Eschatology, and the Privatization of Providence," *Science and Christian Belief* 2 (October 1999): 117–30.

37. See Garrett Hardin, "Ecology and the Death of Providence," *Zygon* 15 (March 1980): 57–68.

38. See James A. Monroe, *Hellfire Nation: The Politics of Sin in American History* (New Haven, CT: Yale University Press, 2003), chap. 12, esp. 370.

39. John Kobler, *Luce: His Time, Life and Fortune* (New York: Doubleday, 1968), 5.

40. J. William Fulbright, *The Arrogance of Power* (New York: Random House, 1966), 20, quoted in Robert T. Handy, "The American Messianic Consciousness: The Concept of the Chosen People and Manifest Destiny," *Review and Expositor* 73, no. 1 (Winter 1976): 57.

41. Walter Russell Mead, *Special Providence: American Foreign Policy and How It Changed the World* (New York: Routledge, 2002), 141, 142.

42. Gary B. Nash and Julie Roy Jeffrey et al., *The American People: Creating a Nation and a Society* (New York: Harper & Row, 1986). The quotes are from 17, 40, 42, 441, 423.

43. For a defense of Christian providential historiography, see Scott H. Moore, "Christian History, Providence, and Michel Foucault," *Fides et historia* 28 (Winter/Spring 1997): 5–14. Even the so-called Calvin school of Christian historiography rejects an overtly providential reading of history. See the comment by George Marsden in Ronald A. Wells, *History and the Christian Historian* (Grand Rapids: Eerdmans, 1998), 11. For an excellent example of Christian history, see Steven J. Keillor, *This Rebellious House* (Downers Grove, IL: InterVarsity Press, 1996). For a very helpful survey of these issues, see Karl W. Giberson and Donald A. Yerxa, "Providence and the Christian Scholar," *Journal of Interdisciplinary Studies* 11 (1999): 122–39.

44. Peter Marshall and David Manuel, *The Light and the Glory* (Grand Rapids: Fleming H. Revell, 1977). One of the ambitions of the conservative Christian wing of the homeschooling movement has been to develop a history of the United States that returns providence to its proper role. For an example of a popular homeschooling text that achieves this, see Mark A. Beliles and Stephen K. McDowell, *America's Providential History* (Charlottesville, VA: The Providence Foundation, 1991).

45. Marshall and Manuel, *The Light and the Glory*, 26.

CHAPTER THREE

On the Question of Preferentiality in Liberalism and Liberation Theology

Reinhold Niebuhr once said that the doctrine of sin is the only Christian belief that can be empirically verified, but something similar can be said about the way history occasionally falsifies a political doctrine. Concerning the fate of communism, providence seems to have shown its hand. Not too long ago, that claim would have been controversial. For millions of the party faithful, communism and its various socialist spin-offs embodied the hope that a godly society, minus the belief in God, could be foisted upon the earth. Since the fall of the Berlin Wall, history has irrevocably demonstrated the falseness of communist ideology. The desire for freedom that swept through that wall has opened up a nearly constant chatter about the end of history and the inevitability of democracy, but there has been little theological discussion about how God is working through America to direct these events.

Francis Fukuyama's thesis concerning the end of history, which he articulated not long after the fall of the Berlin Wall in 1989, has been much maligned. What is wrong with his thesis is not that he thinks the future belongs to democratic capitalism. Rather he sees this future as a secular triumph of a technologically satiated consumerism over spiteful sectarian strife.[1] Fukuyama thinks it is progress when people devote themselves to economic gain rather than the obscurities of theological doctrine. Christians can admire Fukuyama's attempt to imagine the end of history, but American Christians can only wonder at his neglect of the role of faith in the spread of freedom across the globe. What Fukuyama missed is that the triumph of democracy sets the stage for the birth of a truly global Christianity, an argument I make in detail in chapter 6.

Many theologians still stubbornly resist drawing any theological conclusion from the fact that American-style democracy, with its Christian roots,
provides the political horizon for as far as any global forecaster can hope to
see. Theologians have rushed to make various judgments about the dangers
of globalism, but for the most part they have refused to join a remarkable
number of scholars across the spectrum of fields and viewpoints who have
come to the consensus that some form of democracy coupled with some
kind of market capitalism represents the destiny of global politics. Indeed,
many theologians act as if this political development is something to be
regretted rather than celebrated. While providence does not coincide with
progress—that is, God's patient labor in history cannot simply be identified
with what works, so that success becomes a criterion of God's favor—neither
is success necessarily a criteria for God's displeasure either. To suggest that
God is always on the side of the victors would be blasphemous, but it would
also be nearsighted, as well as perverse, to think that the massive transformation of global politics says nothing about God's intentions for world history.
The doctrine of providence invites us to take the risk of reading history, and
it seems apparent to most observers that we have come to a point where history affords a pretty clear text.

So why is there such reluctance by many Americans, not to mention
those who peer at America from other shores, to offer any providential reading of America's global mission? One of the main reasons, I want to suggest,
is that providence raises the divisive question, in the American context, of
favoritism. Liberalism is, in its classical sense, the commitment to a political
order that is governed by impersonal rules. Democracies, with their faith in
the common people, are committed to meritocracy. Only at the founding of
America was the time just right for a group of leaders who were at once aris-
tocratic and meritocratic; since then, meritocracy has been the rule.
Democratic societies put their faith in procedures that make economic and
political advancement open to everyone by minimizing the advantages of
birth, education, and wealth. Although Adam Bellow has heroically
attempted to defend the poor reputation of nepotism—favoritism shown to
a relative—most Americans speak the language of a level playing field and
equal opportunity, even if their practices do not always reflect their rhetoric.[2]
Some of the most divisive political scandals of American history have
involved the abuse of patronage systems, and hiring practices in all segments
of the American economy have become increasingly regulated and bureau-
cratized in response to meritocratic pressures. When an American suspects
that he or she has been passed over for reasons of favoritism, a lawsuit is
quick to follow.

I am not denying that Americans are frequently hypocritical about blind
hiring practices and level playing fields. Few institutions follow procedural

fairness in any consistent fashion. It is even harder for individuals, in their personal relationships, to operate by the principle of fairness. If one has tried to be friends or has worked closely with someone who is truly Kantian in his equal regard for everyone, one will quickly come to the conclusion that something of fundamental value is missing in the relationship. Fairness might be the law of the land, but it is not the stuff of friendship.

Fairness is, however, the substance of contemporary liberal understandings of providence. We expect our political leaders to balance the claims of competing interest groups while appealing to the broadest audience, and God should do nothing less. John Rawls, the great theoretician of American fairness, has articulated the rules of democracy by picturing what he calls the veil of ignorance.[3] He imagines the founders of a democratic state sitting behind a veil, stripped of any knowledge about what kind of family, education, income, or religious beliefs they might have. This self-imposed ignorance would force them to make political decisions from the standpoint of utter neutrality and objectivity. Not knowing what station in life they might be born into, they would naturally devise a political system that establishes a completely flat playing field. Nobody would be favored based on any personal or hereditary characteristics. Everyone would be treated equally.

Of course, politicians do not operate this way. Democracies are especially prone to special-interest groups and the influence of the wealthy. Nevertheless, Rawls argues that public policy makers should act as if they were behind a veil of ignorance. Politicians should not take into account any preferences based on personal history but should instead act according to principles that everyone can accept. In a word, politicians should be as fair as God. It is hard to know which came first: liberal democracy or liberal versions of the doctrine of providence. Liberal theologians have long pictured God as acting in a position similar to Rawls's original ignorance. God stands behind a veil, willfully suspending any knowledge of our personal attributes and thus dealing with everyone with the same evenhandedness, especially when it comes to God's relationship to nation-states. According to liberal theology, God does not take into account particular histories of virtue or the potential for promoting good in the world embodied in national histories. God, in other words, does not play favorites. If anyone is special, then everyone is.

Liberal political philosophy is not the only symptom of our inability to imagine that a good God can exercise preferential judgments. One of the most popular religious philosophies in the twentieth century was process philosophy. Founded by an English logician and mathematician, Alfred North Whitehead, it caught on only in America, under the leadership of Charles Hartshorne. Process philosophy rejects the traditional portrait of God as all-knowing and unchanging. Instead, God is a part of the world and has only limited power in pulling the world toward the good. There is, in fact, no absolute good toward which history is heading. Every entity, from inanimate objects to people, has its own most appropriate good, a level of existence where it maximizes its relationship to the world in freedom and self-fulfillment. Environmentalists like process philosophy because it emphasizes the way in which everything is related to everything else. Nothing stands alone, including God. In the hands of some process thinkers, God is the world's conscience, sternly reminding us of our obligations to others and encouraging us to live up to our potential. In the hands of other process thinkers, God is more like a cosmic cheerleader, praising our progress and sympathizing with our pain.

The process God is nothing if not nice, which is to say, fair. Process philosophy, in fact, subjects God to the forces of democratization, distributing the divine power to everyone. In political terms, God is a master proceduralist who shows no favoritism. God is so fair, according to process philosophy, that God prefers to soften God's image by relating to the world through persuasion, rather than direct intervention. Accordingly, God never acts unilaterally. Indeed, God is the ultimate multilateralist, given that God coordinates the actions of a network of entities in order to urge the world toward peace and harmony. Just as democracies resist locating decision making in individuals and prefer to think that a decision can be the product of a series of group discussions, process philosophy does not think of God as a decision maker. Instead, God sets goals, frames the agenda, and makes priorities, but God then sits back and lets us do all the work. God is a manager, assigning tasks to others while assessing the outcomes. While such delegation doubtlessly compliments our egos, it hardly renders providence more comprehensible, or trustworthy. Who wants to think about life as a political convention where God is working behind the scene and every delegate is occupied with urgent activity even though the candidate has already been chosen?

Process philosophy also models God's relationship to the world upon the laws of science. God is thus portrayed as having a uniform relationship to the world. That is, God's relationship to every entity at every time is exactly the same. God does not throw dice with the universe, for process philosophers, because that would give some creatures a better chance at success than others. God gives each creature the same possibilities as any other. Indeed, God extends the same benefits to inanimate objects as well as living beings, because God does not want to show favoritism of any kind. Creatures, because of their differences in levels of apprehension, take something different from God for their own purposes, but God's purposes remain resolutely the same for all. God does not treat us differently, which means that God treats us with a bit of indifference. God is, in other words, supremely fair.

While it is a popular move by theologians to apply the principles of liberal proceduralism to the doctrine of providence, popular Christianity in America has been unmoved by such metaphysical constraints. American Christians know better than to think that the inscrutable ways of providence can be reduced to the idea of fairness. If that were possible, then Ludwig Feuerbach would be right that religion is nothing more than a projection of cultural ideals from earth below to the heavens above. Americans believe in democracy, but they also believe that God acts in the world in decisive ways, and they know how to hold these two sets of beliefs together without confusing them with each other. That is, God is not a democrat—the divine power is not dependent on the ratification of a majority vote—even though God surely favors democracy, given all the other political options humans have devised.

Connecting God to democracy is one thing, while connecting God to capitalism is another, even though democracy and capitalism, especially in America, are themselves intrinsically connected. This latter point is an important one for American history and is often overlooked. Americans not only created a unique form of democracy, they also transformed capitalism. According to T. H. Breen, the period leading up to the Revolutionary War witnessed a politicization of the marketplace.[4] Providence was the intellectual idea that brought Americans together, but consumer goods were the material means by which Americans recognized their shared destiny. When colonial Americans rose up in support of the punished Bostonians, who had dumped the English tea into the Boston Harbor, resistance to English commercial control grew steadily in each of the colonies and a new nation came into being. The pursuit of happiness through consumption and the pursuit of salvation through the free exercise of religion were united in one political revolution.

Of course, capitalism is capable of succeeding on its own terms without being in need of the blessing of the church. The question remains, however, as to the role capitalism plays in God's providential orchestration of human history. A generation ago, scholars like Michael Novak and Robert Benne, in reaction against those who wanted to give socialism one last push over the top, defended capitalism as the economic form that most closely incorporates and protects the various Christian virtues of freedom, the integrity of the individual, the value of sacrifice, and hope for the future.[5] While it would take not a small library to hold all the books devoted to Christian socialism, the idea that there might be something like a Christian capitalism still strikes many people as a self-contradiction. Perhaps the strongest argument in support of capitalism is that it provides the best means for the creation of wealth and subsequently the best opportunity for the poor to improve their material conditions. Redistribution programs have the unintended consequences of empowering the state, which leads to an inefficient use of economic resources and thus a lower standard of living for everyone. Redistribution programs are also co-opted by the middle class and, even when they help the poor, they decrease the incentive for creativity and responsibility, which are the very virtues that capitalism cultivates. Novak is clear about the task of capitalism in a global economy: "The task is to arrange our institutions so that all the poor of the world may exit from poverty."[6] Critics of capitalism often have no answer to capitalism's capacity to create wealth, and so they are forced to deplore its spiritual poverty, but the alternative—socialization of industry and state control of the economy—is likely to have even more dire spiritual consequences. Rejecting capitalism for its spiritual poverty while neglecting its achievements in pulling so many people out of material poverty is simply too easy.

Capitalism is not only good economics. It can also be good politics. Richard John Neuhaus has been outspoken in defending capitalism as the best way to preserve democracy and thus as an important complement to Christianity. Neuhaus is the author of the important declaration, "Christianity and Democracy," which was adopted by the Institute on Religion and Democracy in 1981. Neuhaus follows the lead of Pope John Paul II, who in his encyclical *Centesimus Annus* (1991) affirmed the morally positive role businesses play in creating wealth for societies and the subsequent good of limited government, the protection of human rights, and the rule of law. Neuhaus admits that the Bible does not offer a blueprint for a Christian form of political order, just as he admits the limitations of democracy and capitalism. Nevertheless, capitalism appears to be a necessary (but not sufficient!) condition for democracy, and thus it warrants critical approval. The document, written at the height of the Cold War, begins and ends with the declaration that Jesus is Lord. More controversially, it also suggests that, on balance, America has been a force for good in the world.

On the issue of an American providence, however, the document is very careful. America has a singular responsibility in the present world-historical moment, but it is not a new Israel. God has made no special covenant with America. "However, because America is a large and influential part of [God's] creation, because America is the home of most of the heirs of Israel of old, and because this is a land in which his church is vibrantly free to live and proclaim the Gospel to the world, we believe that America has a peculiar place in God's promises and purposes."[7] Neuhaus offers a definition of what it means for America to be *under God* that is congruent with the Calvinistic understanding of providence. "Under God" means "first of all, a nation under judgment." He calls on American Christians to be stewards of democracy, and emphasizes how America is the "primary bearer of democratic possibility in the world today." Nevertheless, Neuhaus resists the language of chosenness, preferring instead simply to speak of America's "peculiar place in God's promises and purposes." To the extent that being chosen can imply that America supersedes Israel, that language should be resoundingly rejected. However, even Neuhaus's substitute phrase of "a peculiar place" resonates with the concept of being chosen for a special purpose.

Capitalism, Christianity, and democracy are sufficiently intertwined that pulling one out of the equation might leave all three undone, to everyone's detriment. Neuhaus ends his document with a strong statement: "The debate is between those who do believe and those who do not believe that there is a necessary linkage between Christian faith and human freedom."[8] Such comments no doubt will make a lot of readers nervous, and I do want to acknowledge that good reasons exist for the hesitancy of theologians to once again plunge into the relationship between providence and America. Theological reflection on providence has been swept aside by the rightful admiration of Northern hemisphere theologians for the insistence by Southern hemisphere theologians that world history is not identical to the history of the wealthy and the powerful. History might be written by the victors, but God stands with those who have been swept aside or are just barely hanging on. Liberation theology embraces preferentiality with the same passion that liberalism rejects it, but the consequences for the doctrine of providence are equally deleterious.

The argument from liberation theology is not just that the Southern hemisphere is as much a part of God's plan as the North. That innocuous claim would brook no disagreement or controversy. Liberation theologians go further than this when they insist that God prefers the poor over the rich. They point to a variety of biblical texts to support their position, but their argument is ultimately Christological. Their ambition, however, is not just to change how we read the Bible. They want to change the course of world history, especially the conflict between the rich and the poor nations of the world. The payoff of their claim that God prefers the poor is none other than a providential reading of history which argues that socialism, rather than capitalism, is blazing the trail of God's march through history.

God prefers the poor, liberation theologians argue, because God became a poor person to suffer on our behalf. Moreover, given that Jesus reveals God's true nature to us, we can conclude that God is not just *like* the poor, but that God *is* poor. It is good to take the humanity of God literally, but to what extent does poverty serve as the best framework for God's providential guidance of history? Is "poverty" even adequate as a conceptual description of God's particular entry into humanity in the event of the incarnation? Jesus certainly spoke in favor of the poor, but to what extent was Jesus himself really poor? The incarnation is a downward movement from the divine to the human, but Jesus was not born into the bottom of the human economy.

Scholars like Martin Hengel and Walter Pilgrim have made a persuasive case
that Jesus belonged to the middle class of his day.[9] The poor were certainly
numerous in Jesus's Palestine, but Galilee was no economic or cultural back-
water. Jesus was born into a two-parent, stable family. As the firstborn son,
he had an inheritance, an education, and a career waiting for him. He was a
tradesman whose carpentry skills were most likely in high demand. He
attracted tax collectors as well as the poor and the sick. Some of his followers
owned their own fishing boats, which would have provided them with a
good living. The crowds who gathered around him might have been full of
the most destitute in Palestine, but his disciples hardly fit that category.
Christianity was never the mass movement of the poor that some of those
on the political left wish it had been. As Christianity began to spread, according to Wayne Meeks, the good news was passed along by merchants and arti-
sans, not beggars and outcasts.[10]

True, Jesus's message was one of liberation for the poor, and he could be
very critical of the wealthy, but as Luke Johnson has argued, "poor" and
"rich" were deeply metaphorical terms in his teachings.[11] Jesus did not reject
material comfort as sinful in itself. He used open feasts to spread his message,
and he even talked about the kingdom of God in terms of the bounty of a
banquet. Indeed, Jesus identified with all classes, types, and kinds of people.
He preached liberation from false worship of wealth as well as comfort from
the struggle with poverty and disease. John R. Schneider, in his careful study
of this topic, concludes that Jesus taught a message of delight, not deprivation. It is "a fundamental biblical theme that material prosperity (rightly
understood) is the condition that God envisions for all human beings. It
describes the condition that God has in view for human beings in eternity.
And it describes the condition that God (circumstances being right) desires
for human beings now."[12] Schneider is careful to distinguish his own position
from the "prosperity gospel" that televangelists frequently preach, whereby
faith becomes a guarantee of financial, rather than spiritual, freedom.
Nevertheless, the gospel of wealth is no more out of sync with the New
Testament than the radical gospel of the left, which recruits Jesus for a wholesale rejection of capitalism as contrary to the kingdom. Jesus preached an
excess of grace that took the form of exuberant celebrations. He envisioned
an affluence that would transform our attitudes about security and selfishness
while offering an unlimited scope of participation and engagement.

I am not denying that Jesus led a frugal life without many private possessions, but poverty was not an end in itself in his ministry. Poverty for Jesus
was a teaching tool, not an ideology. The whole problem with discussing
poverty and Jesus is that poverty is as much a state of mind as it is a lack of
stuff. The Bible thus recognizes the poor in spirit as well as the poor in pocket-
book. The former can be poor with a lot of stuff, while the latter can be free

in their material deprivation. Strictly defined, to be poor is to be subjected to forces that are out of one's control. However much money Judas kept for Jesus and his disciples, Jesus was certainly not restricted by the circumstances of his birth. Jesus was not poor in the sense of being unable to achieve his life goals because of his lack of economic resources. God, too, is not poor in the sense of being unable to accomplish God's kingdom through the struggle of history.

Frederick Herzog, who frequently uses the language of the poorness of God, was one of the earliest North American proponents of liberation theology.[13] His work was sophisticated in its attempt to draw from without merely repeating the insights of his Southern colleagues. Herzog warned other North American theologians against any easygoing appropriation of liberation themes, recognizing that American theology, like the American economy, can consume great amounts of imported products without undergoing any observable change. Nevertheless, he insisted that the Holy Spirit is speaking to the North through the theological labors of Southern theologians. What is ironic, then, is how Herzog had to go to great lengths to deny the central insight of liberation theology—an insight that is also the central argument of this book. Liberationists think that theologians must reflect on their own particular historical trajectories if they want to do justice to the movement of the Holy Spirit. Liberation theologians, in other words, are committed to a providential reading of the history of their own nation-states. They did not always make the doctrine of providence explicit in their works, but it is the foundation of their favoritism for the poor, and Herzog was very explicit about resisting its importation into the North American theological scene.

On a theoretical level, the extent to which liberation theology is dependent on the doctrine of providence is undeniable. The equation of salvation with liberation is, as John Milbank has argued, fueled by a belief in an "economic providence," a "purely immanent process" that unfolds according to the logic of social forces.[14] The doctrine of providence also plays a more practical role in liberation theology. Although there is more theology in Latin America than the liberation variety, liberation theology cannot be understood outside of its geopolitical context. From the beginning, liberation theology was an attempt to give voice to a specific region and its unique concerns. This does not keep liberation theologians from universalizing their method; they typically insist that social location is crucial for every theological project. Regardless, their social location is certainly crucial for their attempt to synthesize a Marxist view of political liberation with a Christian view of salvation. Liberation theologians intend to liberate Latin American theology from the dominance of European models and methods. Their theology, in other words, is thoroughly providential.

Liberation theologians, however, are uncomfortable talking about providence directly. They argue that this doctrine has been used to keep the poor in their place. They mask their concern with providence by talking instead about what they call a "unitary view of history." By this, liberationists mean that God does not work through a level of history that transcends the economic, social, and political spheres. There is only one history: the history through which God calls us to join in the divine labor. If history is unitary, then Christians cannot just work for a supernatural good. The kingdom of God is not laid over reality like a thin veneer of glossy comfort. What we do here and now is what God is using to build a kingdom that is very much a part of this world.

The unitary view of history is expressed by many non–liberation theologians as well. It is, arguably, not an innovative theological move; instead, it is just plain good theology. Certainly, the unitary view is necessary for the full development of the doctrine of providence. Neuhaus, in the book *Time toward Home*, wholeheartedly embraces the unitary view of history. "I look for the vindication of myself in my historical particularity, and of the American experience of which I am a part. . . . All of history is *Heilsgeschichte*, salvation history. All history is the history of redemption. There is not a sacred history and then a secular history. There is one, universal history to which God has irrevocably committed himself."[15] Although Neuhaus can speak in much the same way as the liberationists, he has a very different political agenda, one that causes Herzog much discomfort. Herzog accuses Neuhaus of turning American history into a means of divine revelation. A more accurate statement would be that Neuhaus is trying to do justice to a providential reading of American history.

Herzog is perceptive enough to recognize that the liberationist view of history, which he commends for its emphasis on the concrete and the economic, is the same view that lies behind America's particular affinity for the language of providence. It is a view of history that other nations share as well. It would be interesting, for example, to compare America's sense of mission with the chosenness of the Polish nation. Poland has a long history of interpreting in a messianic light its relationship to other nations. The Poles threw back the Turkish invasion in Vienna in 1683 and stopped the Red Army at the gates of Warsaw in 1920. More than through military victories, the Poles see themselves as having been chosen to suffer on behalf of the Catholic faith. Poland was often occupied, surrounded by hostile forces, betrayed by friends, and conquered by enemies, yet the Poles stood fast in their faith, and it was not just any kind of faith. Poland was chosen to purify the Catholic faith—hence its motto, *Polonia semper fidelis*—and represent it in its fullest form. This "Christ of the nations" played an especially important role in world history as the last line of defense against Russian communist atheism.

The election of Cardinal Karol Wojtyla as pope in 1978 struck most Poles as a vindication of their faithfulness. John Paul II was immersed in Polish messianism as a young man, and it has shaped his papacy. Polish providentialism legitimated his efforts to turn the tide against communism. In John Paul II, Poland has indeed fulfilled a very special role in global history.

Perhaps his special relationship to Polish providentialism has led John Paul II to be skeptical of liberation providentialism. If the Latin American view of history had more Calvin and less Marx, liberation theologians would probably get into a lot less trouble. Marx's view of history is little more than a secularization of the Christian theme of providence. Marx substitutes the socialist state for the inevitable triumph of the kingdom of God, economic liberation for spiritual salvation, the proletariate for the church, class warfare for struggle with satanic forces, and the laws of leftist economics for the law of grace, all in an attempt to reduce the spiritual to the material. Latin American theologians were drawn to a Marxist reading of history not only for its socialist economics but also for its emphasis on the working class as the agent of historical change. They modified the traditional understanding of providence as the idea that God sustains and supports everything and everyone by arguing that God directs history by working most closely with those who have the greatest economic needs.

Much is still to be learned from liberationist interpretations of providence. Liberationists rightly insist that providence should not be minimized as a mere footnote to the doctrine of creation. Providence also should not be subsumed into the divine attribute of omnipresence. God might be everywhere, but God always works "here" in order to move us to a "there." To move too quickly to generalize God's work as a universal presence is to miss God's plan for history. All of this is common currency in liberationist discussions of providence, but Herzog has nothing but contempt for any attempt to apply this providential theology to the American context. "We can agree with them on a unitary view of history defined on *God's terms*. Some of us, however, vehemently disagree with the unitary view of history defined on Uncle Sam's terms."[16] In his view, there is no positive role for America to play on the world's stage, given God's antagonism toward our power and wealth.

If a unitary view of history for North America can only lead to mischief and self-delusion, the only option is for us Northerners to read our own history in terms of the Latin American concept of God's "preferential option for the poor."[17] In terms of our own moral responsibility, much can be said for the preferential option for the poor. The preferential option is God's command to us. That is, God would have us give the poor a place of priority in our lives. If the category of "the poor" is interpreted broadly enough, it might also make sense to say that God gives them preference, given that God sides with all those who are sufficiently poor in spirit as to desire comfort in his arms. It is not clear, however, that this concept is an adequate description of how God works through history. Globalized markets, for example, are the best way of raising the standard of living for most people, but open markets also tend to benefit the wealthy disproportionate to their benefit for the poor. Does that mean that God cannot work through market capitalism to help the poor?

God works through history to achieve the final consummation of God's wishes, which is a kingdom that will reorder our priorities and reestablish our lives in their proper perspective. To accomplish this task, God places agents, both individual and collective, into a position where they can do what God wants. How God chooses and arranges such agents is at the heart of the mystery of God's plan. The basic fact of God having chosen Israel is the starting point for theological reflection on providence. We cannot get behind this choice, no matter how much our minds resist it, to a reason that supersedes it. To try to find such higher ground—that is, to try to explain why God organizes the distribution of grace in this way—would be to demote Israel to the status of an example or an illustration and thus deprive Israel of her unique role in world history. God has his own preferences, so specifying what God can and cannot use to achieve his purposes is misguided.

God moves nations by working through history, not against it. By definition, the poor are not effective agents of significant historical change. Even Gandhi's movement had the backing of wealthy friends, and those who marched to the sea for salt were well educated in his philosophical and political agenda. Martin Luther King's movement had the institutional support of the black churches and drew from the burgeoning black middle class, as well as sympathetic Northerners. The children's crusade in the Middle Ages and the peasant's revolt during the Protestant Reformation were truly eruptions of the poor into history, and they disappeared without a trace.

The poor *are* agents of God's grace (as opposed to being agents of significant historical change) precisely because they are occasions for the nonpoor to open themselves to aiding others. The poor need our gifts, and this need is one of the means by which God puts grace into play in our lives. The neediness of the poor does not mean that the poor cannot themselves be givers. In fact, the poor are more dependent on a giving economy than the well-off, who ordinarily give only token or symbolic gifts to each other, because they have no dire material needs. What the well-to-do need most, however, is to realize just how much they need others. To be poor in spirit or to become like a child—what the Gospels require of those who want to follow Jesus—is to open oneself to what others can give to you as an expression of how God gives us everything we need. The poor thus give the wealthy the opportunity to give real (as opposed to merely symbolic) gifts and to receive in return relationships that transcend the capitalist economy of exchange. After all, it is easy to give—giving is an expression of strength and power—but hard to learn how to receive. To receive is to acknowledge our weakness and to risk being transformed by others as their gifts draw us out into relationships of mutual obligation and moral responsibility. To live your life so that you are not dependent on others might be one version of the American dream, but such a life is a Christian nightmare. If we are not open about our need for what others have to give us, then how can we be receptive to God? Giving to others is practically impossible to do in such a way that it does not appear condescending or patronizing. That is, giving is impossible to do gracefully, which is why it must be an act of grace, not a triumph of the human moral will.

Latin American theologians reject the economic language of development because of its acknowledgment of the "dependence" of the South upon the North. Liberation theologians put their hope in the possibility of the poor gaining economic independence from the North, just as these theologians have struggled for intellectual independence from their European roots. Charity is, for the liberationists, a poor substitute for the kind of structural transformations in Latin American economies that would result in the radical redistribution of wealth. The problems entailed in charity, however, cannot be solved by passing responsibility for the poor from individuals to governments. Indeed, giving developing nations more power to nationalize their economies is precisely the wrong policy, according to most economists today. Developing nations need to adopt policies that promote investment and growth rather than the restriction of capital.

God's providence is productive of change, not reiterative of the past. Developing countries need not repeat Western history by climbing the ladder of industrialization in order to participate in the global economy. Bangalore call centers demonstrate how economic growth can take new and surprising forms. The poor need opportunities more than charity. Hernando de Soto, a Peruvian economist and a widely hailed public policy thinker, has demonstrated that the world's poor have much greater assets than economists ever suspected.[18] The value of their savings is many times greater than all the foreign aid these countries have received since 1945. The problem of their lack of economic growth lies in political corruption that inhibits investment and inept legal systems that do not protect property rights. Economist William Easterly concurs.[19] Forgiving the debts of third-world governments—an act of charity promoted by Bono, the pope, and the Dalai Lama—can backfire by serving to perpetuate those countries' internal problems. Debt forgiveness enables an entrenched class of government officials to siphon off economic rewards from the hard work of the poor. Easterly points out that debt forgiveness has been in place for twenty years, and its record is not good. It encourages further patronage and corruption rather than responsible fiscal policies.

Forgiving the debts of poor countries might seem like a proper extension of the gospel ethic from the realm of the church to the arena of international relations, but charity works best on an individual level. Charity is not without social significance. Nations cannot grow economically any more than individuals can grow morally in isolation from each other. The idea that rich nations should give to the poor with no expectations for some kind of return on that gift is as irresponsible as an individual giving away money without any thought to its use. Not only do the poor obligate the wealthy by drawing them into relations of giving, they also have obligations to use those gifts wisely. Gift relationships are reciprocal, no matter how asymmetrical the power relations are. If the poor are not to become chronically dependent on the gifts of the well-off, they have to be open to learning how to turn those gifts into the power to earn their way into giving something back. The same general principle holds true for poor countries.

Liberation theologians are not to be faulted for trying to imagine how God is providing North Americans with opportunities to work for global justice. Americans do have a responsibility to work for a global culture where the oppressed and impoverished can flourish. Where liberation theology goes wrong is in its rush to replace the power of markets with the practice of forgiveness. Moralism of this kind actually promotes a cheap forgiveness compared to the costs of working for democracy and open markets. God has brought America to a position where, in spite of our complacency, we are forced to act on behalf of others. Giving away money is not the only or even the most important sacrifice we can make. Liberating Iraq, for example, will benefit the Iraqis more than us. It will also, of course, benefit us, because we must change the world in order to be able to survive in it.

When the preferential option for the poor is used as the hermeneutical key to history, a drastically dualistic view of North and South results. The implication is that nothing good can come from America, because America is run by the wealthy, not the poor. The North is to find its destiny in the history of the South, not in its own strengths and weaknesses. In chapter 6 of this book, I argue that the Southern hemisphere is playing a leading role in the world, but it is a role that has to do with the globalization of Christianity and not the spread of socialism.

Liberationists have been misled by Marx to confuse the end of history with its means. The liberation of the poor is one of the basic indications of the kingdom of God, but the poor do not have the power to make justice happen on their own. If the poor did have that kind of power, the society "they" created would exclude "others" who disagreed with them and thus would hardly be just. The fact that "the poor" is a political category that requires some form of representation in governmental and civic institutions means that justice will always be a contested notion. A basic lesson of postmodernism is that the moral debate over justice cannot be resolved by an appeal to a universally rational principle. The question of justice is less about moral philosophy than it the source of legitimate political authority.

Providentially speaking, liberation theology gambled its fortunes on the future of socialism and appears to have lost the bet. With the electoral defeat of the Sandinistas, the continued dwindling of Cuba's political status and economic fortune, and the general bankruptcy of socialist systems across the globe, liberation theology is in an undeniable state of crisis. The high hope that a church of the poor could provide an alternative to transnational structures of capitalism is in definite disarray. Even the staunchest supporters of liberation theology now discuss the extent to which the poor themselves can be oppressors, cooperating with and perpetuating various forms of prejudice and violence. The poor, merely by virtue of their economic status, do not necessarily embody Christ's cruciform presence in the world.

Nevertheless, radical critics of capitalism like Daniel M. Bell Jr. remain confident that "God has chosen the crucified people as a vehicle of the Gospel and out of them God is building a new community."[20] For Bell, the poor become a sacrament of salvation when they advance the cause of justice. But how do they "build a new community"? Is this process of building a new community spontaneous, or does it take work, money, power, and political connections? Is the new community a merely spiritual affair, an invisible church, or does it exist within the network of institutions that compose a political economy? Bell admits that there is now a consensus among liberationists that structures of civil society are essential for Latin America to move forward.[21] Without institutions that mediate between the government and the people, advances in education and the distribution of wealth will be negligible. To transform society, the rule of law needs to be reformulated from the top down. Systems need to be put in place that promote financial investment and individual savings. People need to have confidence in their collective future in order to make the plans necessary for economic growth. Civil society is something that America has been particularly good at cultivating, and the relationship of robust civil participation to capitalism is strong and deep. Bell, however, does not explain how the new community of the church of the poor can be sustained without some recognition of the virtues of democracy and capitalism.

The more liberationists accept the need for limited government, civil society, and the creation of wealth through capitalism, the less radical they sound. It should be no surprise, then, that some of the most recent liberationists are moving away from political theory altogether in their search for a radical critique of all things American. Joerg Rieger, a student of Herzog, admits that liberation requires a productive imagination as much as economic redistribution. The project of liberation theology becomes one not of breaking the class barriers to economic wealth but of breaking through the imagination and into reality. The imagination that needs to be broken belongs, for Rieger, to the wealthy, not the poor. We wealthy North Americans need the poor more than they need us. We need to imagine what their lives really are like in order to have any hope of changing our own lives.

Rieger thus reconstructs providence in psychoanalytic terms: "History as the history of God's liberation of the oppressed aims at a reconstruction of the past in relation to the present in terms of the reappropriation of what has so far been repressed in the history of the victors."[22] The poor live by hope, he argues, and thus they are open to God's movement in history in ways that the wealthy are not. The wealthy in turn can learn to wait upon God by attending to the poor. It is in the poor that the powerful find God. So far, so good. But Rieger's point is more ominous. He reads the past as the subconsciousness of a traumatized humanity, so that our collective memory needs to be forced to retrieve what we have repressed. He is not so much interested in the poor for their own sake but as the means by which the modern bourgeois self can be overthrown. By retrieving the poor, middle-class Americans will be forced to rewrite the past, which is historical revisionism on a massive scale. The idea that history is the story of the triumph of the poor over the wealthy is the great "imaginary" foundation of all forms of radical political thought. It is an alternative—before the fall of communism, it was the most powerful alternative—not only to the story of capitalism but also to the Christian view of providence.

NOTES

1. Francis Fukuyama, *The End of History and the Last Man* (San Francisco: HarperCollins, 1992), esp. 197–98, 316. In a recent essay, Fukuyama recognizes that the war against terrorism is civilizational, a topic I return to in chapter 6. See Francis Fukuyama, "Their Target: The Modern World," *Newsweek*, December 17, 2001.

2. Adam Bellow, *In Praise of Nepotism: A Natural History* (New York: Doubleday, 2003).

3. John Rawls, *A Theory of Justice* (Cambridge, MA: Harvard University Press, 1971).

4. T. H. Breen, *The Marketplace of Revolution: How Consumer Politics Shaped American Independence* (Oxford: Oxford University Press, 2004).

5. Michael Novak, *The Spirit of Capitalism* (New York: American Enterprise Institute, 1982); Robert Benne, *The Ethic of Democratic Capitalism: A Moral Reassessment* (Philadelphia: Fortress Press, 1981). Also see the discussion in Charles Taylor, *Religion and the Making of Society* (Cambridge: Cambridge University Press, 1994), chap. 10.

6. Michael Novak, "Catholic Social Teaching, Markets, and the Poor," in Doug Bandow and David L. Schindler, eds., *Wealth, Poverty, and Human Destiny* (Wilmington, DE: ISI Books, 2003), 59. For documentation on the success of capitalism, see Johan Norberg, *In Defense of Global Capitalism* (Washington, DC: Cato Institute, 2003).

7. The document has been reprinted in *First Things* 66 (October 1996): 30–36 (http://firstthings.com/ftissues/ft9610/documentation.html).

8. Ibid.

9. Martin Hengel, *Property and Riches in the Early Church*, trans. John Bowden (Philadelphia: Fortress Press, 1974); Walter Pilgrim, *Good News to the Poor: Wealth and Poverty in Luke-Acts* (Minneapolis: Augsburg, 1981).

10. Wayne Meeks, *The First Urban Christians: The Social World of the Apostle Paul* (New Haven, CT: Yale University Press, 1983).

11. Luke Timothy Johnson, *The Literary Function of Possessions in Luke-Acts* (Missoula, MT: Scholars Press, 1977).

12. John R. Schneider, *The Good of Affluence: Seeking God in a Culture of Wealth* (Grand Rapids: Eerdmans, 2002), 3.

13. Joerg Rieger, ed., *Theology from the Belly of the Whale: A Frederick Herzog Reader* (Harrisburg, PA: Trinity Press International, 1999), 271, 345.

14. John Milbank, *Theology and Social Theory* (Oxford: Basil Blackwell, 1990), 245. For a helpful discussion of Milbank on this point, see D. Stephen Long, *Divine Economy: Theology and the Market* (New York: Routledge, 2000), 245–50.

15. Richard John Neuhaus, *Time toward Home* (New York: Seabury Press, 1975), 64.

16. Rieger, *Theology from the Belly of the Whale*, 155.

17. For a helpful evaluation of this phrase, see Richard John Neuhaus, ed., *The Preferential Option for the Poor* (Grand Rapids: Eerdmans, 1988).

18. Hernando de Soto, *The Mystery of Capital: Why Capitalism Triumphs in the West and Fails Everywhere Else* (New York: Basic Books, 2000).

19. William Easterly, *The Elusive Quest for Growth: Economists' Adventures and Misadventure in the Tropics* (Cambridge, MA: MIT Press, 2002).

20. Daniel M. Bell Jr., *Liberation Theology after the End of History* (New York: Routledge, 2001), 168.

21. Ibid., 68.

22. Joerg Rieger, *Remember the Poor: The Challenge to Theology in the Twentieth Century* (Harrisburg, PA: Trinity Press International, 1998), 170.

CHAPTER FOUR

Resident Advisors vs. Resident Aliens:
9/11 and the Persistence of American Providence

"God Bless the U.S.A." is not only a slogan; it is also a song. And it is sung in churches across the nation. Written by Lee Greenwood in 1984, the song achieved the status of an anthem after 9/11. True to its genre, it is a bit jingoistic and saccharine, invoking an America where "the flag still stands for freedom and they can't take that away." The refrain of the song goes to the heart of providential America: "And I'm proud to be an American where at least I know I'm free. And I won't forget the men who died who gave that right to me." The refrain goes on to connect sacrifice, obligation, and love in what is almost a call to arms. When I first heard this song in church, sung by a high school student, I thought he crooned that he would not forget "the man" who died to set us free. He might have. I was shocked when I found the lyrics on the Web and realized my mistake. I was not upset at the idea of taking time in church to thank the veterans who have died in America's wars. A religion that preaches Christ sacrificed cannot ignore the deaths of those who give their lives for their nation. These Americans are motivated by a love for freedom that is born out of the freedom we find in Christ.

What shocked me was that I thought the song was more Christological than it is. I thought the song was making an explicit connection between American freedom and Jesus Christ—"the man"—who died to set us free. It *is* making that connection, of course, but in a much more subtle way than I expected. It is "the men" who died in battle who hold the place, so to speak, of the cross. According to the song, they give us our rights, not God. Of course, the words of the song should not be overanalyzed, and the Christians who sing and hear this song during worship services on Sunday mornings would be quick to acknowledge that any rights we possess ultimately come from God. The question remains: What is the relationship between the freedom we have as Americans and the freedom we have in Christ? What is the relation, in other words, between "the men" who died for America and "the man" who died for everyone?

Stanley Hauerwas, who is the best-known theologian in America today, would answer, "nothing."[1] He would agree with the sentiments expressed by the French philosopher Ernest Renan, who once said that a nation is a group of people united by a mistaken view about their past and a hatred of their neighbors. Hauerwas is perhaps best known for his book, written with William H. Willimon, *Resident Aliens*, but he is an extremely prolific writer who scatters his barbed commentary on American Christianity far and wide. He is single-handedly responsible for pushing political theology to the center of the study of Christianity in America, which is ironic because he does not believe in politics—even going so far as to advise his students not to vote. Even more ironic was the September 17, 2001, issue of *Time* magazine that declared Hauerwas "America's Best" theologian. Hauerwas, after all, is the one theologian who most tries to distance himself from even the best that America has to offer. Not since Reinhold Niebuhr—the one Christian thinker Hauerwas and his students love to hate—captured the covers of America's leading magazines has a theologian won these kinds of accolades.[2]

Part of the secret to Hauerwas's success is his populist appeal. He is an icon of the antiacademic crowd, with his disdain for the niceties of scholarship and discourse. He sometimes seems to go against received wisdom simply out of stubborn habit. In all that he writes, he brings a chunk of the frontier mentality of folksy exaggeration and noisy revivalism to the study of theology. Hauerwas also frequently thumbs his nose at the church for being an institution too quick to compromise with the world and too frequently more full of itself than the gospel. He thus appeals to the antiauthoritarian rebel at the heart of every American. Paradoxically, however, he relishes in blasting away at American patriotism and the ideology of individualism that undergirds so much of American history. Such iconoclasm makes him exasperating to more traditional Evangelicals, but it also makes him more alluring to the liberal academy. His rhetoric is thus an artful show, with enough bark to entice the most jaded of churchgoers and enough bite to annoy those who would just like to pass on by.

He seems to relish in administering his own particular brand of shock therapy to the church in America. Hauerwas insists that the American church is all but lost in the thickets of patriotic nationalism. In fact, the case can be made that the key to his entire theology is his anti-Americanism. Hauerwas has influenced a whole generation of theologians who make quick work of consumerism, patriotism, nationalism, and popular culture. His critique of all things American makes him so much more at home with liberals than conservatives. By continuously thumping on this theme, he is able to gain a larger academic audience than would ever listen to a more traditionally Evangelical theologian. Indeed, without his constant critique of everything American, he would be in danger of looking just like another Evangelical theologian. The key to his success, then, is the following formula: He urges the cultural elite to take traditional theology more seriously while at the same time assuring them that their left-leaning cultural and political assumptions can remain untroubled. Hauerwas's denunciations of America permit liberal Christians to sound as angry and alienated from popular culture as fundamentalists without requiring liberals to join an Evangelical church.

Hauerwas's tricky prose masks a complex relationship to American providence. He insists that all theology—indeed, all thinking—is fundamentally particular, yet he is allergic to the American penchant for thinking about the world in terms of itself. Ironically, Hauerwas is honest and open about the forces that have shaped his own religious outlook. He often talks about being raised Texan, to the extent that he even says he has a "Texan epistemology."[3] Perhaps this helps to explain his relationship to America, for as much as he claims his Texan heritage, he rarely acknowledges his dependence on the wider American context. He credits his Texan background for teaching him about the limitations of the Enlightenment model of the self-created individual. People have particular identities, Hauerwas insists, just as reason itself is shaped by the contours of narrative. Social location is everything. One might think that this emphasis on story and particularity would lead Hauerwas to meditate on the inevitable way that America has shaped his thinking, but the opposite is the case. When Hauerwas talks about America, he is clearly talking about a symbol, rather than trying to reflect on anything concrete and real. America symbolizes everything that is wrong in the modern world. America is the opposite of everything that Christianity must defend.

Hauerwas wants American Christians to choose between America and Christianity. This portrait of the contemporary Christian situation is woefully uninformed by sociology. Rather than addressing the fact of our multiple loyalties and showing us how each loyalty should be subordinated to (but not obliterated by) a greater good, Hauerwas uses the rhetoric of divided loyalties, as if we must constantly choose between the one and the many. I would argue that a more Augustinian account of Christian morality makes better sense of our fragmented lives. The choices God presents to us are not between an absolute good and a relative good, because all goods in this world are relatively situated with regard to the absolute. Our loves are disordered, but that does not mean that we should love only God. We love God by loving the things of the world in the right way. We find God through our love of family, our calling in the world, our support of friends, our care for the sick and elderly, our charity to the poor, even our love of nation, all of which are shaped by our participation in the church. We do not have to choose between church and nation any more than we have to choose between church and family or church and vocation.

Hauerwas's pride in having no theory of the state is probably his most frustrating rhetorical maneuver. This gloating is a bit disingenuous, because he clearly operates with an implicit, even if inchoate, political theory that he makes explicit when convenient. Reading him is like watching a magician who refuses to pull the rabbit out of the hat even though you know that's where he put it. He is thus able to make grand and sweeping claims about American sins with regard to consumerism, patriotism, capitalism, and individualism, but he refuses to elaborate on how Christians can improve the political order. When pressed, he complains that a theory of the state only encourages states—just as voting only encourages politicians—and nation-states need no encouragement. His idea that the church should be a counter-polis begs for sociological elaboration and support, and his understanding of Constantinianism borders, at times, on the simplistic and absurd. Yet he puts on a great enough show even if he wears some of his tricks on his sleeve.

In the end, one is left with a whirlwind of theological activity that is prototypically American in its quirky ambivalence about authority. Hauerwas rejects the authority of reason, the government, common sense, and (for the most part) the natural law, but he longs nostalgically for a time when churches could tell you who to marry, what job to take, and how to spend your money. Perhaps this tension over authority is as deep as one can go in Hauerwas's theology, the shaky foundation of this rabid antifoundationalist. If so, it makes for some fascinating reading. Each of his essays has an aphoristic quality, packing a punch that swings so wide as to stir up quite a mess before it hits its target. I hope that I have made it clear that, as much as I disagree with him, there are very few theologians I would rather read.

In *Resident Aliens*, he repeatedly insists that American Christians live in a colony, outpost, or isolated island in the sea of capitalism. Baptism transfers our citizenship "from one dominion to another." The idea of a Christian culture is, he suggests, "touchingly anachronistic." Freedom in a democracy is "the tyranny of our own desires." Christians who try to transform the world end up making faith in God private or irrelevant, because they give conventional political ideas only "a vaguely religious tint." Hauerwas can state that "God, not nations, rules the world," which leaves the impression that he does not think that God rules the world through the work of the nations. Although his language of resident aliens signals a retreat from the world, he insists that Christians use the church to launch an assault on American values. Above all, patriotism is to be avoided: "Merging one's personal aspirations within the aspirations of the nation, falling into step behind the flag, has long been a popular means of overcoming doubts about the substance of one's own life."[4]

Hauerwas treats theology not as an abstract discipline but rather as a combination of skills that can be learned only by going to church, so one would expect an extended discussion from him about the Christian skill of reading history providentially. He does pay lip service to providence. "The church is the colony that gives us resident aliens the interpretive skills whereby we know honestly what is happening and what to do about it." His subsequent reading of history, however, merely repeats the typical bromides of the left. Americans, he laments, "really do want to run the world, to set things right, to spread democracy and freedom everywhere. We really want to believe, and even Jesse Jackson wants to believe, that America is different from other nations. Tragically, none of this is true." He concludes, "Our grandest illusions about ourselves led to the greatest horrors of our history."[5] America's "best theologian" has absolutely no sympathy for the oldest American theological tradition.

Hauerwas scatters arguments high and low, so it should not be surprising that he can be accused of being inconsistent. One of his most dominant inconsistencies is his evaluation of democratic freedom. R. R. Reno perceptively argues that, by encouraging Christians to step back from political processes, Hauerwas replicates the liberal differentiation of church and state. "Hauerwas' conservativism with respect to the church—one cannot become too deeply enmeshed in the church—produces a liberalism with respect to all other forms of power."[6] Hauerwas is caught in the dilemma of presupposing the very freedoms that he emphatically denounces. He insists, like most communitarians, that democratic freedom is bad for communities like the church. The freedom to choose forces us to choose being a consumer in everything that we do, including going to church. Yet Hauerwas appeals to our freedom in asking us to act heroically by rejecting American influence on the church. He wants Christians to exercise their freedom of religion by withdrawing their support from the very nation that has dedicated itself to establishing and protecting religious freedom.

As a Methodist, Hauerwas is even further enmeshed in the American commitment to religious freedom. Hauerwas has long insisted on the importance of sanctification. Individual effort, guided by grace, can achieve some degree of holiness in this world. Part of that holiness, he thinks, entails a rejection of the corrosive effects of American democracy. Hauerwas thinks Christians should be actively engaged in the world; he just does not think that democracy is the proper channel for that engagement. If American Christians should not delight in being American, yet they should work for the coming of the kingdom of God, then it follows that they should strive to become more international instead, supporting transnational institutions in the attempt to build an alternative to liberal democracy. Hauerwas should argue that Americans need to become citizens of the world, but this would entail more of a political theology than Hauerwas is willing to articulate. Hauerwas does not envision any constructive political correlate to his ecclesiology. The best way to do politics in a democracy is to do theology; the best way to change the world is to go to church.

Hauerwas does read history providentially, but he offers only half the story of God's relationship to America. That is, he holds America to its side of the covenantal bargain while, at the same time, denying it any special blessings from God. After 9/11, one would think that this harsh treatment of America's role in the world would be a hard sell. If, as it is often said, 9/11 was born in the prisons of Egypt, then America surely has a stake in promoting democracy abroad.[7] Christianity and America are sufficiently intertwined that it seems inappropriate at this point in our nation's history to argue that the church should withdraw from civil society. Yet that is the horn that Hauerwas keeps blowing, no matter how much it sounds like a call to retreat.

Hauerwas is a great rhetorician, but his timing is off. Preaching the incompatibility of church and nation after 9/11 just sounds wrong. It sounds wrong because it is wrong. America needs Christianity, and Christians need America. Part of Hauerwas's problem is that he equates democracy with the inevitable triumph of liberal secularism. This overly intellectualized account of democracy does not do descriptive justice to the ways Christianity has flourished in America. As philosopher Jeffrey Stout has noted, "Every Christian is free to affirm God's ultimate authority over every political community, including his or her own, whether or not others agree. Indeed, Christians who make this affirmation are bound to infer that Christ is now ruling democratic political communities providentially, no matter who acknowledges or fails to acknowledge his authority."[8] For Hauerwas, Christians have provided too much support for the American political system, but the truth is that democracy needs more theological support, not less. Far from being resident aliens in America, Christians are resident advisors. Christians can reside comfortably in America because their faith provided the foundation for the success and the shape of the new nation. Christians, however, should not become too comfortable, because they have an obligation to keep America on a steady course.

When Hauerwas argues that "Christians must withdraw their support" from any political system that "resorts to violence in order to maintain internal order and external security," he is being either disingenuous or irresponsible.[9] When Christians go to church on Sunday mornings, they drive on government-paid roads to a tax-exempt institution that depends on the fire and police departments for safety. Should Christians refuse to pay that part of their taxes that goes to the police and the military? Hauerwas does not say.

Even his cherished ideal of pacifism is thrown around more as a quixotic gesture than a concrete platform of effecting change. In an era without the draft, it is too easy to say that one is a pacifist without having to face the pressure of a government demanding our direct participation in war. Surely Christians should work for peace in the world, but the very term "pacifism" denotes an absolute principle that trumps every other moral concern. A better term than "pacifism" for believers would be "peace first" Christians, which suggests that Christians strive for peace but do not make a god out of it.

Hauerwas rejects the idea that he is "sectarian," but his rhetoric points in no other direction. Stout is right to argue that "commitment to democracy does not entail the rejection of tradition. It requires jointly taking responsibility for the criticism and renewal of tradition and for the justice of our social and political arrangements."[10] The church breeds hypocrisy and sloth— it is as fallen as any human institution—but there is no reason to blame that on democracy. One can support democracy without being a secular liberal.

Christians can contribute to America—indeed, Christians should be responsible advocates of the American project of freedom—precisely because the idea of America is so dependent on a flexible doctrine of providence. Christians have as much or more to say about that than any other group. America needs skilled practitioners in providential hermeneutics. What has become more apparent to me, in the shadow of 9/11, is the extent to which the political left—Hauerwas included—still relies on the rhetoric of providence, even while rejecting its status as a Christian doctrine. The use of providence in polemical disputes, as well as the enlistment of providence to explain American tragedies, has a long history in American theology. Providence not only brought the young nation together but also was the chief polemical tool for partisan debate, especially in the 1790s, when America began to divide into two political parties. National unity was so cherished that the very idea of political parties was anathema to many. Providentially, God had guided America through the Revolution in order to be a blessing to the world, but how could the new country take on such a fantastic task if it were so terribly divided? Federalists and Republicans alike appealed to interpretations of Providence to put their political enemies on the other side of God. The polemics came to a climax with the War of 1812. As John Berens has shown, Federalists took the war to be a chastising of America for the sin of departing from Washington's virtuous policies. Federalists thought Madison was unduly influenced by France—they thought it unnatural for the United States to be allied with this infidel nation—and thus defended dissent as the best expression of God's will. Republicans defended the war with equally intense providential rhetoric. When battles were lost, Federalists claimed that God was punishing America for embarking on an unjust war in the first place. When battles were won,

Republicans talked of a holy crusade. In the summer of 1814, a British expedition seized and burned Washington. Federalists thought the Madison administration brought on this tragedy, while Madison and his supporters saw their successful escape from the burning capital as a stroke of divine favor. Besides, the destruction of Washington was just what the nation needed to provoke it into decisive action.

The debate over the War of 1812 is an example of just how explosive providential rhetoric can become. In a recent book, edited by Hauerwas and one of his colleagues at Duke University, Frank Lentricchia, providential rhetoric can be heard exploding with a bang. Lentricchia, a professor of English, sets the tone for *Dissent from the Homeland: Essays after September 11* by providing the obligatory list of America's sins: Tokyo, Hiroshima, Dresden, and Vietnam.[11] This is fair enough, but then he writes, "In view of these criminal facts of American history, the largest obscenity of all is the howl of American self-pity in the wake of September 11." Lentricchia is a literary critic turned novelist, so I have to take him at his word: American shock at 9/11 was more obscene than what America did to Hiroshima. Perhaps he could be forgiven a bit of hyperbole, but Lentricchia then announces the agenda for the book: "All of the essays are united in the belief that America is threatened by the most powerful enemy in its history, the administration of George W. Bush."[12] The purplish hue of this little bit of hyperbole has turned black-and-blue.

At best, this volume takes an apocalyptic tone that mimics the American surprise at the terrorist attacks on the homeland. The authors almost appear to be saying, "If Americans were shocked by the destruction of the World Trade Towers, then we will show them that we are even more outraged by their shock." The assumption that America was due for a bout of divine judgment locates this volume in the providential tradition it otherwise wants to undermine.

In his contribution to the volume, Hauerwas chides President Bush for wanting it both ways. Bush, says Hauerwas, wants America to be religious, but Bush does not want the war on terrorism to be a religious war. This seems like an unbearable contradiction to Hauerwas, but from the perspective of American providence, it makes perfect sense. America's mission is rooted in the Christian sense of national vocation, but the purpose of that mission is not to force others to convert under the duress of military threat. The religious substance of America's providential history suggests that America's wars abroad should be for the sake of spreading freedom, not spreading the faith. Of course, political freedom is both an appropriate expression of Christian faith as well as a mighty means of enabling Christians to spread their faith. Hauerwas is probably thinking of the rhetoric of Manifest Destiny, which tied the providential tradition to the idea of a holy crusade for American expansion. As I argued in chapter 2, however, Manifest Destiny was at best a heretical offshoot of the more dominant tradition of American providence.

Hauerwas resents Bush's portrait of a faithful nation because Hauerwas is convinced that America is godless. The problem is that Hauerwas gives the impression that he would like to keep it that way. America is beyond redemption. If Christians were to try to save our country, they would risk losing their own souls. Hauerwas holds up pacifism as the only alternative to vengeance and equates all patriotism with idolatry. "God bless America," he declares, "is not a hymn any Christian can or should sing"—unless, he adds, "it is understood that God's blessings involve an element of judgment."[13] Here is the nub of the matter. Hauerwas is willing to grant some aspect of the providential tradition, but only on the condition that judgment be included. Self-criticism, as well as the acceptance of God's judgment, has always been a part of America providence. Hauerwas, however, appears to be cheered by the idea that God will judge America with unreserved harshness. He cannot, however, have it both ways: He cannot say that America is not special—that is, that America has not been blessed by God and given a unique role to play on the global stage—but that, nonetheless, America will incur God's wrath. These two sides of the providential tradition need to be thought together. The judgment follows from the blessing, unless, that is, Hauerwas thinks the analogy is not to Israel but to Sodom and Gomorrah, which were the target of God's displeasure but not, in any special way, God's favor. In sum, Hauerwas can hold America to exacting moral standards only if he himself believes, deep down, that America has been chosen to play a providentially significant role in world history.

Perhaps Hauerwas might agree that America has been chosen by God, but only to the extent that it has been chosen for scorn. America is not a new Israel but a return to the wayward Israel that broke God's heart. Actually, the analogy that Hauerwas and other contributors to this volume use is with Rome, not Israel. The analogy with Rome is a popular one in scholarship these days.[14] For the English theologian John Milbank, America is like Rome in most ways except that it is much worse, and thus America is exempt from some of the positive things the Apostle Paul said about respecting political authorities. The modern nation-state is beyond such concessions, for Milbank, because it exists only to serve the market (Milbank is a socialist). Milbank ignores the various ways that democracies support civil society, from tax exemptions for nonprofit organizations through funding for the arts, to take just two examples. Milbank, like Hauerwas, considers all nation-states to be illegitimate. "Pure liberty is pure power," he writes, "whose other name is evil."[15] He can recognize no positive relationship between Christianity and modern nation-states, nor can he see any positive outcome to the extension of free markets across the globe. Democracy, not Muslim fundamentalism, is the true source of terror in the world.

Milbank thus has no providential interpretation of how democratic nation-states have preserved the common goods of sinful humanity by providing political order and stability. Like radical Protestants who think the Holy Spirit left the church after the triumph of Constantine, only to return with the Anabaptists, Milbank thinks God withdrew his hand from political affairs with the rise of modern nation-states and will return to history only when they are replaced by some form of global Christian socialism. Democracy is a blank on Milbank's providential slate.

Democracy gives people the freedom only to express themselves sinfully, for Milbank. No better example of this distorted freedom can be found, for Milbank, than in the response of Americans to 9/11. He begins his essay wondering, incredulously, "why there was such outrage on such gigantic scale." The scale of the *outrage*, not the scale of the *destruction*, draws his attention. In a classic move of blaming the victim, he traces the origin of terrorism to the American Civil War, and he accuses American government officials of harboring "a hidden glee" over the attack. He then, with not-so-hidden glee, compares "George Bush's terrifying address to Congress" to "Hitler's announcement of the Third Reich."[16]

The second Gulf War has brought out the best and the worst in America, so perhaps Milbank can be excused for his excitable prose. Nevertheless, it is worth pausing here to remember exactly what Bush was saying while Milbank was comparing him to Hitler. Speaking to an audience of Iraqi immigrants in Dearborn, Michigan, President Bush stated an Enlightenment ideal that was worthy of Immanuel Kant: "The desire for freedom is not the property of one culture. It is the universal hope of human beings in every culture." The president can speak with such confidence because he combines the Enlightenment heritage of optimistic humanism with the evangelical fervor of an altar call. Given the fact that the American version of the Enlightenment—which was shaped by Lockean empiricism and the rationality of the market, rather than Voltaire and the virulent anticlericalism of the French Enlightenment—was deeply theological, this evangelical Kantianism, if I can coin a phrase, makes a lot of rhetorical sense. That President Bush combines the Enlightenment dedication to the universal kingdom of reason with the Evangelical pursuit of a universal kingdom of God accounts for much of the outrage over the second Gulf War that could be heard from university professors, who tend toward philosophical relativism and religious skepticism.

What I am calling President Bush's Evangelical Enlightenment or enlightened Evangelicalism should be given careful scrutiny, but scrutiny of the right kind. The problem is not that this theology of foreign affairs depends upon the use of military might. All diplomacy must be willing to use force as a last resort. The problem, for Milbank and Hauerwas, is that Bush reaches deep into America's religious past in order to revive a sense of mission and purpose in this time of crisis. For Milbank, the American appropriation of the Old Testament as a guide for foreign policy is completely unacceptable, primarily because Milbank is so firmly against the "terrible symbiosis arising between Zionism" and American Protestantism. Even more than Hauerwas, Milbank rejects the idea that God "arbitrarily prefers one lot of people to another (as opposed to working providentially for a time through one people's advanced insight—as Maimonides rightly understood Jewish election); and as if he really and truly appoints to them, not just for a period, but for all time, one piece of land to the exclusion of others."[17] So here is the heart of his rejection of American providence: his support of the Palestinians against the state of Israel.

Milbank is perceptive in realizing that American providentialism, by borrowing from the history of Israel, affirms Old Testament history as an eternal template that cannot be altered or destroyed. American providentialism, that is, does not displace but instead acknowledges the literal promises God has made to Israel, which is why Evangelical Christians are among the most dedicated supporters of Israel. Milbank rejects all of this by arguing that God's election of Israel was only symbolic and temporary. Israel might have earned God's favor for a limited time by its "advanced insight," but God does not play favorites for long. By turning God's promise of a homeland to Israel into a metaphor, Milbank undercuts the ground of special providence, which leaves only the most general providential reading of history.

Milbank thus aligns himself with a particularly invidious version of supersessionism, one of the oldest and most tragic Christian heresies. Christianity, for Milbank, is truly universal because it is not tied to place and time. Judaism, and America as well, represents an impediment to a fully international socialism because of its particularism and exceptionalism. One-world government is the logical outcome of Milbank's "biblical and Platonico-Aristotelian metaphysical legacy common to Christianity, Judaism, and Islam."[18] Milbank is on a quest for a radical rethinking of the common philosophical assumptions shared by the monotheistic faiths, but the result is far from orthodox theology.

Without some sense of the special vocation of democracies, these scholars are left with making the case for moral equivalence between America and the terrorists. Milbank thus can write that "the United States has deployed the terrorizing and murder of civilians . . . as a primary instrument of military and political policy." Rowan Williams, the Archbishop of Canterbury and a leading Anglican theologian, echoes this sentiment by claiming that America allows "random killing *as a matter of calculated policy*" (italics his).

For Williams, in fact, talking about the evil of terrorism is useless. The theological category of evil is bound to lead us astray because it "lets us off the hook."[19] In the dark aftermath of 9/11, Williams seems to be saying, not only are we all sinners, but we are also all terrorists. Williams also thinks that terrorism is a matter for the police, rather than the military. He fears that calling the war against terrorism a "war" gives too much dignity to the terrorists, as if naming the fact that they are our enemy could somehow raise their profile and credit their cause.

Jean Bethke Elshtain, in the most systematic and judicious analysis of the war against terrorism—where she concludes that it meets just war criteria—provides a rational alternative to these essays. "Confronted with an aggressive foe preaching hatred of any and all things Western," she observes, "many have responded with a disturbing strain of Western self-loathing." She is especially appalled by those who minimize the differences between terrorism and warfare. "Whereas classic warfare is the continuation of politics by other means, terrorism is the destruction of politics by all possible means." In times of crisis, making distinctions, rather than collapsing them, is crucial. The contributors to *Dissent* blur categories in order to spread the guilt, while Elshtain insists on the importance of moral clarity. An example of this confusion is the frequently stated comparison between the hijackers and Timothy McVeigh, a comparison that is meant to show that Islam is no different from Christianity. Elshtain demurs. "McVeigh no more represented Christianity than they represented Islam, some Muslims told us. But this is one more of the strained and flawed analogies that have proliferated in the wake of September 11. Timothy McVeigh never claimed to be acting in behalf of Christianity."[20] Such moral equivocations permit Muslims to evade the hard choices that confront them in the modern world.

What is most striking to me about all of these essays, besides their virulent anti-Americanism, is that they persist in reading 9/11 providentially. There is no reluctance here to use this tragedy as a metaphor for deeper meanings, even though decades of discussion about the Holocaust should have taught us to resist instrumentalizing the unspeakable by turning it into an opportunity for polemical grandstanding. Susan Willis, for example, takes this occasion to criticize the flag waving that followed 9/11. She calls the flag "an empty signifier" but then turns around to argue that the flag is indeed full of meaning, but what it signifies is racism pure and simple. Her evidence for this charge is her assertion that "most black and Hispanic neighborhoods have been relatively flag free." She thus sets out to deconstruct the flag, but she cannot resist a detour to deflate the heroic status of the rescue workers, many of whom gave their lives trying to save others. Many Americans, she complains, "fail to realize that New York City's firefighters—like its police force— are almost exclusively white."[21] This seems like an inordinately onerous example of a non sequitur.

Wendell Berry also hurries to turn 9/11 into grist for his environmentalist mill. He emphatically declares, "The time will soon come when we will not be able to remember the horrors of September 11 without remembering also the unquestioning technological and economic optimism that ended on that day." This is obviously an example of wishful thinking, in that Berry thinks Americans of the future will look back at 9/11 as the beginning of their acceptance of his own ideas about the limits of technology. Also jarring is Frederick Jameson's use of the now worn and tired but once-fashionable language of social construction to argue that America "invented bin Laden." Jameson also draws from the French philosopher Jean Baudrillard (and at the same time shows how low postmodernism has sunk) by insisting on "the essentially aesthetic nature of the attack."[22] Americans were moved by the disaster, he suggests, because it was such a mesmerizing spectacle. The terrorists were not trying to kill us, he implies. They were just trying to get our attention in the only way they knew how: by entertaining us.

Peter Ochs, one of the nation's foremost scholars of Judaism, contributes the one essay that avoids all of these problems. It is surely no coincidence that Ochs is profoundly in touch with the providential aspects of his own Jewish tradition and thus is more sympathetic for the plight of all Americans in this time of crisis. Ochs brings to bear on America's reaction to the terrorist attack Jewish responses to the destruction of ancient Israel's temples. The parallel is richly suggestive. The magnitude of the destruction of the World Trade Center is such that its interpretation will shape the future course of American history. Even the contributors to *Dissent* acknowledge this by demonstrating an apocalyptic proclivity to read 9/11 as a harbinger of the end of American imperialism. With the exception of Ochs, the contributors read 9/11 as absolutely revelatory in showing the world America's true nature, which is vengeful and self-deluded. Ochs, by contrast, embraces America providentially by drawing on the parallels between America and Israel. He is thus able to express sympathy for those killed in the attack while also articulating a hope that God will use this event for the world's good.

Unfortunately, the viewpoint of American providence in *Dissent* is so taken for granted by liberals in higher education that it hardly attracts notice. Another example of such political analysis is a book with the catchy title *Captain America and the Crusade against Evil*, by Robert Jewett and John Shelton Lawrence. They observe, right from the start, that the rhetoric of a chosen nation "is no longer used by sophisticated Americans," although "the values and emotions associated with such ideas continue to exercise their power." The authors survey nearly every military conflict in America's long history and blame them all on the doctrine of providence. They use the comic book *Captain America* as a paradigm of what they think is the basic American myth of world redemption. By caricaturing American providence as a thinly disguised justification for holy crusades, they are unable to make any constructive distinctions between Islamic fundamentalists and Christian conservatives. "Each side views its anger as blessed by the deity, which thereby absolutizes zeal and jihad and eliminates normal restraint." American super-heroism is nothing but a threat to democracy. Even though their tone is apocalyptic, espying providential rhetoric behind every American misstep, they cannot resist appealing to the very doctrine they blame for all the world's evils: "The American sense of mission, scorned by cynics, secular realists, and disappointed idealists alike, needs to be transformed rather than abandoned."[23] American providence is okay for these authors as long as it does not involve us in fighting for what we believe is right.

Political leftists were not the only ones to read the terrorist attack in terms of God's just punishment. Jerry Falwell offered just that interpretation during an appearance on the *700 Club* on September 13, 2001. His comments were widely reported and strongly condemned in the media: "I really believe that the pagans, the abortionists, and the feminists, and the gays and the lesbians who are actively trying to make that an alternative lifestyle, the ACLU, People for the American Way, all of them have tried to secularize America. I point the finger in their face and say: 'You helped this happen.'"[24] The irony is that, on a literal level, Falwell is right. Many Muslims view America as the epitome of sexual excess and licentious behavior. America is the enemy of Islam not just because America is Christian but also because America is so immoral, from a Muslim point of view.

Falwell's remarks were greeted with as much vitriol as Boykin's. Indeed, it is hard to know which of these men most offended the media, one for arguing that God is on our side and the other for arguing that God has punished us because we are not on God's side. Falwell tried to stem the tide of the backlash that was swallowing his remarks and spitting out his reputation by appearing on CBS's *Good Morning America* to apologize for his lapse of good judgment. He had "missed the mark," he said.[25] Falwell was, in a way, wrong. Nobody is to be blamed for the terrorist acts—certainly no Americans, of any moral or political position—except the terrorists themselves. Nonetheless, Falwell was saying nothing especially different from the contributors to *Dissent*. For Falwell, God sometimes uses our enemies as a justifiable scourge, in order to awaken us from our moral slumber. For the contributors to *Dissent*, God permitted the terrorists to punish us for the sins of imperialism and consumerism. Both of these arguments belong to the same theological tradition, but one of them was taken to the cleaners while the other ended up in a respectable book that will line the shelves of libraries across the nation.

Religious studies scholars might be expected to see the parallels between the way political leftists and Christian fundamentalists have conceptualized the significance of 9/11. Instead, they have drawn the parallel between

Falwell and the terrorists themselves. This is the point of Bruce Lincoln's book, *Holy Terrors*. Lincoln thinks that all religions are mere masks for the attainment and display of power, so he is naturally drawn to the events surrounding 9/11. After analyzing the rhetoric of Sayyid Qutb, Mohamed Atta, and Osama bin Laden, Lincoln turns his attention to Christian fundamentalists. "Although they struggle against an endogenous and not a foreign enemy, the perspectives of Pat Robertson, Jerry Falwell, and the American religious right are similar in most other ways." Lincoln also sees a strict parallel between the rhetoric of President Bush and Osama bin Laden: "Both men constructed a Manichaean struggle, where Sons of Light confront Sons of Darkness, and all must enlist on one side or another, without possibility of neutrality, hesitation, or middle ground." Their speeches thus "mirror one another." Of course, bin Laden highlights the religious motivations of his call for terrorism, while Bush, in Lincoln's view, uses religion "in subtle, but revealing ways." According to Lincoln, when Bush talks about "killers of innocents," he is making an allusion toward Herod's slaughter of the innocents in Matthew 2.[26] Lincoln thus accuses Bush of encoding a providential view of America into his announcement of the war against terrorism. I do not think one has to be that subtle to see that President Bush is drawing from American providence, but I also do not see the moral equivalence between Bush's rhetoric and the ranting of bin Laden.

My criticisms of the way the political left has used 9/11 is not meant to suggest that there should be no critical commentary on this event. I am only suggesting that not all commentary is of equal moral value. I heard from many people in the academy that 9/11 would mark for them the end of postmodernism, which is, I think, a worthy sentiment. Gene Edward Veith, in one of the best books on this topic, *Christianity in an Age of Terrorism*, makes exactly this point. Veith rejects the idea that the airplanes were thunderbolts thrown by God from the sky. Nevertheless, a lesson remains to be drawn from the tragedy. "Suddenly all of the moral relativism, the pop-cultural shallowness, and the cynical posing of postmodernism seemed irrelevant." Veith is a Lutheran, and from the perspective of Luther's theology of the cross, the terrorists "invariably hold to a theology of glory."[27] Luther understood the attraction of a theology of glory, just as Luther understood the allure of legalistic religions. Thus it does not surprise Veith that after 9/11, conversions to Islam in America skyrocketed, with some reports estimating the number of new converts at thirty-four thousand. What Veith worries about most is whether America has the spiritual resources to combat the spread of Islam, with its strict code of conduct and its solid pillars of faith. Christianity promises freedom and demands inward transformation, which is a hard combination to achieve. Freedom is easily abused, and personal transformation is hard work. Veith also worries about those who say that the real lesson of 9/11 is the need to fight intolerance and religious zealotry everywhere. Some liberals want to Talibanize Christian conservatives and absolutize secularism.

Christians, especially those from a Lutheran perspective, understand how easily religion leads to self-righteousness and arrogance. The solution is not to repress the spiritual longings of the heart. Christians need to do a better job of articulating the uniqueness of the Christian faith in its call for repentance and personal transformation. A passage from Luke, where Jesus is teaching about the meaning of suffering, is important: "Or those eighteen who were killed when the tower of Siloam fell on them—do you think that they were worse offenders than all the others living in Jerusalem? No, I tell you; but unless you repent, you will all perish just as they did" (13:4–5). Mourning is difficult, but even more difficult is the command that mourning include repentance.

A providential view of America is dependent on the covenantal theology of the Puritans, who put into practice Calvin's argument, as exemplified by his nearly theocratic ambition in Geneva, to bring heaven to earth—or at least to transform some parts of the earth into communities suitable for heavenly living. This does not mean, however, that Americans have nothing to learn from Luther. If Calvinism resulted in a drive toward social transformation that could prove to be politically radical, Lutheranism, under the rubric of the two separate kingdoms of God and man, resulted in a more skeptical attitude toward making the rule of God into the rule of humanity.[28] Lutheranism, in other words, could lead to political conservativism or indifference, but it could also give rise to an ironic awareness of the sinfulness that renders the Calvinist's task—for all practical purposes—impossible. Americans, precisely because of their Calvinist heritage, are not adept in the ways of irony. American optimism, coupled with a sense of divine purpose and hope for the future, can be met with skepticism or even cynicism, but it takes a more refined sense of history to use the tricky trope of irony. Even the staunchest critics of American providentialism are typically humorless in their rejection of any special spiritual status of the American experiment. Critics can brandish the sword of cynicism or cut with the knife of skepticism or even lash out against American arrogance with an axe of outrage, but rarely do such critics know how to handle the slight but deadly dagger of irony.

Irony requires a great deal of sophistication; it is an almost godlike view of events, because it sees the inevitable outcomes of which historical actors are unaware. Irony is a pattern that is only discernible, in other words, from afar. It takes a long or transcendent view of history. Hauerwas resists any role for the theologian to stand outside of the church in order to survey the lay of the secular land. Theologians are to focus their sights on building up the church and thus leaving secular culture to itself. Hauerwas has a Calvinist concern with building up the kingdom that precludes a Lutheran employ-ment of irony. Nonetheless, his frequently shrill criticisms of American capi-talism and democracy are in need of precisely that trope. Reinhold Niebuhr is the great theologian of irony, perhaps because Niebuhr had an apprecia-tion for both the strengths and the limits of American providence. For Niebuhr, America can believe in the innocence of its own messianic mission only if it is blind to all of its many weaknesses. Such blindness is a prerequi-site for any nation's understanding of providence. Niebuhr does not con-clude that America has done no good for the world. On the contrary, and this is where Niebuhr works his ironic magic, the good America has done is made possible by the ignorance Americans gladly embrace. We are so innocent of history, Niebuhr suggests, that we do not realize all of the many pitfalls that await our imperial ambitions. Our innocence, in fact, keeps us from naming our ambition as a species of imperialism. Yet that very same innocence allows us to avoid many of the faults of empires of the past. We actually believe we can do good in the world. We have pursued what the political sci-entist Andrew J. Bacevich has called a "strategy of openness"—with the intention of creating a more integrated world by eliminating barriers to trade, capital, and ideas—with a level of aggression necessary to confront resistance.[29] Only a naive belief in ourselves could permit us to promote such idealism at a cost that would keep other nations from even trying. What saves us from doing more damage than we end up doing is our individual-ism, which keeps us from articulating a coherent social vision of our inten-tions in the moral arena. Our very respect for freedom, in other words, both fuels our overseas endeavors and inhibits us from developing the kind of ideology that could result in global domination. We are much too morally fragmented to think that we can run the world morally, although we are just pragmatic enough to think that we could do a good job running the world economically.

Without a sense of irony, fundamentalists on both the theo-political left and right are tempted to see menacing forces behind every historical event. If every nation has its own peculiar neurosis, surely America's is the tendency for providence to turn to paranoia. Timothy Melley has written a fascinating book about the culture of paranoia that grips much of America. Paranoia is a parasite on the civic body that shows no favoritism to the political left or right. It is charming, in a way, that our collective fantasies most typically take the form not of the lust for land or the quest for power but of the fear of con-spiracy. The obsession with who shot JFK is but one example of what Melley calls "the empire of conspiracy." Rather than talking about seemingly intractable political problems, Americans have a favorite pastime of asking a question along the lines of, "Who do you think is really in charge of . . ." or "What do you think really happened to . . ." Melley attributes this American sport to anxiety over our own beloved belief in individualism. We think we are a nation of individuals, yet we firmly believe that corporations control everything we do and that a handful of powerful companies run the U.S. government.

Melley argues that Americans are actually so conformist that we need to invent conspiracies that put our individualism in peril in order to muster the passion to try to save it. He calls this "agency panic."[30] A less convoluted explanation might be termed "providence panic." Purveyors of the doctrine of providence taught Americans to read between the lines of history, looking for the ways that the hidden force of the divine will secretly guides America to its destiny. The habit of this kind of reading remains in post-Christian American, but the decline of providential thinking forces us to fill in the blanks with stories that do not concern God. If we believed that history is a random series of events, we would not look for patterns that signal some secret source of control. We have overthrown God as the agent of providence, but the result is that we have thrown ourselves into a fit of paranoid fantasies. Our diminished sense of providence renders us more subjected to forces out of our control. Consequently, we grant enormous power to the CIA, FBI, ACLU, NRA, the Mafia, fundamentalist churches, or the liberal media. We have just enough Christianity left in our civil religion to lead us to read between the lines, but we have no plot to tell us what to find.

NOTES

1. I am drawing here from two of my articles: "The Very American Stanley Hauerwas," *First Things* (June/July 2002): 14–17, and "A Voice Cursing in the Wilderness," *Reviews in Religion and Theology* 10 (February 2003): 80–85.

2. Hauerwas and his students typically accuse Reinhold Niebuhr of lacking an ecclesiology, but they miss the extent to which Niebuhr rejects the idea of America as a substitute for the church. Niebuhr has what we can call a negative ecclesiology, although he does not take Hauerwas's step of turning the church into a kind of nation.

3. See Gloria H. Albrecht for a good discussion of Hauerwas's Texan epistemology, in *The Character of Our Communities: Toward an Ethic of Liberation for the Church* (Nashville: Abingdon Press, 1995), 31.

4. Stanley Hauerwas and William H. Willimon, *Resident Aliens* (Nashville: Abingdon Press, 1989), 12, 16–17, 32, 38, 43, 78.

5. Ibid., 146, 159, 159.

6. R. R. Reno, in *The Blackwell Companion to Political Theology*, ed. Peter Scott and William T. Cavanaugh (Oxford: Blackwell Publishing, 2004), 314.

7. It should be noted that the correlation between poverty and terrorism, widely argued by liberals, is false. The hijackers of 9/11 were not poor. Moreover, Alan B. Krueger, a professor economics at Princeton, and Jitka Maleckova, a professor of Middle Eastern studies at Charles University in Prague, have carefully explored and refuted the notion that deprivation breeds terrorism. See their article, "Does Poverty Cause Terrorism?" *The New Republic*, June 24, 2002, 27–33.

8. Jeffrey Stout, *Democracy and Tradition* (Princeton, NJ: Princeton University Press, 2004), 103.

9. Stanley Hauerwas, *Christian Existence Today: Essays on Church, World, and Living In Between* (Durham, NC: Labyrinth Press, 1988), 15.

10. Stout, *Democracy and Tradition*, 152.

11. Some of the following discussion is taken from my review of *Dissent from the Homeland* in *Reviews in Religion and Theology*, 11/2 (April 2004): 227–31.

12. Stanley Hauerwas and Frank Lentricchia, eds., *Dissent from the Homeland: Essays after September 11* (Durham, NC: Duke University Press, 2003), 5.

13. Ibid., 8.

14. See two volumes, both edited by Richard A. Horsley: *Paul and Empire: Religion and Power in Imperial Society* (Harrisburg, PA: Trinity Press International, 1997), and *Paul and Politics* (Harrisburg, PA: Trinity Press International, 2000). Of course, on one level, that of a straightforward reading of history, the analogy between America and Rome is limited, if not fatally flawed. Not only were the imperial ambitions of Rome completely different from the global responsibilities of America, but the Romans viciously persecuted Christians, which makes it especially obnoxious to compare Rome to a predominantly Christian America. More particularly, to the Evangelical Christian community, which includes President Bush, the arguments of theologians like Hauerwas and Milbank make little sense. I still value the account of church history taught to me by the Evangelical church of my youth. It involved three basic stages. The early Christians were persecuted, but God chose Constantine to save the church and conquer paganism. [See Robert Louis Wilken, "In Defense of Constantine," *First Things* (April 2001): 36–40.] The Reformation purified the medieval church in order to set free the Word of God for a renewed mission of proclamation. Finally, America, for all of her faults and limitations, has been chosen by God to spread Christianity across the globe, thus fulfilling the great commission. The straight and narrow line that can be drawn in this account from Constantine, through the Reformation, to America, would no doubt send shudders down the spines of the liberal critics of the Bush administration, whether they are Christian or not. This approach exudes all of the rhetoric of a line drawn in the sand, daring anyone else to cross it. It traces a story that would need to be supplemented by many other lines to make it convincing. Although today I see this line as full of ellipses that delete much of the richness and variety of church history, I find it to be a more persuasive account of the workings of the Holy Spirit through history than the account of those who think capitalism and the birth of nation-states sold Christianity down the river.

15. Hauerwas and Lentricchia, *Dissent*, 65.

16. Ibid., 63, 64 and 67.

17. Ibid., both quotes on 71.

18. Ibid., 81. For further analysis of Milbank, see my essay, "Stateside: A North American Perspective on Radical Orthodoxy," *Reviews in Religion and Theology* 8, no. 3 (June 2001): 319–25.

19. Hauerwas and Lentricchia, *Dissent*, 79, 30, 27.

20. Jean Bethke Elshtain, *Just War against Terror: The Burden of American Power in a Violent World* (New York: Basic Books, 2003), 145–46, 152, 136.

21. Hauerwas and Lentricchia, *Dissent*, 124, 122, 121.

22. Ibid., 37, 59, 61.

23. Robert Jewett and John Shelton Lawrence, *Captain America and the Crusade against Evil* (Grand Rapids: Eerdmans, 2003), 3, 24, 324.

24. Transcript of Pat Robertson's interview with Jerry Falwell on the *700 Club*, September 13, 2001, available at www.pfaw.org/issues/right/robertson_falwell.html.

25. See Michael Naparstek, "Falwell and Robertson Stumble," *Religion in the News* 4 (Fall 2001): http://caribou.cc.trincoll.edu/depts_csrpl/RINvol3No3/RINVol4No3.htm

26. Bruce Lincoln, *Holy Terrors: Thinking about Religion after September 11* (Chicago: University of Chicago Press, 2003), 60, 20, 27, 29.

27. Gene Edward Veith, *Christianity in an Age of Terrorism* (St. Louis: Concordia Publishing House, 2002), 86, 34.

28. Lutheranism is also more skeptical about the eschaton. Article seventeen of the Augsburg Confession condemns any speculation about a worldly form of the Kingdom of God prior to the resurrection of the dead.

29. Andrew J. Bacevich, *American Empire: The Realities and Consequences of U.S. Diplomacy* (Cambridge, MA: Harvard University Press, 2002).

30. Timothy Melley, *Empire of Conspiracy: The Culture of Paranoia in Postwar America* (Ithaca, NY: Cornell University Press, 2000), 6. One of his poorest examples of a conspiracy mentality is his unfair reading of Leo Strauss's "Persecution and the Art of Writing" (1952).

CHAPTER FIVE

A Particular Theory of Providence

Of all Christian doctrines, providence should not be discussed in general terms alone. Providence asks us to read history in a particular fashion, which suggests that providence itself cannot be treated in a general way. "General providence" is actually a technical term, which means God's regular mode of operating in the world, as opposed to God's special acts that we perceive as miracles. I argue in this chapter that God's providence is best thought of as always special and particular, not regular and general. General providence tends to portray God as the hidden cause behind all events, rather than the agent who is driving history forward toward a specific end. This might not seem like much of a difference, but the two kinds of providence can lead to two kinds of religious response. General providence suggests a rhetoric of presence rather than action. The rhetoric of presence invites a meditative response to God's design. The rhetoric of action invites participation in the divine drama. By emphasizing God's action in history, I do not mean to insinuate any regions of time or space in which God is absent. God is thoroughly present in the world, but God is present as a personal agent, not an impersonal force. The God of the Bible, as revealed in Jesus Christ, is not a diffuse field of divine energy pervading all matter as a kind of subatomic glue. God is dynamic, intentional, and purposeful. God is present everywhere, but God works in a very personal way.

The doctrine of providence holds together the doctrine of creation and the doctrine of eschatology. God is not yet done with the world, but God is here and now directing all things to their proper end. When providence loses this orientation toward the future, it can turn into a merely general scheme.

Jonathan Edwards understood that providence is always particular: "The work of creation was in order to God's works of providence. So that if it be inquired which of these two kinds of works is the greatest, the works of creation or God's works of providence, I answer providence because God's works of providence are the end of God's works of creation as the building of an house or the forming an engine or machine is for its use."[1] Edwards speaks often of God's grand design, but he keeps this design in the proper perspective of God's particular historical aims.

In the American context, any particular reflection on providence must start with Calvin. The central doctrine of Calvinism, the sovereignty of God, entails a strong confidence in providence. The Westminster Confession of Faith (1649), which sets the theological standard for the Presbyterian Church, states, "God, the great Creator of all things, doth uphold, direct, dispose, and govern all creatures, actions, and things, from the greatest even to the least, by his most wise and holy providence, according to his infallible foreknowledge, and the free and immutable counsel of his own will, to the praise of the glory of his wisdom, power, justice, goodness, and mercy."[2] This is a theological mouthful, and it led to long debates about primary and secondary causes, as well as ordinary and extraordinary means. Westminster's interpretation of providence implies an interrelated set of propositions involving predestination that did not always sit well with many American Christians. Calvinism makes the fall a product of God's foreknowledge, emphasizes how God chastises the chosen for their sins, and insists that God hardens the hearts of the wicked.

Although Westminster followed the great theme of providence with an affirmation of free will, many people today find the minor theme hard to hear in the Confession. To Calvinists, however, providence was far from being a paralyzing doctrine of fate. Providence took the shape of a covenant, and the covenant demanded the active participation of believers. Providence was thus a call for social revolution, not quietistic escape. Nevertheless, the social critic Christopher Lasch is right to point out a subtle but crucial shift from the dark pessimism associated with the traditional belief in providence to the bright optimism assumed by the modern notion of progress.[3] Christians looked to providence most often to help explain why history was not going their way. Calvinists especially assumed that they would not live up to God's expectations, and thus God would need to punish them. Providence was more about judgment than promise. By the nineteenth century, promise had prevailed over judgment.

What makes the liberal doctrine of progress so radical is its rejection of limits altogether. Progress is, in Lasch's words, "the promise of steady improvement with no foreseeable ending at all."[4] For Lasch, Adam Smith, not John Calvin, lies behind the modern stake in progress. Only if our desires are insatiable and infinite can capitalism work, and capitalism works by promising not an end in the sense of a fulfillment to our desires but their perpetual refinement as we are taught to want more and more. Progress expects the world to keep getting better and better as expanding economic forces create new ways to both incite and satisfy our limitless desires.

Progress is so troubling for Lasch because it assumes that the undisciplined appetite is the engine of material improvement rather than the source of social chaos. Lasch wonders how we can learn to live humbly within the limits of our finitude if we think that economic growth has no end. By defining providence in opposition to progress and then connecting progress to capitalism, Lasch can hold out the hope for recovering the doctrine of providence only with the overthrow of capitalism. His own analysis of progress repeats the providential theory encapsulated in premillennialism, which expects things to get much worse before they have any chance of getting better. For Lasch, capitalism is inherently flawed because it tries to vanquish the very limits that make us human. Consequently, in order to succeed, capitalism must become increasingly inhuman, even as it promises to make every human wish come true. Lasch cannot imagine that capitalism can correct itself, or that open markets, coupled with democratic forms of government, might provide the freedom necessary for Christianity to reform itself. He also cannot imagine that providence might be linked to the promised land as well as divine judgment.

Lasch can oppose providence and progress only if he downplays the role of postmillennialism in nineteenth-century America. Postmillennialism occupies an odd conceptual space in the history of providence, because it lies between the strict Calvinist view of history and modern-day secular optimism. Postmillennialism is not popular today, because it is trumped by premillennialism among Christian conservatives and replaced by secular optimism among liberals. In the nineteenth century, Christians felt compelled to reform American society because they sensed the nearness of the kingdom of God. Arguably, some form of postmillennialism is necessary not only to do justice to the history of providence in the Old Testament but also to give impetus to the emergence of a global Christianity that is spreading as rapidly as capitalism itself. In the next chapter I sketch a providential view of the future of this coordinated triumph of democratic capitalism and Evangelical Christianity.

Postmillennialism is out of favor in theological circles today in part because of overtones of triumphalism. The idea that the reign of Christ will occur before the final judgement can be taken to mean that human effort can bring about the kingdom of God. The logic of postmillennialism, however, does not necessarily entail a view of history that minimizes God's contributions while maximizing human effort. Postmillennialism is certainly optimistic, but it is optimistic about the direction of history as that direction can be ascertained in the present, not about the strength of human nature unaided by grace. Postmillennialism reminds us that the kingdom of God is continuous as well as discontinuous with human history. It thus suggests an ultimate coordination of human politics with the coming kingdom of God. That is, the political sphere can anticipate the greater glory of the heavenly governance of God. This is a historical hope with biblical roots, but it gained credibility with the triumph of Constantine, the first Christian emperor of Rome.

Constantinianism is the term theologians use when they want to suggest that another theologian has compromised with worldly powers and corrupt politics. No doubt, my attempt to recover the doctrine of providence will be subjected to that charge. Strictly speaking, Constantinianism is not attributed to Constantine himself, but to Eusebius, bishop of Caesarea. Eusebius did not know Constantine personally until he attended the Council of Nicaea in 325, and he never had more than a few personal contacts with the emperor. Nevertheless, Eusebius was convinced of Constantine's cosmic importance, and he set out to write his life in a mixture of panegyric and narrative history.[5] That Eusebius thought he was living in the climax of history allowed him to attempt something new in Christian theology.

Of course, the pagans also believed that the gods worked through history, but their collective will was hidden in the course of events, and their decisions were capricious and subjected to manipulation. One of the Greek deities was Tyche, whom the Romans identified as the goddess Fortuna. When the pagan Julian, nephew of Constantine, inherited the Roman throne in 361, Christians understandably became anxious about the possibility of a return to the age of persecution. They expressed that anxiety in the city of Caesarea by destroying the temple dedicated to Tyche, which was the only pagan temple still remaining in that city. The great Cappadocian theologian Gregory of Nazianzus applauded the riot. He thought it was appropriate that Christians turn their anger against a symbol of chance and luck.[6] The pagans had their gods, but their gods made historical events seem more arbitrary, not less. Christians refused to go back to a time when religion taught that history was ruled by random forces and thus life was a throw of the dice. Julian's death, in battle against the Persians, was widely celebrated by Christians as an affirmation of their view of divine providence over the pagan acceptance of the tragic battle between the passions of the gods and the ambition of men.

Origen had already argued that the Roman Empire was a providential boon to Christianity, brought into being to facilitate the spread of the gospel. Christians before him could not imagine what Eusebius now saw—how a political ruler could imitate the rule of God in heaven. Eusebius was inspired to make this imaginative leap by Constantine himself, who understood his rule to be part of God's providence. Constantine felt called by God to be of service to the church, but he did not see any contradiction between that service and his obligations to the state. Instead, they were united aims under the one providence of God. Church and state could work together to ensure a harmony in this world that would reflect the harmony above. This fusion of altar and sword is often taken as a betrayal of the pacifistic message of Jesus, but both Constantine and Eusebius were appalled by the way pagans had ritualized and thus celebrated the spilling of blood. Both saw the Christianization of the Roman Empire as a victory for peace and not war. In the orations he gave praising Constantine, Eusebius drew a parallel between Constantine and Christ. Christ came at a time of peace. The Roman Empire was a gift from God meant to be the outward sign of the new kingdom that Christ was inaugurating. Constantine had returned Rome to its peaceful purpose, bringing Rome and Christianity—"two roots of blessing"— together to further the mighty plan of God.[7] A true empire, for Eusebius, presupposes monotheism. Under Constantine, the Roman Empire became the true version of itself for the first time.

Augustine would have none of Eusebius's court theology. What pirates do with one boat, he argued, the Romans do with a navy. One is called brigandage, the other empire.[8] Of course, Augustine wrote at the end of the Western half of the Roman Empire, when the barbarian invasion was being blamed on the Christians and the Empire did not appear to be providing much hope for peace. He had to make the case that the destiny of Christianity was completely different from the fate of the Empire. He is sometimes read as separating the kingdom of God from the kingdom of humanity to such an extent that he problematizes the doctrine of providence. This is going too far. John Von Heyking has argued against the idea that politics, for Augustine, is a postlapsarian response to sin. Political order is a natural good.[9] The political city of humanity is but a shadow of the city of God, but the two are constructively related nonetheless. After all, the city of God is a *city*. It is structured, and its structure cannot be completely dissimilar to the kinds of structures we experience in earthly cities. If we are resurrected as bodies, then we will be part of a political body in the heavenly city. It follows that our political organizations now are not totally unrelated to what we will someday become.

Augustine rejected the idea that divine providence raised Rome above the level of the average empire, but he also criticized those pagans who argued that Rome had seen better times before the coming of Christianity. When he had completed ten books of *The City of God*, he encouraged one of his students, Paulus Orosius, to write his own treatise in support of his position. Vandals had driven Orosius from his home in Portugal around 412, so he knew firsthand about Rome's troubles. Nevertheless, Orosius came to the conclusion that pagan kingdoms prior to the coming of Christ, including Babylon, Macedon, and Carthage, let alone Republican Rome, were far worse than Christianized Rome. Orosius was convinced that Christianity had brought peace to the world and that Imperial Rome was the agent of that peace. Republican Rome was a period of tremendous warfare, broken only by the interlude of peace that coincided, Orosius points out, with the birth of Christ. Only Christian monotheism achieved the worldwide unity that pagan Romans could never impose without brute force. For Orosius, the empire allowed him to survive as a refugee. "No matter where I flee, I find my native land, my law, and my religion."[10] Rome had come into its own in service to the church.

The idea of Christendom was, in the minds of many Christians, equivalent to the idea of peace and freedom. Like Orosius, Dante Alighieri (1265–1321) lived during a tumultuous time. The bitter power struggles of the Italian states led to his exile from Florence in 1301. He naturally came to the conclusion that independent cities could not control their own citizens. In his *Monarchia*, he looked back to the Roman Empire as a political unity sufficiently comprehensive to guarantee the peace necessary for humankind to achieve their God-given potential. For Dante, the Roman Empire had a providential mandate. Without the universality of Roman law, the atonement of Christ could not have had its global impact. Dante argues that the human species as a whole has a purpose that transcends "the capacity of any one man or household or village, or even of any one city or kingdom." Humans were created to perform a variety of intellectual tasks, but the full measure of human success requires universal peace. "The human race is at its best when most free." This freedom, for Dante, is not abstract and individual. Indeed, the necessity for one ruler and one kingdom follows from the definition of providence. Providence harmonizes human wills with the divine plan, just as a universal kingdom makes concord possible by subjecting humanity to one political authority. Providence wants what is best for us, and "mankind at its best depends upon unity in the wills of its members."[11] Such singular unity demands a singular authority. The direction of providence thus must be toward global political unity or, in Dante's terms, monarchy. After all, Dante points out, God chose to enter into human history in the incarnation at just that point when the world first saw a glimpse of universal peace in the reign of Augustus.

Providence gets its worldly and political direction from the Old Testament. The Bible is about election: God chooses Israel; Israel does not choose God. The distinction is crucial for the doctrine of providence. Nations inevitably worship gods of their own making, projecting their prowess onto the heavens so that their notions of providence amount to little more than self-congratulations. That God chose to side with one nation means that God chooses to bring all nations under one divine rule. God has a universal purpose for Israel that is more than but not less than political.

Thus, God acts through other nations in order to assure the destiny of Israel. Assyria, for example, becomes "the rod of my anger" (Isa. 10:5). Israel's bondage in and deliverance from Egypt especially serves as a kind of code for what God is doing with the nations.

The story of Joseph is often taken as the key scriptural attestation to the doctrine of providence. God works in mysterious ways, but God does get the job done! In this story, God is with Joseph, and thus God keeps one step ahead of Joseph's brothers. The brothers wish evil on Joseph, but God turns that into good (Gen. 50:20). The story is dramatic because God works behind the scenes as a personal agent and not an impersonal force that can be directly observed. God is the writer, director, producer, costumer, and scenic designer of the story, so much so that God is never eclipsed by Joseph, the play's star. The Joseph story was thus far more than a secular tale with a little bit of God thrown in for good measure. As André LaCocque, explains, "A trivial story of envy and jealousy becomes a parable of Jewish destiny in the world. A notion of election and providence, of vocation and divine direction, permeates the narrative and gives it its ultimate dimension that leaves far behind its other qualities of entertainment or as a portrait of mores."[12] The story of Joseph shows God directing human actions, no matter how sinful, toward a good conclusion.

The Joseph story works on the individual and social level simultaneously, because it is about both Joseph in particular but also Israel in general. According to many scholars, the Joseph story was written or edited during the postexilic or Second Temple period, after the Babylonian exile. When Israel as a nation collapsed, God had to be discovered in a wider context. Providence became crucial for Israel precisely at this time of tragedy and rebuilding. Significantly, Israel had to acknowledge that non-Jews played very important roles in history. Israel experienced divine deliverance in the Exodus, the wilderness wandering, and the conquest of Canaan, but Israel also experienced God's continuing guidance in the exile in Babylon. Just as Joseph's forced relocation to Egypt became his refuge and a blessing to his brothers, the exile in Babylon, the story suggests, would eventually work to the good for the people of Israel.

That Israel understood itself to be chosen by God does not mean that providence depends upon a certain chronological interpretation of Israel's history. Israel did not experience history first and then develop a doctrine of providence after the fact.[13] Any nation or group has a sense of history precisely because they are already in the act of interpreting it even as they live it. Time is not the framework for all of our experiences; narrative is. Stories are how we understand ourselves and the time we live in. In this sense, providence is the way in which Jews and Christians experience time. Other cultures and other religions structure time differently. Nations, families, and the myriad organizations we belong to all contribute their own narratives to the story we make of our lives. We do not just live in providence—we occupy many narratives, overlapping and conflicting with each other—but there is no other theological notion of time. For Christians, history tells a story, and providence provides the guidelines for how to read that story. Providence is just another word for time.

Scholars argue whether Israel had a sense of an ultimate goal of history that extended beyond its own national concerns. The question seems inappropriate. All history concerns the story of Israel. True, Israel does not treat providence in an abstract manner. There is very little speculation about a divine plan, a timeline on which all events can be plotted. The Prophets of the Old Testament are much more practical than that. They retrieve Israel's past in order to speak to its present as well as its future. The Prophets seek conversion, not prediction. Of course, the Prophets do make predictions in the sense of forecasts of what is to occur, but they also restate God's promises, which can be fulfilled in a number of different ways in the short term but point to an ultimate fulfillment that includes all of creation.

God's promises are not just for Israel. The covenant with Noah was universal and thus demonstrates how Israel understood its relationship to God to be embedded in an inclusive horizon. Although Israel mediates the relationship of all nations to God, nations are also given their own space and histories somewhat independent of Israel. As the Apostle Paul put it, "From one ancestor he made all nations to inhabit the whole earth, and he allotted the times of their existence and the boundaries of the places where they would live, so that they would search for God and perhaps grope for him and find him—though indeed he is not far from each one of us" (Acts 17:26–27). In the end, all nations will be blessed by God. "On that day Israel will be the third with Egypt and Assyria, a blessing in the midst of the earth, whom the LORD of hosts has blessed, saying, 'Blessed be Egypt my people, and Assyria the work of my hands, and Israel my heritage'" (Isa. 19:24–25). Like Isaiah, Amos chastises those who would interpret providence in an arrogant manner. "Are you not like the Ethiopians to me, O people of Israel? says the LORD. Did I not bring Israel up from the land of Egypt, and the Philistines from Caphtor and the Arameans from Kir?" (Amos 9:7). Israel is chosen to lead the nations, but the nations do have their own histories. However, those histories will make full sense only when they converge in the end with the story of Israel.

Even in the midst of the destruction of their nation, Israel maintained its confidence in God's governance of the world. Other nations can try to thwart God's plan, but their efforts will not avail. "Band together, you peoples, and be dismayed; listen, all you far countries. . . . Take counsel together, but it shall be brought to naught; speak a word, but it will not stand, for God is with us" (Isa. 8:9–10). God allows other nations to hold enormous power, but it is only temporary and for the instruction of Israel. The best example of this is Cyrus, the founder of the Persian Empire. God speaks clearly about Cyrus, saying, "He is my shepherd, and he shall carry out all my purpose" (Isa. 44:28). Cyrus is designated as God's anointed, a term otherwise reserved for Israel's kings or priests. God uses Cyrus to subdue the nations (Isa. 45:1). If God could so commission and reward Cyrus, a pagan idolater, how much more is God guiding America in its relationship to Israel and beyond?

That God chose Cyrus might be some justification for arguing that God has chosen to work through George W. Bush, but that does not answer the question of what God is doing through the president. Critics of the president argue that he is bringing God's judgment upon the land. God does work through the crises that confront nations. "Does disaster befall a city, unless GOD the LORD has done it?" (Amos 3:6). Amos is addressing Israel, but his point extends beyond that particular context. All nations exercise their power at the prerogative of the one true King. "The king's heart is a stream of water in the hand of the LORD; he turns it wherever he will" (Prov. 21:1). It would be shortsighted, then, to infer from the lack of philosophical speculation in the Old Testament that Israel's understanding of providence has no implications for God's relationship to every nation's history. Providence is always particular, in the sense of determining the meaning of the specific events that compose one nation's history, but providence also implies a goal that transcends every individual interest. The Old Testament gives little reason to go seeking divine revelation outside of this history, but it gives every reason to think that God guides the histories of other nations, if only in order to make them converge with this one.

Of course, for Christians, the history of Israel comes to a climax in the life of Jesus Christ. No other modern theologian has been so careful about keeping the focus of theology on the particularity of God's election of Jesus Christ than Karl Barth, so it would be appropriate to see what he has to say about providence. Karl Barth's theology is often criticized for being too severe in its treatment of God's lordship and our obedience, but in his discussion of providence, we see another side to his great vision of God's sovereignty. Some readers get hung up on Barth's insistence that God is absolutely singular, complete, and whole, from which Barth infers that God does not need us in any way. Nonetheless, God chooses to create us, and God also chooses to stay with us after the creation. God acts in history as the One who gives us freedom by demanding our obedience. Providence is the "co-ordination, integration, and co-operation"[14] of our lives into the divine. In his discussion of the doctrine of providence, Barth shows how God grants us true freedom by determining our lives according to God's will. God makes us a partner in the divine plan.

Karl Barth develops his theology of providence in the context of the doctrine of creation, but he is careful to distinguish between the two. God created the world at one particular time, but God guides history at every point of time. Providence is not just a corollary of creation, as if what God did at the beginning of time is to set in motion the laws that govern all subsequent time. This is the mistake of deism: It collapses providence into creation. Providence is how God works in history in order to bring time to a radically new fulfillment. The end of history is much more than a repetition of the act of creation in the beginning. Barth pays particular attention to the story in Genesis of God resting at the end of creation. For Barth, this means that the work of creation came to an end; likewise, it suggests that something new was about to begin.

The distinction between creation and providence is crucial in order to resist the tendency of some theologies to turn the doctrine of providence into a general theory of history. If providence is subsumed into a universal account of God's relationship to the world, then providence will be little different from speculative philosophies of historical change. Theology is always particular for Barth, precisely because we know God only in the unique person of Jesus Christ. Providence thus must be Christologically construed. God does not work through history according to human or natural laws. God works through history with the wounded yet glorified hands of Jesus Christ. A neutral providence reduces God to a universal principle that can be applied to every case, but that is precisely the problem. A neutral providence is one that is under our control. We can use it as a key to the hermeneutics of history. The result is a natural theology that justifies humanity's ways to God, rather than accepting God's way to humanity.

Barth cautions us against trying to pin down the precise ways in which God is at work in specific times and places. Providence is not a hypothesis, opinion, or postulate, he states over and over again. General providence is meaningful based on the special providence narrated in the Bible. Barth clearly was concerned about the abuse of this doctrine by German Christians during the rise of Nazism, given that he refers to providence as one of Hitler's favorite words.[15] He warns against beginning with a general principle about God's relationship to the world because such general principles tend to be wide enough to justify or rationalize any kind of nationalism or other sinful behavior. Providence is nothing other than the form that faith takes in our relationship to history. Providence thus must begin with Christ. Nevertheless, Barth goes so far in advising restraint, modesty, and caution in the use of this doctrine that he nearly undermines his own insistence on its importance.

Providence is grace, and so it is out of our hands. It is the time God gives the creature in order to allow the creature to participate in God's unfolding of the divine purpose. This means, for Barth, that God is never absent in any part of history. History is thoroughly providential. Barth makes this point by explaining that there is only one history, and that is the history of God. Barth thus anticipates the position of liberation theologians on the unitary view of history. There are not two histories running parallel to each other. This is a hard piece of theological wisdom, but Barth drives his point home. When we find ourselves forsaken by God, he explains, it is not that there is another history out there in which God is really present, and thus we can trust in that time as a contradiction to our own misery. Humans have only the one time of their lives, and God is in that time by determining it providentially. "There are certainly two standpoints from which the being of man and God's dealings with him may be seen and understood. But it is not the case that these confront and continually contradict one another. The case is rather that the standpoint of creation history is lit up by that of salvation history."[16] The time we live in is always dark. We cannot look inward for a subjective guarantee of God's presence. Yet we can look at the time of the Bible as our time too. The thin line of biblical narrative cuts a large swath through history. Indeed, there is only this one line of time. All other lines are nothing but mirrors of it.

The image of the mirror is, in fact, one of Barth's favorite ways to describe providence. The original covenant, founded in God's election of Jesus Christ, is not to be found among the artifacts of history. History reflects God's action in Christ, but that reflection is but a mirror image. We must be careful not to identify the history of our own time with salvation history. Barth's theology of providence can provide a corrective to those Christians who imply, by their rhetoric of America as the new Israel, that American history is sacred script. God, not any nation or national history, is the object of providence, and no nation can take the place of Israel. America's history must be read in the light of the Old Testament, but America does not shine with a light of its own. Barth liked the idea of reading current history as a "mask of God," and America in this sense can truly be called one of God's masks.[17]

The language of masks and mirrors might seem to evacuate human history of any ultimate meaning. That language can seem to denigrate the history we live in as nothing more than a repetition of the history recounted in the Bible. Contemporary events are less real than biblical events and have their own reality only insofar as they reflect the reality of God's mighty deeds. Barth is, however, a dialectical thinker. Thus he also insists that history is our home. We are more than just pilgrims. "Even as God's creatures, and within the world of other creatures, caught up in the great drama of being, we are not in an empty or alien place. It is not God's fault if we do not feel at home in our creatureliness and in this creaturely world."[18] We can accept the passing of time because God too has passed this way, redeeming time by becoming one of us. Indeed, Barth insists that God is found not just in the extraordinary or exceptional events of history. God "loves the law-abiding bourgeois as well as the nomad."[19] The victories of common sense, he says, are God's victories as well.

Another potential limitation of Barth's doctrine of providence is his placement of it within the context of his concern with theodicy. Since the Enlightenment, theologians and philosophers have passionately focused on the question of how God can allow evil in the world. Christians should rejoice that even in the midst of evil God is present, but skeptics use the fact of evil to deny God's providence. Barth does not resist the temptation to defend providence from the charge of evil. He calls providence a great "Nevertheless" that we say in spite of the confusion and emptiness of history. In other words, we do not read providence directly from historical events. History is not transparent to God's will. Providence is our faith that, even given the vanity of history, nevertheless, God is there. It is no coincidence, then, that the volume of *Church Dogmatics* that discusses providence contains Barth's longest and most systematic treatment of the problem of evil, which Barth addresses under the rubric of "God and Nothingness." The problem is that when providence is treated in the context of the problem of evil, it becomes just the kind of hypothesis to be tested that Barth despised.

More wise than the connection of providence to theodicy is Barth's decision to discuss heaven and angels in this same volume. Providence is not just an earthly matter. That God rules the heavens means that God does nothing less on earth. One of the traditional titles for Christ, after all, is King. Jesus Christ is not only the Messiah, the King of Israel, but also the ruler of the kingdom of heaven. Angels administer God's will and thus are the chief agents of divine providence.

Nonetheless, Barth did not think that God chooses specific nations in order to hurry along the coming of the kingdom. God's only concern with the nations is how they reflect God's just rule. God does not deal "with one state but with his state, the just state in all national states."[20] Barth was proud of his homeland, Switzerland, for its humane traditions, but he did not believe that Christians should give their stamp of approval to any particular political party. All of his political experiences warned him against treating providence as a skill of historical interpretation. The great majority of German intellectuals celebrated the outbreak of World War I, which taught Barth that providence can be subjected to the most tortured distortions. In fact, his rejection of natural theology—the attempt to begin with human knowledge in order to work up to knowledge of God—sets the context for his suspicions of providence. He saw providence as the misguided effort of Christians to find God working in one's own historical situation. This is misguided because we always read God wrong when we begin with reading ourselves.

Despite his suspicion of any association of providence with nationalism, Barth's own life demonstrates just how inescapable the providential reading of history is for Christians. He demonstrated tremendous wisdom in his early insight into the destructive and idolatrous nature of the Nazi Party.

More controversial was his political decision to oppose the Cold War by siding with neither Russia nor the United States. He rejected cheap anticommunism and, in fact, refused to hurl his great "No" to the East. He could speak with great enthusiasm about democracy: "The claim that there is a similarity or dissimilarity between all forms of government and the Gospel is not only well-known, but wrong. That one can go to hell in a democracy and be saved during mob-rule or in a dictatorship is true. But it is not true that as a Christian one can just as seriously support, want, and strive for mob-rule or a dictatorship as for democracy."[21] But he could not bring himself to condemn communism with the same passion. Emil Brunner was right to challenge Barth in 1948 to denounce communism in the same manner that he had denounced the Nazis. Barth remained throughout his life a humanist and a liberal in terms of being deeply suspicious of how social systems deprive individuals of their freedom.[22] As a liberal, he should have sided with America against the Soviet Union. That he did not suggests that Barth invested so much of himself in rejecting the Nazis that ever after he could not take the risk of thinking that God had embraced one nation for a universal good. Unfortunately, there are still those today who portray Barth as a political leftist whose theology was a thinly disguised mask for revolutionary political change. For Barth, a democratic state can be an allegory of the Word of God, but nations do not proclaim the gospel; only people can do that. Nevertheless, an allegory is better than an outright lie.

Barth's breakthrough point is that special providence has precedence over general providence. Unfortunately, this is precisely the opposite of what most theologians think today. As Maurice Wiles has stated, "What is conceptually questionable, morally dubious and dangerous in practice is the notion of particular events as occasions of specific providential activity on the part of God. . . . I don't think many thoughtful people, even among firm Christian believers, really believe in the idea of special providences. But they feel guilty about not doing so."[23] Wiles argues that, once special providence is given up as a remnant of the superstitious imagination, there are only two alternatives. One can say that God's providential activity is absolutely universal, so that God's actions lie behind every action in the world, or one can deny providence altogether.

Wiles attributes the universal position to Kathryn Tanner. Tanner's position, by tracing every action directly and immediately to God, undercuts our ability to single out some acts as having a special providential character. The best way to understand her complex position is to see what she rejects. "One might try to get a sense of the sort of world God wants to bring about by isolating principles and precedents to be found in the Bible, then using this information to defend the rightfulness of one's intentions and acts as a response to present circumstances," she writes. According to her view of providence, however, "the emphasis on God's active and free sovereignty makes at least the application of those principles and precedents problematic. The force of precedent in particular is undercut; God may be working differently now than before."[24] Her emphasis on the immediate presence of God in every event severs providence from its biblical roots and makes of it an expression of acceptance, perhaps gratitude, but hardly a skill of historical interpretation.

Special providence can seem to trivialize the actions of God by portraying the divine as more interested in the minutiae of everyday life than such things warrant. This rejection of special providence, however, is based on a mistaken image of God. If God were one of us, then God would be crazy to be more interested in the things we do than we ourselves are. God would be the ultimate multitasker, or the absolute computer, processing information faster than the speed of grace! But God is not like us. God's agency is completely different from ours. Any form of providence makes sense only when God is understood to be absolutely unique. There is only one God, and the very nature of God is to permit no other gods to exercise rule in the universe.

The denial of special providence these days often goes under the banner of open or relational theism. Evangelical theologians John Sanders and Clark H. Pinnock have developed the most cogent and sophisticated account of an open God, and they have been heavily criticized in the Evangelical community for their efforts.[25] They are sincere Christians and brilliant theologians, among the best Christian minds of the day, but they are still wrong. The root problem is that open theism wants to make God look more like us. Sometimes this model argues for God's omnipotence and omniscience, only to suggest that God is self-limiting. God exercises self-restraint in order to give us freedom. This is logically inconsistent, because it suggests that God is so in charge of the world that God can step back from the world in order to achieve God's purposes. Either God really does step back from the world, in which case there is no providence, or God's step back is just a feint, in which case God is not self-limiting. Only if God is one of us does God need to limit the divine power in order to empower us.

At other times, open theists argue that God's nature entails vulnerability and change, which risks reducing God to an agent in the world who is an awful lot like us. Traditional theists note that God's level of operation in the world is totally different from our own, so that God's agency and ours cannot compete. God does not replace human causation in the world, creating robots to do his bidding, but neither does God withdraw from the world and observe us from afar. God works in the world in a mysterious way that affirms our freedom. According to the terminology of classical theism, God is the primary cause of all things, but God does not obliterate the secondary causation that we can test through scientific observation. A classical doctrine of providence would avoid both extremes of humanizing God by making

God an agent like us (proponents of open theism would argue that they are doing justice to the anthropomorphic images of God in the Bible) or dehumanizing God by portraying God as the immediate cause of every event. God's providence is more mysterious than both of these alternatives allow. For Tanner, God controls everything in a general way, but I would rather extend Barth's insight by suggesting that God controls everything in a special way. If one begins with general providence, then it becomes hard to distinguish God from fate or from the scientific laws of nature. But special providence does not mean that God lets nature roll along according to its own laws, only to intervene with the occasional miracle. All of God's action in the world is special in the sense that it is based on the biblical history of Israel and the Father's care for the Son. All of God's action in the world is also personal in that a triune God, and not a distant superpower in the sky, guides history and nature alike. General providence can seem like a tempting model for all of providence because of the regularity of natural events, but scientists have long rejected the closed mechanical system of nature based on Newtonian physics. It is no longer adequate to say that God macromanages human history while micromanaging nature, given that nature is as open and free as history. Chaos theory shows how large patterns of events are dependent on singular situations that cannot be predicted or anticipated, and quantum theory demonstrates the complexity, if not the uncertainty, of the smallest of atomic events. Certainly our devotional understanding of God's actions in the world will differ from scientific and historical examinations of various events, but there is no reason to begin with natural law as a model for how God works through history, just as there is no reason to reduce God's role in history to a manager and motivator of free actors. God is in charge of both history and nature, and God's governance is complete and final, yet God's governance includes the blessing of human freedom and the integrity of human action.

What special providence properly highlights about God's authority is that it encompasses the political authority of rulers and the ruled. Christians hope for the eventual "conversion of the political into the cosmic," as Aidan Nichols puts it, which implies that nation-states have more than an incidental role to play in sacred history.[26] The biblical view of nations is determined by the history of Israel, but it is also framed by the first and the last books of the Bible. The story of the Tower of Babel (Gen. 11) explains how God ordained cultural pluralism as a restraint on evil. God saw that limitless human freedom is dangerous. Humanity was not ready to exercise the power of speaking one language. God dispersed the builders of Babel by confusing their tongues. Henceforth, pluralism would become an aspect of the human condition; nations would emerge with the potential for grave misunderstandings and mortal combat. As a consequence of the pride that resulted from the fall, pluralism is hardly seen as a good in itself, but it is also not understood as a barrier to divine providence. Thus there is a constructive tension between Gen. 11 and Rev. 7:9–12, where John sees a great multitude from every nation standing before the throne of the lamb. Clearly, human beings are more than their national identity, but nations comprise the humanity that God will save in the end.

No political theologian has done more to stress the importance of political history to God's plan than the Anglican Evangelical theologian Oliver O'Donovan. O'Donovan has been accused of developing a reactionary defense of Christendom, and thus of being a modern-day Eusebius, but his thought is much more profound than that. All theology is political for O'Donovan, but not in the sense of having political consequences. Theology is political because a real analogy exists between divine and human rule. While Augustine set out to unmask the political achievements of antiquity, such acts of suspicion today are too easy and thus degenerate into cynicism and apathy. Political engagement is both risky and necessary; even being politically passive is a decision with consequences. O'Donovan's project is ambitious and cannot be easily summarized, but the scope of his thinking should be noted: He wants to reinstate Western politics within a theological horizon. Church authority, contrary to Hauerwas, cannot be limited to the church alone. Neither can church authority be limited to the office and structure of church hierarchy. Political activity should be given a positive and not just critical theological account, and that account must begin with Israel.

The reason we can speak of human political authority, according to O'Donovan, is that God has asked us to speak of God's authority in terms of the divine rule. True, the New Testament does not address its audience in terms of a nation or a polis. The books of the New Testament were written to believers scattered throughout the Roman Empire in order to bring them into the new community of the church. As a universal message, however, the Gospel cannot be understood apart from the role of nations in the Old Testament. When the Bible proclaims that the Lord is King, it really means it. Politics and theology are thus inseparable. God's authority is absolute and unique, but it is not irrelevant to how humans organize themselves politically. God is King; human kings are such only metaphorically. The hope of Israel, after all, was for land, not otherworldly salvation. All nations will one day be reflected in the light of that hope. As an Anglican, O'Donovan comes from a tradition that still uses a coronation rite, which points to the unity of church and crown, but his point is more general than that. Secular political arrangements have only the authority that God grants them. Secular governments cannot stand on their own. Even the best democracies must offer their citizens more than a mirror of themselves, which means that democracies can never meet their citizens' deepest political needs. The secular thus stands under God's judgment and awaits transformation in God's kingdom.

To be alienated from political authority is to be alienated from ourselves and from God. Such alienation is the rule today, when cynicism about political authority reigns. For O'Donovan, this state of affairs is not inevitable or even natural, because God has given us the resources to reinstate political authority on its proper basis. That foundation is, in a way, the doctrine of providence. As O'Donovan states, "YHWH's kingship is not a creation *ex nihilo* but an act of providence, keeping faith with creation once made. It is, therefore, true to say that the goodness of his authority lies in the fact that it demands what is recognizable—but not recognizable as a reflection of the worshippers' *wills*, rather as a calling to their *fulfillment*."[27] The fusion of human and divine authority is given to us as a guide in the history of Israel, but it also functions as a horizon for eschatology. It is the *telos* that drives all nations beyond themselves in a quest for true authority.

Political authority can be understood providentially because biblical history provides us with the tools to interpret the origin as well as the destiny of the nations. For O'Donovan, the advent of Jesus Christ is crucial, but the incarnation cannot be separated from the covenant that Jesus came to renew and fulfill. The authority of Jesus is in continuity with the emergence of a body of law under God's kingship over Israel. Of course, God does not need this body of law in order to rule over Israel or any other nation, for that matter. God's kingship did not cease when Israel was carried into Babylonian captivity. Even governments that are illegitimate from the point of view of God's demand for justice can carry out the divine will. As O'Donovan explains, "If Israel's experience of government is to be taken as a model for other societies, then we must allow that divine providence is ready to protect other national traditions besides the sacred one."[28] God's rule was conceived by the Israelites as international in scope, and its aim was nothing less than global peace. God's special providence for Israel does not preclude more general (but nonetheless not less special!) providential direction of other nations.

In Babylon, Israel found itself under the dual rule of the true God and a foreign king, which is still the situation that all of God's people find themselves in today. Political dualism, however, is not the destiny of the faithful or the nations. God is still King, and Jesus's proclamation of the kingdom shows that "he did not recognize a permanently twofold locus of authority." For Christians, Jesus mediates God's authority, so that the Davidic monarchy is reconstituted under his leadership. O'Donovan can go a long way toward Hauerwas's position when asserting "the true character of the church as a political society."[29] The point of the church, however, is not to withdraw into its own political sphere. It is to work toward the transformation of the political by keeping its focus on the eschatological horizon of the end of dual authority. O'Donovan can talk at times as if baptism confers all the political identity a Christian needs. Nevertheless, if it was God's intention to preserve

Israel under the divine rule during the Babylonian exile, then it follows that God is preserving Christians in their nations today. Nations have legitimacy as vehicles of God's plan, but they should restrict their authority in order to provide room for the growth of the true kingdom that will one day supplant them.

For O'Donovan, governments are authorized by the rule of Jesus Christ, but only for minimal purposes. As O'Donovan writes, "The responsible state is minimally coercive and minimally representative."[30] The purpose of the ideal government is limited to what O'Donovan calls "judgment." Governments are at their best when they apply God's law in order to attain justice. They should not invent law on their own. It follows, for O'Donovan, that the court, not the legislature, is the paradigm of all true governance.[31]

Nicholas Wolterstorff has criticized O'Donovan for his parameters for the proper role of governments today.[32] For Wolterstorff, there is no reason to think that states cannot be more ambitious than O'Donovan allows. Wolterstorff takes issue with this classically liberal (conservative, to use contemporary terminology) view of the state. The details of domestic policies can be endlessly debated, but from a providential point of view, it is hard to deny that limited government seems to be the wave of the future. O'Donovan's argument about government, however, is theological. From a Christological point of view, as much authority should be given to the church as possible, so that the state guarantees religious freedom but does not usurp the role of the church. This is what America, at its best, has accomplished.

My questions for O'Donovan are not Wolterstorff's. I am more interested in his providential reading of history and his view of eschatology. The destiny of society is to be transformed, O'Donovan states, but the destiny of rulers is "to disappear, renouncing their sovereignty in the face of his [Christ's]." This is clear enough, but the tricky point is to sketch out the biblical plan of the transition from the one to the other. How can we imagine the ultimate political triumph of Jesus Christ? How will nations give up their power, and how can societies be transformed without human rulers leading the way? For O'Donovan, the proper unifying element in international relations is law, not government. Empire is the name he gives to nations that overreach themselves and thus work against God's providence. But are all empires the same? And how does one acknowledge the role of empires in providence, given one of O'Donovan's theorems: "That any regime should actually come to hold authority, and should continue to hold it, is a work of divine providence in history, not a mere accomplishment of the human task of political service"? O'Donovan goes so far as to acknowledge the way modern liberalism develops the legacy of Christendom through its emphasis on freedom and justice. He also correctly notes that the substance of Christendom was mission: "It was the missionary imperative that compelled the church to take the conversion of the empire seriously and to seize the opportunities it offered. These were not mere opportunities for power."[33] So how is the American empire extending the virtues of Christendom and how should Christians seize upon it in order to spread the gospel?

O'Donovan's defense of international law, it should be noted, does not mean he necessarily disagrees with the Bush doctrine of preventive war. In a sophisticated account of the just war tradition, he shows how preventive wars must be defended by demonstrating a grave danger for not going to war. International authority can retain its legitimacy only if it is able to act effectively in times of crisis. That has not been the case in recent years with the United Nations. "Just as private citizens may tackle and detain a mugger in the absence of the police," O'Donovan explains, "improvising a form of government where the official form is not at hand, so a nation may improvise international justice where international authority is not capable of enacting it."[34] Unilateralism is not always bad, though in order for it to be good it must be aimed at achieving new configurations of international cooperation and consensus.

If the Lordship of Jesus Christ is truly global, if the desire of nations for true authority will one day be fulfilled in history, and if God's covenant with Israel is eternal, then the most important task of theology today is to offer a biblically sound interpretation of the relationship of the church to international politics, the fate of nations, and the purpose of limited government. All of these subjects can be addressed under the rubric of globalism. Inspired by O'Donovan, and in an attempt to add to and even complete his theological project, I propose my own vision of the true nature of globalism in the next chapter.

NOTES

1. Jonathan Edwards, *A History of the Work of Redemption*, ed. John F. Wilson (New Haven, CT: Yale University Press, 1989), 118.

2. *The Constitution of the Presbyterian Church (U.S.A.)*, part 1: *Book of Confessions* (Louisville, KY: The Office of the General Assembly, 2002), 126.

3. Christopher Lasch, *The One and Only Heaven: Progress and Its Critics* (New York: Norton, 1991). For a more positive assessment of the relationship between providence and progress, see the appendix.

4. Ibid., 47.

5. Averil Cameron and Stuart G. Hall, trans., *Eusebius, Life of Constantine* (Oxford: Clarendon Press, 1999).

6. For an account of this story, see Jaroslav Pelikan, *Christianity and Classical Culture: The Metamorphosis of Natural Theology in the Christian Encounter with Hellenism* (New Haven, CT: Yale University Press, 1993), 160. For a fascinating discussion of the relationship between providence and gambling in American history, see Jackson Lears, *Something for Nothing: Luck in America* (New York: Viking, 2003).

7. Eusebius, "From a Speech on the Dedication of the Holy Sepulchre Church," in Oliver O'Donovan and Joan Lockwood O'Donovan, eds., *From Irenaeus to Grotius: A Sourcebook in Christian Political Thought* (Grand Rapids: Eerdmans, 1999), 58.

8. Augustine, *City of God*, trans. Henry Bettenson (New York: Penguin Books, 1972), 139.

9. John Von Heyking, *Augustine and Politics as Longing in the World* (Columbia: University of Missouri Press, 2001). Also see Donald X. Burt, *Friendship and Society: An Introduction to Augustine's Practical Philosophy* (Grand Rapid: Eerdmans, 1999), 145.

10. Paulus Orosius, *Anti-Pagan History*, from the selection in O'Donovan and O'Donovan, *From Irenaeus to Grotius*, 167.

11. From the selection in O'Donovan and O'Donovan, *From Irenaeus to Grotius*, 415, 419, 422.

12. André LaCocque and Paul Ricoeur, *Thinking Biblically: Exegetical and Hermeneutical Studies*, trans. David Pellaur (Chicago: University of Chicago Press, 1998), 389.

13. John Rogerson, "Can a Doctrine of Providence Be Based on the Old Testament?" in *Ascribe to the Lord: Biblical and Other Studies in Memory of Peter C. Craigie*, ed. Lyle Eslinger and Glen Taylor, Journal for the Study of the Old Testament Series 67 (Sheffield: JSOT Press, 1988), 531.

14. Karl Barth, *Church Dogmatics*, III/3, *The Doctrine of Creation*, trans. G. W. Bromiley and R. J. Ehrlich (Edinburgh: T. & T. Clark, 1960), 41. For commentary, see Kathryn Tanner, "Creation and Providence," in *The Cambridge Companion to Karl Barth*, ed. John Webster (Cambridge: Cambridge University Press, 2000), chap. 7.

15. Barth, *Church Dogmatics*, III/3, 33.

16. Ibid., 40.

17. Ibid., 21.

18. Ibid., 48.

19. Ibid., 161.

20. Quoted in Frank Jehle, *Ever Against the Stream: The Politics of Karl Barth*, 1906–1968, trans. Richard and Martha Burnett (Grand Rapids: Eerdmans, 2002), 2.

21. Ibid., 95.

22. For this point, see Haddon Willmer, "Karl Barth," in *The Blackwell Companion to Political Theology*, ed. Peter Scott and William T. Cavanaugh (Oxford: Blackwell, 2004), 132.

23. Maurice Wiles, "Providence," *Epworth Review* 21, no. 1 (January 1994): 81.

24. Kathryn Tanner, *The Politics of God: Christian Theologies and Social Justice* (Philadelphia: Fortress Press, 1992), 106.

25. Clark Pinnock et al., *The Openness of God: A Biblical Challenge to the Traditional Understanding of God* (Downers Grove, IL: InterVarsity Press, 1994), and John Sanders, *The God Who Risks: A Theology of Providence* (Downers Grove, IL: InterVarsity Press, 1998). Also see the fascinating revival of cosmic warfare theology and a consequent critique of classical notions of providence in Gregory A. Boyd, *God at War: The Bible and Spiritual Conflict* (Downers Grove, IL: InterVarsity Press, 1997).

26. Aidan Nichols, *Christendom Awake: On Re-Energizing the Church in Culture* (Grand Rapids: Eerdmans, 1999), 71.

27. Oliver O'Donovan, *The Desire of the Nations: Rediscovering the Roots of Political Theology* (Cambridge: Cambridge University Press, 1996), 32. Also very helpful is Craig Bartholomew, Jonathan Chaplin, Robert Song, and Al Wolters, eds., *A Royal Priesthood? The Use of the Bible Ethically and Politically: A Dialogue with Oliver O'Donovan* (Carlisle, UK: Paternoster Press, 2002).

28. O'Donovan, *The Desire of the Nations*, 73.

29. Ibid., 93, 159.

30. Ibid., 233.

31. Oliver O'Donovan and Joan Lockwood O'Donovan, *Bonds of Imperfection: Christian Politics Past and Present* (Grand Rapids: Eerdmans, 2004), 207–24

32. Nicholas Wolterstorff, "A Discussion of Oliver O'Donovan's *The Desire of the Nations*," in *Scottish Journal of Theology* 54, no. 1 (2001): 87–107.

33. O'Donovan, *Desire of the Nations*, 193, 46, 212.

34. Oliver O'Donovan, *The Just War Revisited* (Cambridge: Cambridge University Press, 2003), 135.

CHAPTER SIX

On the Two Globalisms and the Destiny of American Christianity

"Globalization" is a term that is as vague and malleable as "postmodernism." You can find anybody saying anything about it, which makes it seem like a postmodern phenomenon. Among the cultural elite, globalization has become a dirty word, having been dragged through the mud in the wake of America's ascent to its status as the world's sole superpower. Like most dirty words, its meaning is very slippery. Although it has a very contemporary sound, globalization is as ancient as the silk road. Today, the growth of networks of economic interdependence raises the dreams and fears of a one-world government. Like all economic systems, the global economy cannot be left to function without some kind of governance. A world economy requires world order.

Leftist critics of American foreign policy dream of global peace and harmony, while ignoring the fact that free trade is one of the best means of preventing war. Nevertheless, even free trade is not enough to keep international competition in check. The European balance of power has kept the world's leading nations in various wars for over half the years since 1500.[1] What is needed is strong international leadership, in addition to open markets and democratic governments. Joseph S. Nye Jr., an assistant secretary of defense in the Clinton administration, has pointed out that an inequality of power can provide the context for peace and stability better than the elusive quest for a precarious balance of powers.[2] What shape the Pax Americana will take—and not the triumph of global capitalism, which has already occurred—is the real question raised by this singular word.

Capitalism was global long before America entered the scene, but America, because of the bounty of its land and the habits of its citizens, has taken that economic system to unlimited heights. Marxists are right at least in regard to one thing: Capitalism has inherently global ambitions. After all, open markets and political freedom are concrete aims that presuppose an international scope. "Globalization" has become a catchword for all that is bad about the world economy only because "socialism" is a word that nobody takes seriously anymore. When it became obvious that socialist governments could not advance the prosperity of their citizens, the only thing left for political radicals was to bemoan the expansion of American values and influence. The leftist criticism of globalization is ironic, if not hypocritical, because activists on the left hoped for a world government based on socialist principles well before they turned on globalization as a pernicious form of homogenization and a cover for the imperial export of Western values. Communism's own global ambitions were a distortion of Christianity's expectation of a just end to history, but communism could not deliver the goods. It is hard not to come to the conclusion that, as far as free trade is concern, the leftist critique of globalism is a case of sour grapes.

Critics of globalization see America hiding behind every international trade, and they portray America as a more insidious threat to the world than communism ever was. This portrayal is especially prevalent in Europe, where, as Jean Bethke Elshtain observes, "Anti-Americanism is the form that nationalism takes in many European countries."[3] Anti-Americanism functions to unite many Europeans, but it is more than that. Anti-Americanism is so passionately irrational that it can only be described as a new religious movement, the dogma of the antiglobalization left. Jean-Francois Revel has documented its fanatical extremism in his home country of France.[4] The French were not content to call America a superpower, so they coined the term "hyperpower." It sounds a bit like hyperbole, which fits the French tendency to see America as all superficial style without any intellectual substance. Revel attributes the exuberance of anti-Americanism to a psychological disturbance along the lines of an obsession, which makes sense, especially when one realizes that America's superpower status can be attributable to European mistakes. America has entered the world scene largely because of what Europe has done or what Europe has left undone.

More substantially, Revel demonstrates how the Blame America First reflex is a visceral rejection of everything associated with liberal democracy in favor of everything associated with socialism. His documentation of how the liberal media and cultural elites have been more charitable toward the communism of the Soviet Union than the liberal democracy of America is shocking. Revel attributes this double standard to irrational prejudice, but it is worth looking a little bit deeper for a rational explanation. The only factor that could explain this discrepancy in the treatment of Russian communism and American capitalism is the role of religion in the two nations. The Soviet

Union was given a pass because it represented the culmination of the modern faith in progress. America was treated so much more harshly because it was an obstacle to the secular dream of a united and enlightened humanity. More specifically, America was and is often abused because of its claim to have a providential relationship to God. The good is always the object of ridicule in this fallen world, and a nation that thinks it has been chosen to achieve good on a global scale is especially susceptible to the most virulent forms of scapegoating.

So much criticism for a nation whose highest goal, apparently, is to amuse and feed the rest of the world. Globalization gets caricatured as the triumph of Disney and McDonald's, but if America were so predictable in its exports, it could hardly have such threatening success. Globalization is better thought of as the economic form that corresponds to the metamorphosis of all cultures into pluralistic societies. America is poised to become the most global empire the world has ever seen precisely because it has the most pluralistic culture in the world. American provides the cultural substance for globalism because America is itself a microcosm of the globe. American culture is open, inclusive, dynamic, and adaptive. Everyone can be American while still maintaining something of their own national identity. American globalization works because it provides a carefully crafted menu of options that is perfect for every occasion. It is not just Disney but a thousand television channels and not just McDonald's but the chance to eat sushi, steak, and sauerkraut in the same restaurant that are the engines of American capitalism. Leftists are simply wrong when they say that Americanization equals homogenization. They are confusing American capitalism with Russian communism.

Some critics of globalization defend good old-fashioned national interests, but others want a global culture that stands for environmentalism, feminism, and the radical redistribution of wealth. That is, they do not mind a global culture; they just do not want that culture to be shaped by American corporations. It is almost as if leftist critics would not mind if everyone were watching the same movies, as long as those movies were independent, low-budget productions or plaintive pieces of French philosophizing rather than American action blockbusters. In other words, leftists want the global culture to fit their understanding of high rather than low culture, even though high cultures are, by definition, elitist and serve to unite the ruling classes.

Marxist Antonio Negri offers an example of this confusion. He is not sure whether to celebrate or lament the fact that national identities have been so scrambled that "we continually find the First World in the Third, the Third in the First, and the Second almost nowhere at all."[5] National sovereignty, according to Negri, has been transformed into a global cultural empire, with its headquarters in Hollywood but confined by no geographical boundary. The new empire, in other words, is American in spirit but not limited to

America in the flesh. This causes problems for leftist agitation. How can an empire that possesses no territorial specificity be fought, let alone defeated? If there is no wizard behind all the glittering machinery of the new empire, how can he be exposed? True, America has the most to gain in this new world order, but Negri himself points out that European dominance was a peculiarly modern phenomenon while American hegemony takes a postmodern form. If the outline of modern empires was clear enough, the postmodern empire is blurry and cannot be equated simply with American national interests. When the new global empire is everywhere, it is also nowhere, and political conflict is best replaced by the pursuit of economic productivity.

Significantly, Negri acknowledges that along with the growth of the first truly global Western empire (that is, Rome) came the first truly transcendent alternative to empire (the church). Rome and Christianity, empire and church, are in equal parts completely opposed to each other and completely inseparable. It is, in other words, impossible to conceive of them independently. Empires demand ideological uniformity, but Christianity stood outside of Rome's authority even as it took advantage of Rome's roads. Yet the pagan foundations of Rome faltered, and Christianity provided a stronger justification for European unity. Negri does not think the church can pull the same trick today, but he does hope to find something like a Christian response to empire. "Given that the limits and unresolvable problems of the new imperial right are fixed, theory and practice can go beyond them, finding once again an ontological basis of antagonism—within Empire, but also against Empire, at the same level of totality."[6] In other words, protest against globalism must come from within the very forces that have created globalism in the first place. There is no absolute exterior to capitalism anymore. Just as Rome provided the roads that led to the spread of the religion that eventually checked its impulses and finally replaced it, Negri hopes that global capitalism today will likewise give birth to forces that will lead to its own demise. By his own analysis, though, globalism knows no limits, so his hope seems like wishful thinking. I suggest in this chapter that only the church can play the role of globalism's *other*, precisely because the church is both inside and outside of Western capitalism. Christianity is the source of much of globalism's success, so only Christianity can be sufficiently inside of this economic process in order to divert it away from its own most destructive tendencies. Only the parent can tell the child when enough is enough, no matter how big the child has grown.

The problem that Negri expounds can be simplified considerably: Global harmony can be achieved only with the spread of a universal culture, but the only nonreligious candidate for a truly global culture is the American consumerism that leftists love to deride. The best bet for global peace is global prosperity, which can come only with open borders and mutual trade, which are precisely the goals of American foreign policy. Sometimes critics of globalism want nation-states to have the power to protect their own local interests, but such arguments support the defense of national sovereignty, the very thing leftist critics most bemoan about the United States. True, Hollywood functions as a form of soft American power, spreading American values, but this does not guarantee perpetual American supremacy. It does not even guarantee that other countries will like us, given that American culture is simultaneously loved and abhorred. Furthermore, many analysts think that the spread of technology will result in a decrease in American hard power, because the Chinese might come to dominate the Internet, for example, and poorer nations will be able to have quicker access to technological information.

While critics rage against American power, others predict our slow decline. Some political scientists think that America does not have the will to play the global cop. Charles A. Kupchan predicts that the European Union will become the next global power.[7] George Soros thinks that America is fated for oblivion at the rate we are going, while Robert Jay Lifton opines that there is a "malignant synergy" between the United States and Al-Qaeda. Emmanuel Todd is already talking about what the world will be like "after the Empire," when our predator behavior will leave us in reckless disregard of our profligate spending, which remains, he argues, our chief weakness.[8] (One might think our weakness is more evident in our inability to persuade even the smallest nations to cast a symbolic vote in our favor at the United Nations.) Scholars in this camp can be called declinists, and they typically want America to return to an isolationist foreign policy. Unfortunately or not, the undeniable reality of the spread of American culture means that there is no turning back from America's deep involvement in global affairs. Nevertheless, triumphalism is not a better attitude than isolationism, given that nothing lasts forever, especially in the information age.

It is just as likely that globalization will bring a new age of competition as cooperation. True, many analysts predict that national borders will become increasingly virtual as transnational and nongovernmental organizations grow in power. Nevertheless, nation-states will not necessarily vanish. On the contrary, nations will have to work all the harder to protect their interests. Limiting competition to the economic sphere is an advance from the age of world wars, but there is no guarantee that open markets will bring to an end the need to protect national boundaries. The rise of terrorism indicates that policing borders will become more important, not less, in the future. Suppressing terrorism will also require cooperation between countries, which is why policy makers like Nye have been critical of President Bush.[9] There are certainly good reasons to work with allies to achieve common goals, but such alliances can do as much to entangle nations in regional conflicts as to support world peace. For Nye, the problem is whether America can use its soft power overseas to develop the kind of cultural consensus that makes the use of hard power effective, when it is needed at all. Thus Nye argues that America must maintain democracy at home if it is to be admired overseas. In fact, whether other countries follow our political example or not, our democracy is the source of our strongest "soft" power. If America does decline, it most likely will be because of an internal loss of direction rather than an external challenge to our might. If America were to completely lose its sense of a providential calling, then there would be no point to its worldwide leadership, and calls for isolationism would be impossible to ignore. The culture wars at home are as momentous as any wars we might fight abroad.

If we export democracy abroad, then we have to know why we value it at home. As I have argued throughout this book, democracy is a theological good, firmly rooted in Christian principles. It is hard to remember just how much criticism Ronald Reagan took when he began working to support the spread of democracy abroad. Clinton followed this policy, which had widespread support until the invasion of Iraq rejuvenated antidemocratic sentiment from the left. A number of federal agencies work toward supporting democracy abroad, including the State Department, Defense Department, U.S. Agency for International Development, Justice Department, and the National Endowment for Democracy. More should be done to build democratic institutions in developing nations.

A crucial distinction needs to be stressed, however, in order to avoid romantic notions of world harmony. America cannot always act democratically on the world stage, even as it acts to increase the number of democracies in the world. Globalization requires management, and without some kind of world religion, global management will have to work through the imposition of power rather than the quest for consensus. In the next and final chapter, I examine Carl Schmitt's argument that pure democracies are impossible given the need for a decision (the exercise of sovereignty) in the face of an emergency. Much the same can be said about globalization. A democracy of nations is no less impossible than a pure democracy of individuals. For better or worse, and for the foreseeable future, the United States will have to make the difficult decisions in times of crisis, as with the question of how to handle terrorist states. America need not always act alone, but multilateral actions will likely be increasingly selective.

Declinists often point to the illusory hopes for eternal supremacy of both the Roman and the British empires as exemplary warnings for American aspirations. The British Empire is especially held up as the paradigm of everything that is wrong with a religious sense of national mission. Americans are reluctant to compare their global political situation to that of Britain because it is deeply ingrained into the American consciousness that

Britain is what America is not. Our freedoms came at the cost of rejecting British rule. Nevertheless, continuities between America and England are greater than discontinuities. The American Empire was born at the end of World War II when America took over from exhausted Britain its global role. *Took* is not a bad word, because it lies between *stole* and *received*. Franklin Delano Roosevelt hated the British colonial system because he thought it led inevitably to war as well as the impoverishment of their colonies. In a way, he trusted Stalin and the Chinese nationalist leader Chiang Kai-shek more than Churchill, and Churchill knew it. Americans fought against the Germans and the Japanese, but they fought for the end of every variety of imperialism, which included the British. The British mortgaged their empire for the war effort, and they understood at the end of the war, better than the Americans, that the United States had bought their debt.

Of course, the American Empire was no accident. It was a continuation of policies that date back to Alexander Hamilton's recognition of the need for a strong federal system of economic regulation. Hamilton understood that America would have to become an empire in order to ensure its economic expansion; even Jefferson, Hamilton's staunchest foe, saw imperial expansion westward as necessary for America's future. It was no coincidence that America became an empire at British expense; the American Empire is a continuation of its predecessor, only on a much grander scale.

The British Empire is much maligned, and not only by antiglobalists. Its greatest sin for most Americans was not its global ambitions but the manner by which those ambitions were expressed. Every film about the British Empire shows its representatives condescending to native peoples, completely unaware of their own arrogant and patronizing tone. Even the youngest student of American history is incensed by stories of incompetent and arrogant Englishmen telling the colonialists what to do. For Americans, as I argued in chapter 3, fairness (and its related virtues of honesty, openness, and plain speaking) is the basis of democracy. Americans all speak alike; even the mightiest should not speak with a distinctive tone. To be spoken down to is to be denied one's rights. Democracy affords everyone the right to be treated with some minimal degree of respect. The British Empire, fairly or not, represents in the American imagination not the evils of empire per se but the evils of a society ruled by overt social signs of unbridgeable economic classes.

Niall Ferguson, one of the finest contemporary British historians, has taken a fresh approach to the British Empire by demonstrating its many virtues as well as acknowledging its vices. Perhaps we are sufficiently removed from it—and perhaps Americans are now aware of how difficult imperial responsibilities are—that it can be given a more balanced treatment. Free trade is not a naturally occurring tendency in the world; it is a result of Britain's global ambitions. Critics of imperialism now argue that its effects on the powerful are nearly as bad as its impact on developing coun-tries.[10] One reason they make this argument is that it is no longer clear that the effects of the British Empire on its colonies were as bad as people used to think. Ferguson points to the example of Zambia, whose per capita GDP is today twenty-eight times less than in Britain; the differential in the colonial period was much less, on the order of seven times.[11] The rule of law, coupled with efficient and corruption-free governments, is essential for economic growth, and that is precisely what Britain imposed on its colonies. Lord Curzon, as Ferguson is the first to admit, went too far in declaring "the British Empire is under Providence the greatest instrument for good that the world has seen."[12] Yet the benefits of British rule, as listed by Ferguson, are impossible to exaggerate: the unitive role of the English language, English property law, common law, the spread of Protestantism, English banking practices, team sports, the ideal of a limited state, representative government, and the nearly universal recognition that liberty is a positive good.

The British government ruled roughly a quarter of the world's popula-tion in a remarkably minimal way. Perhaps that is its most lasting heritage. Global governance need not be based on massive military force but rather the spread of a universal culture.

Thanks to the British, globalization is, in Ferguson's elegant word, anglobalization. America continues the British Empire but is shed of its sense of inherent cultural superiority. Indeed, Americans have always felt a little bit inferior to the British and have compensated for their lack of ancient traditions by absorbing everyone else's. The American Empire has been called a British Empire Lite, but it would be better to think of the American Empire as a low-church version of its British parent. That the British Empire was rationalized by an established church while the American Empire has taken the form of disestablished Christianity makes all the difference. Kevin Phillips has demonstrated, in his magisterial work, *The Cousins' Wars*, just how much the American Revolution was a continuation of the English Civil War. Phillips notes that he did not set out to write about religion, but its role in European history surprised him. It is hard to imagine a time when inter-est rates were a matter for theological debate, so hard that many historians do not even try. For Phillips, the story of military revolutions must be told in theological terms. The sixteenth century to the eighteenth (and beyond) saw one long battle between low-church and high-church forces, and the former were fortified by their belief that God's kingdom was their destiny. The result was not only the triumph of America's low-church culture but also the expansion of "political liberties, commercial progress, technological inven-tiveness, linguistic ambition, and territorial expansion."[13] The struggle between America and Britain for world supremacy thus began long before FDR made the dismantling of British colonies a goal of World War II. The

Puritan ambition was not satisfied, after losing in England in the seventeenth century, with winning in America in the eighteenth; the Civil War was also a result of the providential mission that propelled the Puritan consciousness through history. At the end of the Civil War, it was clear that "Cavaliers, aristocrats, and bishops pretty much lost and Puritans, Yankees, self-made entrepreneurs, Anglo-Saxon nationalists, and expansionists had the edge."[14] Britain still had decades of economic growth ahead, but the New World had already laid the groundwork for its own eventual triumph.

As Phillips's work shows, the religious substance of the American Empire cannot be understood apart from the English battles over what it means to have an established church. Theo Hobson has one of the most powerful theological voices in England today, and he has recently published a controversial call for the disestablishment of the Church of England, to which he belongs. While the internal politics of Anglicanism are not my concern here, his criticisms of establishment demonstrate, by way of contrast, how unique American Christianity is. I have been arguing all along that Christianity is a political religion. Hobson is right to dismiss much criticism of establishment as facile, because "all Christianity naturally gravitates towards expecting to be established in some way or other, as its birthright."[15] On the face of it, this remark could be seen as an admission that the church is always sinful and thus ever eager to seek political advantage. More fundamentally, the Christian church seeks not the approval of politicians but the establishment of God. Ultimately, church and state cannot coexist, because the church will someday be the state. Christianity is driven by an eschatological expectation to become the political framework of the whole world. The state needs to be established by the church, not the other way around. Penultimately, however, the church advances the kingdom by shaping social institutions, thereby granting the political order a relative degree of autonomy. Providentially, the church has within it the seed of democracy, but realistically speaking, the church can contribute to and find a home in nearly any political order. Democracy is the fruit that falls closest to the Christian tree because democracy is a universal political form that not only springs from the great Christian theme of freedom but also facilitates the global growth of the church.

An established church runs the risk of prematurely identifying the revolutionary political message of Christianity with the narrow interests of a single state. An anonymously written article in *Harper's New Monthly Magazine*, published in 1858, gets at the heart of the difference between English and American Christianity with an enviable economy of prose: "A national Church is one thing, a national Religion is quite another; and in nothing are they more unlike than in their capacity to awaken the sense of Providence in the breast of a people."[16] Established churches have a lot invested in making the orderliness of the liturgy a reflection of the orderliness of the state. In times of political upheaval, the doctrine of providence can contribute to both the stability and the instability of the state. In seventeenth-century England, providence rallied the low-church Puritans to revolt, but it also helped cement the connection between high-church Christians and the monarchic form of government. Juhn Spurr has noted how providence functioned to associate national continuity with immersion in church tradition. "Anglican preachers dwelt in morbid detail upon the controversy between a wrathful God and an incorrigible nation, and they strove to associate the stability, even the fate, of the country with the reformation of national manners."[17] After the restoration of the monarchy in 1660, according to Spurr, providentialism became the centerpiece of Anglican pastoral work.

Hobson is intent on pointing out that the unique character of Anglicanism—its middle way between Catholicism and Protestantism, which is to say, its Catholicism minus a papacy—is a direct result of establishment. Establishment has worked to check outbreaks of religious "enthusiasm" that would have taken the church in a "sectarian" direction. By substituting the cult of the monarchy for the pageantry of the papacy, establishment has also worked to resist calls for a return to Rome. By freeing the sacraments from Roman control, Anglicanism can embrace them in their highest ritualized forms with a romantic enthusiasm. The Anglican Church is liturgically formal, theologically restrained, and morally serene—the very opposite, and intentionally so, of American Evangelicalism. In Hobson's strong words, "In a permissive society, the established Church is necessarily a permissive Church; otherwise it advocates social policies at odds with the law of the land and becomes a reactionary sect. This is why many liberals fear disestablishment, despite knowing in their hearts it is right: it would jeopardize the Church's commitment to the liberal values of the cultural mainstream."[18] Evangelicals have been tolerated in the Church of England, but just barely.

The fact is that England does not need its church anymore, except when a new monarch is to be crowned or a princess is to be buried. As church attendance has continued to spiral downward, out of ecclesial control, establishment for some has become more important as a way for ensuring that the masses absorb a minimal amount of Christianity through the Christianization of English culture. This is especially important given that the sound of the English language is so beautifully condensed in the Anglican liturgy. When Thomas Cranmer's poetry was exported to America, it risked becoming fetishized as an object of contemplation, because it conveys romantic notions of a homogenous and united culture in addition to the content of the good news. I have argued elsewhere that the church should be a school of public speaking, teaching the rhetorical skills that are required for proclamation.[19] Ideally, the spoken word sacramentally embodies the message of Jesus Christ and demands a kind of hearing that empowers the listener to speak anew, testifying to God's grace. When the spoken word becomes a script to be intoned for its own beauty, it can drown out the need for the laity to find their own voices. Hobson himself laments the sacramental turn that results in "instead of communism, communionism."[20] When the cultivation of liturgy fails to speak to the average Christian, church leaders can become desperate to find something to contribute to public affairs. In England, church leaders have increasingly turned to political moralizing rather than preaching the Word. Inevitably, they draw from the politics of the left in order to prove their independence from the very establishment that gives them a voice in the first place. Anglican leaders thus go to one extreme—predictably radical politics—in order to reject the ecclesial extreme of establishment, when it would be much simpler just to become disestablished.

Hobson holds out the hope that a disestablished Church of England can still fulfill its providential promise by showing Christians of all stripes how to tie together the loose ends of Catholicism and Protestantism into a neat liturgical knot. Anglicanism certainly has a global role to play, but the spirit is moving across the globe in a way that transcends the best efforts of the mainline denominations. A religious revolution is afoot every bit as significant as the globalization of capital. The historian Philip Jenkins has predicted the development of a second reformation of the church that would rival in significance the one that occurred in the sixteenth century.[21] He argues that the future of Christianity lies in the Southern hemisphere (by which he actually includes Asia, Africa, and the Pacific Rim, as well as Central and South America). Christianity is not dead in the North, but it is in need of rejuvenation from the South. Jenkins justifies his forecast by pointing to some startling patterns and trends. The majority of Anglican bishops are now from Asia and Africa, making that church truly global. About one-sixth of Roman Catholic priests currently serving in American parishes have been "imported" from abroad. African priests are necessary to keep the Roman Catholic Church functioning in, of all places, Ireland. Great Britain, which has become increasingly secular, has fifteen hundred missionaries from more than fifty countries working in it. One of the more missionary-oriented African churches is the Nigerian-based Redeemed Christian Church of God, which was founded in 1952. It is active in Europe, England, Germany, France, and the United States. This church makes inroads in the North by ministering to immigrant populations, but it builds on this base to appeal to locals as well. Perhaps most significantly, one can imagine a future alliance between an America still hanging onto its religious faith and a heavily Christianized China.[22]

Christianity is, in a way, returning to its roots by spreading in countries that are economically poor and politically dependent on greater powers.

Consequently, European theological developments, which were focused on defending the legitimacy of faith in response to the critical consciousness of the Enlightenment, might prove one day to be irrelevant to the church. As Jenkins points out, and as Anglicans have found in debates over gay priests and bishops, Southern Christians are much more conservative than their Northern cousins. Southern Christians are moved by the healing miracles of the gospel stories, unembarrassingly embrace the supernatural dimension of faith, and are very conservative when it comes to issues of personal, especially sexual, morality. If Southern Christianity represents the future of the church, then Western-style globalization just might meet its match. Certainly, liberal assumptions about the progressive evolution of faith toward secular ideals, as well as liberationist arguments about the value of using religion to advance a leftist political agenda, are beginning to look more and more like the arguments of an elite few rather than the premises for a theologically sound interpretation of divine providence. Liberal forms of Christianity just might fail to survive the transformations wrought by globalization.

Much of the growth taking place in the Southern hemisphere is a result of the revivalist mentality of Pentecostal churches. Pentecostalism, in its modern form, was born in America—in the Azusa Street revival, Los Angeles, 1906, to be exact. America is more than its birthplace, however. Pentecostalism exemplifies many of the most basic traits of the American religious profile. Pentecostalism empowers laity by encouraging them to develop their own spiritual gifts and to have a direct relationship to God. From the vantage point of mainline Christians, the Pentecostal surrender of rational control and subsequent diminishment of social forms of dignity looks like a loss of honor. For people who have nothing left to lose, however, this submission to a higher power that begins within is a both an egalitarian and empowering process. Even the way Pentecostalism has grown demonstrates its improvisational and spontaneous nature. Pentecostalism spread in Latin America not so much through formal missionary efforts as through Latin American migrants to the United States who attended urban Pentecostal churches and brought that style of worship back home with them. Pentecostalism in Latin America has had great success with the poor and disenfranchised, but like its Northern variant, it has begun moving into the middle class as well.

Bernice Martin has connected to globalization the spread of Pentecostal styles of faith in Latin America. She argues that Latin America has jumped from a preindustrial to a postindustrial economy in a very short period of time. Poverty has been intensified, but so has affluence. Information spreads quickly. American ideas travel as fast as the American dollar. The church has played an increasingly important role in shaping and filtering the spread of American ideas. Pentecostalism is highly syncretistic in the way new information is combined with old practices. While Rome was tightening discipline in

Latin American Catholicism, Pentecostalism was absorbing local folk customs with an American-style ease. Spirit possession, to take but one example, was incorporated into the Sunday liturgy. Healing and exorcism were also Christianized.

Other aspects of American Pentecostalism have had a profound impact on the Latin American scene. Pentecostalism eschews the Calvinistic mandate to postpone all religious rewards to the afterlife. Shaped by the American emphasis on self-improvement, Pentecostalism promises well-being to believers, giving them the tools for immediate improvement in their lives. Little distinction is made between the spiritual and the physical. Faith should mould one's character and lead to material and well as spiritual success. The fragmenting impact of modernization is fought by keeping families together. Pentecostalism thus serves to help Americanize the Latin American poor while also providing them with the tools to fight their oppression. As Bernice Martin explains, "It is not fanciful to see Protestantism as an obvious anti-colonial option for such groups [the mobile poor] in the same way that Islam today appeals to segments of the black populations of North America as a symbolic refusal of colonial Christianity."[23]

If Pentecostalism encourages good work habits and solid family values, it might seem like nothing more than an instrument of American imperialism. Short of believing that the CIA is behind its spread, however, other factors must be given their due. Bernice Martin again is helpful: "Pentecostalism grows because it offers two valuable things: to many, including some of those who gain worldly success, it offers an anchor in the face of dizzying new possibilities; to many more it offers hope and lived solutions to problems arising out of structural conditions which it is beyond the power of individuals to alter."[24] People can see it working, and they judge it by its fruits. It is a pragmatic religious movement and asks for no other criteria by which to be measured. That Northern Christians and secularists alike look down their noses at it is the height of hypocrisy and irony. Pentecostalism is working to create both dynamic community and individual responsibility in Latin America in much the same way that Methodism provided North America with so much hope and energy over a century ago. Pentecostalism, of course, has its roots in Methodism, which traditionally emphasized holiness and sanctification. Pentecostalism urges perfection on its followers and campaigns against vice with the confidence that immorality can be restrained, if not completely cured. After all, moral discipline is a necessary prerequisite for advancement in an impoverished but increasingly dynamic economy. Northern Christians cringe at the strict moralism of Pentecostals, but in a society where social change is constantly accelerating, firm boundaries need to be established to demarcate the believers from the rest of the world. Moral boundaries are thus protective, granting believers the space they need for self-improvement. Perhaps this is what really troubles the American elite about Pentecostalism: It couples a moral absolutism with economic liberation. Moral relativism is the enemy, while true freedom is the goal. This combination of ideas is beyond the grasp of Northern secularists.

Far from being in retreat from the modern world, Pentecostalism is, in the words of the subtitle of a recent collection of essays on the topic, "a religion made to travel."[25] Much of their success comes from the creation of an alternative media, which is further evidence that they are providing a unique source of resistance to American-led globalization. Pentecostals are enthusiastic about technology because it transfers authority from the sphere of the elite to the hands of the masses. The result has been spectacular. In a time representing less than five percent of Christian history, Pentecostals have become second only to Roman Catholicism in numbers (they run around 500 million strong, compared to roughly a billion Catholics). Although many scholars have not adjusted their worldviews to take them into account, others are already talking about how Pentecostalism constitutes a new global culture.[26] Pentecostalism mixes Catholic and Wesleyan spirituality with an emphasis on orality and the rejuvenation of local customs. Even its Protestant dedication to scripture takes on new forms. As Lamin Sanneh, a native of Gambia and professor at Yale Divinity School, has argued, the translation of scripture into local languages in Africa has had a stimulating effect on indigenous traditions. The biblical narrative sanctions and promotes a restructuring and revival of African storytelling, which puts Christianity in a completely different situation from Islam with regard to primordial traditions. As Senneh explains, "The mujahid scholar/warrior holds all the cards in his hands, conceding nothing to the other side, including the idea that the enemy's language might have any scriptural merit."[27] Islam is a language, to the point of nearly deifying the Arabic of the Qur'an, while Christianity deputizes every language to carry the Word of God.

The challenge for Pentecostalism is not further growth. Rather, it is in taking responsibility for the transformations it has begun. Pentecostalism has the opportunity to give voice to a truly global Christianity that penetrates every denominational tradition. At one time, the World Council of Churches gave priority to the theological reunification of Christianity with its theme of "The Unity of the Church—The Unity of Humankind." The unity of humankind was thought to be possible only on the basis of the unity of the church, but by the late 1960s, the World Council of Churches increasingly believed that the unity of the church was possible only on the basis of the unity of humankind. Moreover, the latter unity was to be achieved through social justice, not the work of missionaries dedicated to establishing new churches. Perhaps ecumenism was simply too hard and too idealistic, but the call for social and political change can never replace the demand for Christian unity based on the sacramental reality of the church.

Early Pentecostal leaders were almost utopian about the possibilities for Christian unity, but liberals usurped that theological theme for much of the twentieth century. Nevertheless, Pentecostalism provides some hope for Christian unity because it represents the missiological drive of Christianity. It is able to adapt to new cultural forms because it is so invitational, flexible, and personal. Its strength is also its weakness, however, in that Pentecostalism tends not to hold history in very high regard. A tradition that wants to restore the ancient church must continually reinvent itself. Every generation, by identifying with the New Testament church, begins Christianity all over again. The result is a theology that is completely self-validating. That is, there is no need to appeal to any warrant of plausibility outside of the experience of the Holy Spirit as it is occurring. All of this sets up obstacles for ecumenical dialogue with other traditions that put more value on history, liturgy, and theology. In any case, Pentecostals do have transnational organizational links, regional church structures, parachurch networks, and various mission agencies that provide some of the infrastructure necessary for global acculturation. They also have a commitment to using every available technological means to advance the gospel, and such technologies are the very stuff of global unity.

Expansive and dynamic, Pentecostalism reinforces the virtues necessary for democracy. Indigenous leadership is the key to Pentecostal growth. These churches share another feature with democracies: the emphasis on material prosperity. Many of these churches promise financial rewards in return for strict obedience to the Bible and the church community. North American theologians can be tempted to take an extremely condescending attitude toward prosperity preaching, although, like much of the rest of Pentecostalism, the gospel of success has its origins in America. It is too easy for the comfortable American middle class to dismiss this theology. Christianity has already contributed to American prosperity, so why shouldn't it contribute to Southern success as well? Prosperity preaching can be a distortion of the gospel when it downplays the Christological meaning of suffering. It can even be a kind of magic, promising an automatic return in dollars on the investment of any spiritual capital. Nonetheless, people are frequently drawn to Pentecostal churches during times of personal crisis that often have to do with financial stress. At its best, Pentecostalism fights against global capitalism by shifting the ground on which prosperity rests. Loyalty to biblical principles does promote discipline, and the church provides solidarity. Pentecostalism is every bit as dynamic, individualistic, and expansionistic as global capitalism itself.

Protestantism began with the theme of the priesthood of all believers, but this theme was not developed fully until Christianity came to America. America put the priesthood of all believers to work politically, but this doctrine came into its own in the church only with the rise of Pentecostalism.

David F. Wright has drawn attention to the ways in which Pentecostalism has contributed to the laicizing of Christianity.[28] The improvisational character of charismatic worship works only if it is accepted that all members are equally filled with the Holy Spirit. Pentecostalism is thus appropriately named, because the day of Pentecost witnessed the spread of the Spirit without regard to social, ethnic, or any other distinction of persons (Acts 2:17–18). The Pentecostal movement, in fact, insists that everyone has a spiritual gift that should be exercised on a regular basis. Moreover, the spiritual immediacy of every believer's relationship to God has a democratizing effect on the church. Such immediacy can degenerate into emotionalism and anti-intellectualism, especially when it is defined as incompatible with the theological education required for ordination in mainline traditions. It is certainly a species of antiprofessionalism. Everyone is called to minister to everyone else; the charismatic church is truly a coordination of Christian teaching and democratic political form.

The emphasis on spiritual immediacy can lead to a broadly ecumenical approach to church divisions, but such ecumenism is often purchased at the price of belittling theological doctrine. Moral discipline appears to have emerged as a social marker in place of theological tradition. Some charismatic leaders have noted a parallel with the origins of Christian monasticism, which was "overwhelmingly lay, uninitiated and unauthorized by clergy, and in itself a critique of the urban, Hellenized church."[29] While Pentecostalism has been spreading like wildfire throughout the world, its impact on mainline churches should not be overlooked. As much as its worship style has been criticized for repetitive praise songs and mindless emotionalism, it has served as a model for contemporary worship services in every denomination. The Charismatic movement is even making significant strides in England, as demonstrated by the Alpha movement, developed by Nicky Gunbel in the 1990s.[30] Twenty years ago it probably seemed like the most likely impact of the Charismatic movement on the church would be divisive, but it now appears more likely to be unitive. It is the global wing of the Christian church, poised to put into practice a universal democracy every bit as powerful as its American secular counterpart.

In a fascinating essay on Pentecostalism, Stanley Johannesen argues that the political order that best corresponds to Pentecostal faith is American democracy. While Pentecostals do not have an explicit conception of how to bring religious order to the world, the way they organize their experiences does have political significance. Johannesen argues that Pentecostalism can be defined as a religion without any sense of sacred territorial boundaries. Historically, Pentecostalism took root most firmly among people who were deprived of both economic status and religious tradition. Johannesen contrasts the Pentecostal emphasis on the Holy Ghost with the Roman Catholic veneration of Mary. The Virgin Mary has appeared in several places, but devotion to her is ordinarily attached to a specific site. Mary is not everywhere, in other words. Her devotion is territorial, while being filled with the Holy Spirit is an experience that can happen anywhere and at anytime. Pentecostal churches are often functional and bereft of any religious symbols. Place does not matter, because the Spirit works within the heart. Johannesen even suggests, "The less sanctified a place the more likely it was that a religious feeling impressing itself there was an authentic visitation of the Holy Ghost." Johannesen thus concludes that Pentecostalism is the "final mass-movement phase of a Calvinist 'moment' that has been Christianizing mobile, commercial, and frontier populations since the sixteenth century, most dramatically and typically in America."[31] The church as a voluntary association, the enthusiastic employment of every available technology to promote the gospel, accommodation to a mobile society where people live among strangers, and the reliance on personal testimony as the carrier of truth all find their culmination in Pentecostal worship.

Pentecostalism represents the final logical unfolding of the Protestant ideal of the priesthood of all believers, but it also represents a potential dead-end for Protestantism as a whole. The Protestant Reformation was a great tragedy on many levels, not only because of the resulting wars that took so many lives but also the fragmentation of Christendom that broke apart the body of Christ. Providentially speaking, it is hard to deny that God has worked great miracles through the fragmentation of Christendom. Energy has been unleashed and the gospel preached with a renewed vigor that might not have otherwise happened. Nonetheless, the Roman Catholic Church alone of all churches gives shelter to a theologically coherent and historically consistent principle of religious universality. Because Christian unity is integral to the gospel, the reunification of all Christian churches with Rome must be articulated as one of the primary goals of all evangelization.[32]

If the church of the future is to be more than one global agency among others, it will have to be united. Protestants and Catholics have much work ahead of them. If Pentecostalism needs a better sense of global responsibility and the corresponding ecclesial structures, Catholicism needs more development along the lines of a spirit-filled laity. As Nicholas Boyle, a liberal Catholic humanist, has recently written, "The theology of the spirit, which Hegel rightly saw as the distinctive new impetus which the Reformation gave to human development, the radical following-through of the belief that God speaks in and through us, has more work to do in the Catholic Church than further the charismatic revival. The work of Protestantization—that is the work of Reformation without schism—begun by the Council of Trent and continued by the Second Vatican Council, is not remotely complete yet."[33]

Unity among Christians must do justice to both the sacramental theology of Catholicism and the Protestant empowerment of the laity.

The movement of Catholicism and Protestantism toward each other has already been happening in America, so that it should be said that American-style Christianity is not limited to Protestantism. When Alexis de Tocqueville toured America in the 1830s, he was amazed at how well Catholicism had adapted to democracy. He predicted that Catholicism would thrive in America and the future would be divided between those who completely abandon Christianity and those who return to Rome.[34] What is currently at the cutting edge of American-style Christianity, however, is its more Protestant features. Emotionally charged, liturgically pragmatic, and individually empowering, American Christianity is different from its European ancestors, having been forced at birth to fend for itself. It is tougher, more egalitarian, and experimental in its search for ever new forms of expression. American Christianity is at its best when it empowers the laity. As Nathan O. Hatch has documented, Christianity made America a democracy, while America democratized Christianity.[35] The influence went both ways, to the extent that it is difficult to know where democratic forms of Christianity begin and the peculiar form of American democracy ends. American Christianity is also more this-worldly in its insistence that faith involves the whole person, body and mind. Healing and happiness are not outside the reach of religion. Healing was an essential ingredient in the American revivalism of the late nineteenth century, present in all denominations until the professionalization of medicine drove it to the religious margins. Southern Christians are putting it back in the center of the church again, so that this American export is likely to become an American import, rejuvenating the land of its origin.

Of course, I can be accused of painting a rosy picture of American and Christian triumph. What I am not arguing is that American-style Christianity and American-led capitalism are equal partners in the rise of a truly global culture. Christianity might ride on the back of capitalism as its penetrates the far corners of the globe, but capitalism is not the goal and purpose of history. The kingdom of God might be ushered in by bankers and businesspeople, but it will end up as something greater than they can manage. Indeed, the future of globalization is up for grabs. America is at the mercy of international markets along with all other countries, which is why the church will become more important in the world, not less. Secularization theorists hope for a time when the world will be so united that there will no longer be religious conflict, but what they miss is the extent to which world unity requires some kind of religious justification. Nye emphasizes the extent to which transnational organizations will become increasingly significant players in the era of globalization. For effective action on the international scene, consensus will be necessary, and thus communities that provide the means for determining epistemic agreement will have substantial leverage on political decisions. Communication theorists talk about the "paradox of plenty," which occurs when the quantity of information is overwhelmingly disproportionate to its quality. When we are immersed in a sea of knowledge, we sink without some outside assistance. It is hard to pay attention when you do not know what is worth paying attention to. This is especially true for citizens of emerging nations whose access to information is disproportionate to their training in how to process it. As a result, those communities and organizations that are able to filter out the noise and organize information in productive ways will increase their hold on political power. Contrary to the predictions of secularization theorists, then, the church will become more important as knowledge becomes more democratized. The church will become one of the primary filters of information for several billion people. The question of the future will be not what you know, but whom you trust.

Christianity will be able to compete with consumerism because the church was Hollywood before Hollywood was. That is, Christianity provided the deep structures of the religious imagination for the global reach of what remained of the Roman Empire. Christianity took the convoluted religious desires of paganism and transformed them into a coherent whole, just as Hollywood reflects back to consumers their economic desires sublated into erotic form. Both Hollywood and Christianity are all-consuming in the sense that they do not want to admit that there is any deeper way to get at reality. In this sense, the screen is as wide as the pages of the Bible are deep.

Nye argues that there are different architectures of globalization. The most common is the model of a hub and spokes. This model points to the instability of global designs. The hub has power, but when multiple connections are made between the various spokes, the hub becomes less important. When the spokes can speak to each other, they no longer need to communicate through the hub. If market capitalism and democracy are the hub of globalization, we can think of the spokes as the various religious ideologies that are positioning themselves in relation to the hub for future growth. Christianity extends across the globe, thanks to American revivalism and European and American missionary activity. The question is what would happen if the spokes of Christianity were to becoming increasingly linked, sidestepping the hub. A new configuration of worldwide power would come into being with the potential to transform market democracies.

To think about the global destiny of Christianity must strike most scholars today as only a little bit short of madness, but this is not how it has always been. Arnold Toynbee (1889–1975) once did the kind of history that was as unabashedly theological as it was pretentiously predictive. That he seems to belong to a distant era even though he was still publishing into the 1960s is evidence of how far in just a few short years we have come to marginalizing Christianity in higher education. Toynbee's twelve-volume *The Study of History* put religion at the heart of history. His long view of civilizations mapped their rise as well as their decline. All of this was popular fare in the 1940s and 1950s, but by the 1960s, he was all but ignored by theologians and historians alike. Admittedly, he was not a very good theologian, though the breadth of his historical knowledge was astounding. In his early work, he took a triumphalist approach to Christianity's future. In peaceful competition, he thought, the religion that was most adaptable in its articulations of God's love would win out. He thus predicted that Christianity would overcome its rivals because of its Protestant ability to change institutional form while meeting religious needs. By the late fifties, Toynbee shifted. He now thought that Christianity would win because it was best able to adapt not to God's grace but to other religions.[36] Toynbee was one of the first to argue that all religions are basically the same, and he thought Christians of all people should be the first to recognize this basic truth. World history would bring a convergence of faiths in a higher religious form. The harmonization of religions would be led by those traditions that could purge their own exclusive features. He urged Christians to drop their claims to uniqueness. Christianity has a universal mission, he asserted, but only if it treats its most central dogmas as unnecessary accessories. The baggage it needs to throw overboard in order to ascend higher than other faiths includes its ties to Judaism. Judaism, of course, is always the scapegoat for those who emphasize the universal nature of religious truth, as well as for those who think the universality of providence must eclipse everything that remains stubbornly particular. By disassociating themselves from the "tribal" roots of their faith, "Christians can face the future with confidence."[37]

Toynbee was right to argue that there can be no unity of humanity without a unified participation in God. All civilizations are overtures to the eventual triumph of the church.[38] Nevertheless, the church that Toynbee sees at the end of history looks more like the dog's wagging tail than the nose scenting the way. The church torn away from Judaism would constitute the abolition rather than the triumph of the Christian faith. Though Toynbee did not have his finger on the pulse of divine providence, he was remarkably prescient concerning the way the liberal elite would come to regard religion. His descriptions of the kind of religious ideology needed to pull the world together sound exactly like the kind of religious pluralism that can be found in countless Religious Studies textbooks today. His words, which sounded so radical in the sixties, now sound like common sense, hardly worth uttering. He was a prophet ahead of his time, so much so that it is hard to imagine the time when he really was prophetic.

Toynbee raised a most politically incorrect question concerning which religion would triumph in the global age, but his question is now politically unavoidable. Stephen R. L. Clark, one of the most prolific and provocative of contemporary English philosophers, has admitted the relevance of Toynbee's question. Clark announces one of those truths that is as obvious as it is astounding: "A world state not animated by any corresponding religion could only be imperial."[39] This statement follows from the argument that no cooperation of governments in an international order is possible without some kind of moral consensus about the point of that cooperation. The most likely candidate for a world religion is a mild form of post-Christian humanism, which treats every individual as unique and promotes reason as the arbiter of creedal differences. The most likely candidate, however, is not the most providential candidate. Clark points out that humanism is as creedal as any other religion. Furthermore, the faithful are rarely as dangerous in their pride and ambition as when they think that they are being impartial and reasonable. Clark's summary of such humanism underlines its foibles: "We all agree to disagree, because we have no disagreement worth mentioning: no one is ever wrong, or right."[40] Secular humanism would be the worst form of religious justification for globalism precisely because it would have nothing to offer by way of resistance to the juggernaut of consumerism.

In any case, the billions of believers in the world's various religions are unlikely to want more than a sip of the secular version of Christianity brewed by an American elite. This potion might be heady stuff for academics who want to disabuse their pious students of their narrow religious beliefs, but it will go down like poison to nearly everyone else. So what is the alternative? Hinduism is intrinsically linked to the land of India, even if it has grown outside those borders because of immigration. Buddhism is sometimes put forth as a world religion poised for global expansion, because of its syncretistic potential to adapt to Western beliefs. It can appear to be less attached to the specifics of one historical tradition than the faiths that are rooted in Abraham. Buddhism's very adaptability, however, is its limitation. Many Westerners attracted to Buddhist meditation use it in an instrumental fashion to promote positive thinking and to relieve stress. The metaphysical core of Buddhist doctrine and the rituals of Buddhist practice remain alien and poorly understood by even the most sympathetic Westerners. At one point in history, the Marxist faith in a universal brotherhood of the proletariate seemed like a good advance on the Kantian brotherhood of all those who acknowledge the sovereignty of rationality, but both Kantianism and Marxism now appear to be little more than offshoots of providential theology, minus the doctrine of original sin.

One of the leading contenders for recognition as a global ethic is the protest against the way globalism damages the environment. The idea that the earth is sacred is as old as the first cultures to populate the earth, and it is especially appealing to those who reject the transcendent God of Judaism, Islam, and Christianity. Those three religious traditions, however, are unlikely to dismantle their notions of divine transcendence in order to embrace an earthly goddess. If one of the Abrahamic religions wins the global race, "then it will be obvious that Israel is the source of the world's blessing." Clark goes on: "But something like that is already obvious: no one can understand global society without reference to Israel."[41] Israel is the sign of hope that a particular culture can carry universal meaning. Globalization can avoid tyranny only if some version of Israel's prophetic message is able to spread as rapidly and as thoroughly as capitalism itself. Given the small size of Judaism, this leaves Islam and Christianity to compete for a truly global status as the one, true religion. Providentially speaking, the religion that triumphs cannot do so at the expense of God's ongoing covenant with Israel.

There should be no doubt in anyone's mind that Islam is ready, eager, and willing to compete for global triumph. Such competition, in fact, is built into Islam from its very beginnings. Since the 1980s, as Samuel P. Huntington has documented, Islamic rejection of the West has only increased. The competition is not over territory, which was the coveted prize in the past. Instead, according to Huntington, it is over "broader civilizational issues" such as democracy and human rights. "The underlying problem for the West is not Islamic fundamentalism. It is Islam, a different civilization whose people are convinced of the superiority of their culture and are obsessed with the inferiority of their power. The problem for Islam is not the CIA or the U.S. Department of Defense. It is the West, a different civilization whose people are convinced of the universality of their culture and believe that their superior, if declining power imposes on them the obligation to extend their culture throughout the world."[42] No doubt this sounds extreme to liberals who wish we could all get along, but no amount of wishful thinking will solve the growing divide between Christianity and Islam.

Islamic supersession of Christianity is built into Islam in a much more invidious way than Christianity's relationship to Judaism, especially given the widespread Muslim belief that American versions of Christianity are so utterly co-opted by the corrupt West that they no longer contain any truth. Most Muslim literature on Christianity is meant to bolster Muslim confidence, so it never reaches the English-speaking world, but Kate Zebiri, a lecturer in Islamic Studies at the University of London, has done the West a great service by wading her way through this thicket of prejudice and misinformation. The majority of Muslims, she points out, take the Gospel of Barnabas, an Italian manuscript dated to the sixteenth century and discovered in the eighteenth, to be the truly authentic record of Jesus's teachings. They thus believe that the true Jesus is known only by Muslims. Muslims deride the New Testament because it has multiple versions and translations, in contrast to the Arabic purity of the Qur'an. Jesus is seen as a prophet who failed, especially in comparison to Muhammad's military successes. Many

Muslim writers portray Christianity as being as weak as its prophet. Christianity is doomed to falter and fail in the course of history. Christianity is too flexible to be principled, too diverse to be unified, and too other-worldly to provide the legal foundation necessary for political order. Muslim intellectuals talk about Islam, by contrast, as a "Christianity reoriented toward the world."[43] Islam has its own doctrine of providence, but it places history on a course of inevitable collision with Christianity.

If the history and the destiny of America and Christianity are interwoven, and if Islam represents the greatest contemporary challenge to both democracy and the Christian church, then the war against terrorism is arguably also a war over the future of religion. The problem is not that Islam is a faith that makes no separation between the religious and the political orders. Christianity too is invested in the question of the proper shape of government. The problem is with the kind of political order Muslims think God has planned for the world. In a way, one cannot blame Muslims for turning their backs on democracy. After all, in the eyes of most modern Muslim intellectuals, this is precisely what the West has done by separating church and state. That is, Westerners no longer think that democracies stand in need of any theological support or justification, which proves, to the Muslim mind, that democracies are a purely secular and therefore corrupt form of governance.

Sayyid Qutb (1906–1966), one of the founders of modern Muslim militancy, was the first to develop this analysis of the West.[44] Qutb visited the United States in 1949–51, where he fell into a deep hatred for all things American. He was right to react negatively to signs of secularization, but he was wrong to blame the widening separation of church and state on Christianity itself, rather than on those liberal Christians who were cooperating with the forces of secularization. Qutb misread Christianity as an other-worldly religion, with an absolute dualism between reason and faith. For Qutb, Christianity is not sufficiently legalistic in its approach to religion, and thus Christianity has allowed the very political systems it has created to slip out of the sphere of its own influence. Qutb makes no distinction between secularization and democracy. Even contemporary, less radical Islamic scholars, like the Indonesian scholar Syed Muhammad Naquib Al-Attas, cannot imagine how faith in God can be given political expression in democratic form.[45] From the Islamic point of view, Christianity is not to be commended for paving the way for democracy. Democracies are weak precisely because they do not admit their need for a religious foundation. Christianity's relationship to democracy is only proof of its inferiority to Islam.

For many people across the globe, 9/11 was a wake-up call to the danger posed by Muslim terrorists. The call was muted, however, by the insistence of politicians, scholars, and the established media that Islam is a religion of peace and harmony. Much of this talk sounded condescending, as if Americans and

Europeans had to pat Muslims on the back to assure them that the Americans and Europeans found nothing offensive about their beliefs. Official responses from Western governments were so muted that one could only suspect that the primary aim was to ensure that oil supplies were not endangered by any stray criticisms that would upset the Muslim world. The lack of candor was too much for some people to take. The Italian writer Oriana Fallaci, who lives in New York City, wrote a breathlessly angry treatise against Islam that was also an attack on Western leniency and weakness.[46] But there were even more books telling Americans not to worry, because Islam has no ambitions that could be interpreted as troubling in any way. The American response to 9/11 brought out the best in America, in the sense that there was very little stereotyping, but there was also so much caution and niceness that nobody wanted to subject to critical scrutiny the religious beliefs that motivated the attackers. Most of the media acted as if the terrorists belonged to some fringe group that had nothing whatsoever to do with traditional Islam.

The West was paralyzed in the face of the Islamic threat by its own ideals of multiculturalism and moral relativism. Immediately after the attack, many liberals could be heard—acting like armchair generals—bemoaning what they suspected would be President Bush's overreaction to the terrorists. Bush outsmarted them at their own game, using language that was more politically correct than his opponents could have imagined. What restrained the political left in America from being more critical of Islam was their deeply held sympathy for the Palestinian political leaders who have been conducting a similar campaign of terror against Israel for decades. Islam, which never went through a Protestant Reformation and has no figure in its history to match Martin Luther, has reached a stage where there is widespread consensus that it is acceptable to kill Israeli civilians in suicide bombings. It is a small step from justifying terrorist attacks against Israeli civilians to justifying the bombing of American civilians in New York. For those on the left, evidently, it is too wide of a step to identify the connections between the two and thus condemn both equally.

Immediately after 9/11, President Bush launched a public relations campaign to woo Muslim moderates and to quiet leftist critics who suspected him of wanting to turn the war against terrorism into a holy crusade. The campaign failed on both fronts. His critics did not listen to him, and militant Muslims took his apologetic tone to be a confession of American weakness and hesitation. Muslims will have to figure out how to reform their religious traditions, and they will have to do that on their own, given that they have so little trust in American advice. Their prospects do not look good. A 2002 United Nations report stated that the nations that constitute the Arab League, with a population of over 300 million, annually translate about 330 books, evidence of an inward turn that will be hard to reverse. Arab nations have put their Christian citizens to flight in vast numbers, which also suggests a further sundering of the ways between Islam and the Christian West. In the light of these problems, President Bush's words, delivered at the American Enterprise Institute on February 26, 2003, seem like common sense: "The world has a clear interest in the spread of democratic values, because stable and free nations do not breed the ideologies of murder. They encourage the peaceful pursuit of a better life."[47] Unfortunately, the reaction in the press was immediately hostile. The political left does not sufficiently trust the American form of government to commit itself to recommending its export abroad.

The secular mind is so habituated by relativism that it must cast about in medieval history for evidence that Christianity is just as militaristic as Islam. What is conveniently ignored is that the Crusades were a belated response to over three centuries of Muslim military aggression in the colonization of Christian lands and the mistreatment of local Christian populations. American academicians are usually absolutely opposed to transferring a term developed in a Christian context to a non-Christian one, but an exception is made in the case of the word "fundamentalism." By calling Muslim terrorists fundamentalists, academics can force them into the same group with Christian conservatives at home and thus imply that the problem is really with all forms of religious traditionalism, not just Islam.[48] In fact, the strongest criticism that the liberal elite can muster against Islam is that it fails to separate church and state. This is cheap criticism, of course, because it faults Islam for not upholding the very premise of liberalism. That is, it faults Islam for not being liberal, something Islam has never wanted to be. This criticism also has the added advantage of putting conservative Christians in their place as well. It takes the form of, "There but for the grace of the separation of church and state goes America!" The problem with Islam, I would argue, is not that it has the ambition to unite mosque and state. The problem is the kind of state with which it wants the mosque to unite.

Islam increasingly is the voice of the losers of globalization. As an accelerated form of modernization, globalization demands mobility in thought as well as deed. Cultural assumptions must give way to indeterminacy and hybridity, so that markets can adapt efficiently and rapidly to new demands. If globalization is inevitable, then only those religions that look to the future with the promise of freedom will be able to provide the socialization necessary for full participation in a world economy. This is not to suggest that all fundamentalists are global losers, because there are different kinds of fundamentalism. Only secularists have an interest in grouping all conservative religious positions together under the fundamentalist umbrella. Some forms of fundamentalism can be quite dynamic and progressive in their emphasis on personal responsibility and the need for adapting to market forces.

The broad and inaccurate use of the term "fundamentalism" points to the sad fact that it is nearly impossible in the modern academy to have an open and honest discussion about Islam. Although higher education makes a point of subjecting Christianity to the most stringent and corrosive forms of historical criticism, affirmation and empathy are the name of the game when it comes to studying Islam. Christianity is largely taught in colleges and universities today from an outsider's perspective. The perspective of suspicion is the rule, and the sociology of knowledge is the method. As a result, Christianity is treated as a thin cover for political aspirations of power. Islam, which makes no pretension of *not* being about political power, is treated from an insider's perspective. It is almost as if Islam is holding higher education hostage, because if the tools of historical criticism were fairly applied to Islam, it would not receive a passing grade. I remember raising questions as a sophomore in college about discrepancies between the Qur'an and the Bible, only to be told that Muslims believe their oral tradition to be the truth that the biblical version of events had distorted. A moment's reflection would show the impossibility of this line of thinking. Muhammad was influenced by Christians and Jews who passed on to him garbled forms of the biblical narrative. How he could have received the "real" story in any other way than through divine revelation is impossible to fathom. I was being told to accept the divine origins of the Qur'an and not to ask any messy (i.e., Western, historical, Christian) questions. Devout Muslims do not ask these messy questions either. Muslims believe the Qur'an came from heaven, and scholars are reluctant to point out its historical development and internal inconsistencies. Islam has never had to pass through the fire of philosophical and historical criticism, precisely because that fire was a direct product of the Christian approach to truth. Christianity assimilated Greek philosophy in its universal affirmation of all truth as a gift from God, while Islam has focused its energy on elaborating the legal conditions for a perfectly Muslim state.

One writer who has dared to treat Islam honestly is Serge Trifkovic, whose combined career in journalism, government, and the academy gives him a distinctive perspective on current events.[49] Trifkovic points out that Muhammad, after he failed to convince his fellow citizens of Mecca that he was a prophet, turned to Jews and Christians for acceptance. He thus admonished his followers not to argue with "People of the Book," a title he gave to Jews and Christians in honor of their shared repertoire of biblical stories. Later, in Medina, when his claims were rejected by Jews and Christians, his sayings about them turned more harsh. Muhammad was very clear: "Believers, take neither Jews nor Christians for your friends" (5.51). As he mounted war against the Meccans, Muhammad's revelations increasingly justified the murder of one's enemies. "I will cast terror into the hearts of those who disbelieve. Therefore strike off their heads and strike off every fingertip of them" (8.12). Further revelations made booty and ransom lawful, chastised poets who mocked him in verse or simply provided an alternative to his own religious poetry (37:35–36), and sanctioned the rape of captive women as long as a dowry was paid (4.24). Muhammad also turned against a Jewish tribe in wholesale slaughter, accomplishing what would be called in our day ethnic cleansing or genocide. Muhammad's sayings were also collected in the *hadith*, many of which go further than the Qur'an in glorifying war: "Jihad is your duty under any ruler, be he godly or wicked." "He who dies without having taken part in a campaign dies in a kind of unbelief." "Paradise is in the shadow of swords."[50] Muhammad began as a religious poet but ended as a warlord. As a result, Islam can be defined as a religion in search of an empire.

One aspect of Islam that puzzles Westerners is the status of women. Various revelations conveniently justified Muhammad's expanding household. One in particular states that God gave to Muhammad the wife of his adopted son, by the name of Zayd (33.37). Muhammad evidently noticed her beauty and received from God the command that his son divorce his wife so that he could have her. By the end of his life, he had over fifteen wives, and he used negotiated marriages to cement his relationships with his followers. Allah approved of this: "Men are in charge of women because Allah has made the one of them excel the other" (4.34).

All of this is not to say that there is not aesthetic rigor in the Qur'an, although its style has little appeal to most Westerners. Perhaps the single most significant obstacle for Christian appreciation of the Qur'an is its lack of a fully developed doctrine of sin. Obedience is the essence of Islam, so it is a moralistic faith with little of the subtle fathoming of the fallen will that is so prevalent in Christianity. There is no equivalent to Augustine's *Confessions* in Islam, or the Apostle Paul's understanding of a will divided against itself. Even the portrait of Jesus in the Qur'an—which in no way can be squared with the Gospels, so that one must simply choose between them—empties him of any of the all-too-human features of vulnerability and suffering that make his embodiment of the divine so transformative as well as scandalous. In fact, the Qur'an is contradictory and confusing about the death of Jesus, which has left room for much discussion about whether Jesus only appeared to die on the cross or somebody else took his place.[51] It is as if Muhammad was unable to stomach human weakness. Success and strength are the true characteristics of being chosen by God. Without a theological appreciation for the composite nature of human subjectivity, the Qur'an's account of God's will and humanity's obligations can appear to Christians as one-dimensional and unmoving. It is often pointed out in the Qur'an's defense that it accords respect to the Old Testament and the Gospels; this attempt to bring the Qur'an into the orbit of the Bible is well-motivated but misleading. For Muhammad, there is only one scripture, a heavenly prototype that is found in its pure form only in the Qur'an; all other scripture is full of lies and deception.

While scholars debate the extent to which Islam spread through peaceful trade or military conquest, most traditional Muslims are firm in their conviction that the primary criterion of judging the appropriate means of expanding global Islam is success, not freedom. The Crusades are held against the West as an example of Christian militarism, even though they are an exception compared to the rule of conquest that dominates Islam. Jihad certainly has a polyvalence that renders it difficult to translate, but the media, following the lead of liberal scholars, has been all too quick after 9/11 to claim that it means something more like an inner struggle than an outright war. Certainly the great jihad is to bring one's own will into accord with God's will, but the whole point of that struggle is to extend the domain of influence of Islam. In the words of the great Islamic scholar Bernard Lewis, "For most of the fourteen centuries of recorded Muslim history, jihad was most commonly interpreted to mean armed struggle for the defense or advancement of Muslim power."[52] The struggle against evil in Islam is inseparable from a political and military struggle against the enemies of Islam. The world is thus divided cleanly into two, and the two halves are in continual conflict. There is the Land of Peace (*Dar al-Islam*) and the Land of War (*Dar al-Harb*). The latter lies outside of the borders of the Islamic Empire, or what is left of it since the fall of the Ottoman Empire and the elimination of the caliphate (the caliph was the head of all Sunni Islam and a potent symbol of Islamic unity) in 1924.

Many historians, Bernard Lewis chief among them, have asked the question, What went wrong? Lewis's work is impeccable, but in the hands of some scholars, this question is loaded with assumptions about a golden age of Islam that was mysteriously eclipsed by the rise of the West. True, during the medieval period Islam was the most advanced civilization in the world, because of its expansionistic vigor and religious confidence. Nevertheless, it was not able to capitalize on that wealth and power as Europe marched toward modernity. The question of what went wrong also assumes that Muslims want to be as modern as the Christian West, when in reality, Muslims think *we* have gone wrong, not them. As Lewis writes, "Secularism in the modern political meaning—the idea that religious and political authority, church and state are different, and can or should be separated—is, in a profound sense, Christian. Its origins may be traced in the teachings of Christ, confirmed by the experience of the first Christians; its later development was shaped and, in a sense, imposed by the subsequent history of Christendom."[53] Christianity provoked and defied political authority as it sought a future convergence of political and religious order. Muhammad, by contrast, was, in Lewis's words, "his own Constantine."[54] All civil law is canon law, to use those Christian terms. It is often pointed out that Islam is an egalitarian religion (although not for women), but this does not translate into political terms, where authority is vested with sacred power and obedience is required for both civil and religious reasons.[55]

Whatever the causes, the economic and cultural gulf between the Islamic world and the West keeps widening. Tyranny and poverty feed on each other. Many Muslims blame modernity for their troubles, but it is not that modernity has failed them; rather, they have never tried it. Their religion prevents them from entering the modern world as modern people. Turkey is a good example of this predicament, since Kemal Ataturk was able to modernize Turkey at the end of World War I only at the expense of privatizing Islam and severing the nation from its cultural past. That heroic effort largely succeeded, but it could not be expected of other Islamic nations.

Christians would be wise to have very realistic expectations of Islam, if anything can be learned from the past. Much has been made of the supposedly fair treatment Christians and Jews received at the hands of Muslim, and it is true that "People of the Book" were protected in Muslim lands in ways that Jews often were not in Christian territory. Nevertheless, conquered people were treated as second-class citizens at best. They were allowed to stay in Islamic land only if they agreed to a contract, called *dhimma*, which included paying a poll and land tax to their new Muslim masters. If they failed to pay up, they could be subjected to death or enslavement. Christians could not display a cross in public and had to wear special clothing of some sort. What began as jihad became systematic oppression and ended in the Islamization of much of Eastern Christianity. Bat Ye'or, a British scholar born in Egypt, is the world's leading authority on what she calls "dhimmitude," or the state of oppression under Muslim rule.[56] Islamic law, or *shari'a*, when applied to the conquered, puts them at the mercy of an enormous administrative machinery aimed at their complete subjugation and ultimate conversion. Religion for Islam is indistinguishable from politics, and politics is inextricably related to war. It is one of the great shames of Western Christianity that there is not more concern about the fate of Eastern Christians, for the fact is that dhimmitude worked all too well. Christianity has been nearly driven to extinction throughout the Middle East.[57]

Although there has been a mass exodus of Christians from Arabic lands, the situation, if possible, is only getting worse. Islam has diverse expressions, but Ye'or points out that Islam is becoming increasingly Arabized throughout the world. Middle Eastern countries are a model for the process of Islamization, which entails strict enforcement of Islamic law. Christians cannot contradict testimony from a Muslim in a religious court, and to complain about discrimination in any case is to invite deadly reprisal. Persecution against Christians "is an expressly taboo subject."[58] Liberal academicians are so focused on the situation of the Palestinians that they have no sympathy left over for Middle Eastern Christians. *Shari'a* itself prohibits critical dialogue with a *dhimmi*. *Shari'a* is based in large part on the elaboration of Muhammad's words and deeds in the *hadith*, and this too is taken as a direct revelation of God's will, on par with the uncreated Qur'an. Consequently, any criticism of *shari'a* is taken as blasphemy on the order of mocking Muhammad or rejecting God.

Although the liberal media operates by a conspiracy of silence about the persecution of Christians abroad, the Christian solidarity movement has filled this information vacuum. Activists led by Nina Shea, Paul Marshall, and Caroline Cox have pushed Western Christians to be more aware of the plight of their less fortunate brothers and sisters.[59] The result is a populist, grassroots movement—"Its leaders do not teach or minister to students at Harvard or Yale"[60]—that has taken different forms and led to mixed but promising results. Christian Solidarity Worldwide, Open Doors International, Voices of the Martyrs, and Christian Freedom International are some of the major organizations that lobby on behalf of Christians in Muslim countries and promote freedom of religion throughout the world.

The clash of cultures might seem a bit abstract to people living in America, but in the rest of the world it is only too real. The *Middle East Quarterly* recently reported how the Islamist campaign of violence in Algeria has resulted in some Muslims converting to Christianity. Some Christian converts are attracted to the ministry of healing found in Pentecostal churches. Others are just plain sick of the killing in the name of Islam. One convert said, "Christianity is life, Islam is death."[61] This is why Muslim nations have so much invested in silencing Christian proclamation.

America, in its innocence about Islam, has inadvertently contributed to this clash of cultures by enlisting Muslim aid in the fight against communism.[62] To say that America created Islamic terrorism, however, is to belittle Muslim initiative and Islam's sweeping view of history. Islam is growing peacefully in Europe and America, mainly through immigration and natural population growth rather than conversion, but in much of Africa and parts of Asia, Muslims still take to the sword to expand their territory. The West so far has adopted an attitude of appeasement toward Islam. It remains to be seen how Islam will evolve in the West and whether Western styles of Islam, if Western Islam does become assimilated into the modern world, will have any effect on traditional Islam. Trifkovic could be accused of being alarmist about the Islamic threat to the West, but it is better to be cautious than careless. "To pretend, as the ruling elite does, that Islam is a 'religion of peace,' rather like Episcopalianism, is stupid or deeply dishonest."[63] An example of the weakness of the West is the way in which the war against terrorism has been portrayed as having little if anything to do with Islam, when the current terrorist threat to America comes exclusively from segments of that religion.

Trifkovic argues that secularization since the early twentieth century has shifted the conflict between Christianity and Islam to one between the West and Islam. This gives Islam the advantage, since the West no longer has any theological strength to compare to Muslim dedication and enthusiasm. The threat of Islam is essentially theological, and thus it can be fought in no other way. "The allied nations did not shirk their duty to convert Germany and Japan into democracies after defeating them. In the same way, we have every right to openly evangelize the Islamic nations with not only the gospel of Christianity, but also the 'gospel' of secular democratic thought."[64] Trifkovic makes the controversial point that Islam is at least as dangerous a threat to the West as was communism. To combat it, he advises, Russia should be enlisted as an ally and given more Western support, and Western reliance on oil, which is at the heart of much American hypocrisy about the dangers of Islam, should be drastically reduced.

The political analysts who have been most willing to acknowledge the degree to which Islam is the enemy of America are David Frum and Richard Perle. Their book, *An End to Evil*, is painfully honest about the extent of Muslim rage against America, and their reward is to be pilloried in the press with the unfair charge of wanting to topple every Middle Eastern regime.[65] They speak the rhetoric of foreign policy realism in order to justify a fierce utopianism concerning America's ability to reshape the world in its own democratic image. They are hard-liners who see nothing but freedom at the end of the line. Freedom is not a neutral value, and its export abroad cannot be separated from the work of the Christian church. A global religion like Islam, because it systematically encourages and promotes resistance to American values, must be battled primarily on the ground of ideas. Forcing Muslim nations into democratic political orders can accomplish much good in the world, but it needs to be recognized that this goal is theological as well as political. Islam has to be changed for democracies to flourish in the Middle East, and one of those changes is that Christianity has to be given a fair chance to speak its word.

When that happens, Christianity grows. In 1900, Muslims outnumbered Christians in Africa by a ratio of 4:1. Today, African Christianity equals Islam in numbers and continues to grow at an astounding rate. This story has not been told well in the West. As Lamin Sanneh states, "A skeptical Western audience, fortified with anthropological theory and with a postcolonial sensitivity, will scarcely budge from its view of Christian missions as cultural imperialism and religious bigotry."[66] Africans themselves have found Christianity to be utterly liberating. In fact, Africa is becoming a Christian continent, and it is doing this in a remarkably peaceful fashion. By the end of the first quarter of the twenty-first century, projections estimate that there will be 600 million Christians in Africa, making it the most Christian continent on the planet.

The export of democracy and the expansion of Christianity go hand-in-hand because preaching the gospel is a powerful speech act that threatens societies that do not believe in the freedom of speech. The power of the spoken word is one of the great themes of the Protestant Reformation. The power of the Word for the Reformers was embodied in the deep baritone of Luther, the serene confidence of Calvin, and the purity of the protesting and persecuted anabaptists. The Reformers had different understandings of how the power of the gospel relates to the powers of the world, but they were clear that the Word they spoke was nothing if not an exercise in true liberation. By contrast, mainline Protestant churches and their legitimating theologies too frequently shy away altogether from the question of power.[67] They equate power with exploitation and oppression, and thus they do not want to have anything to do with it. Power is what people outside the church have; in any amount it is absolutely corrupting. Of course, anyone who goes to church knows that power struggles, no matter how insignificant in the greater scheme of things, are as present in congregations as they are in corporations. More importantly, the gospel cannot be presented in a power vacuum. God is powerful, and so is God's Word, no matter how quietly it is spoken. The rhetorical shape of the gospel proclamation changes, because rhetoric itself is the art of adapting a message to changing circumstances. But as long as preaching remains the defining feature of Protestant churches, power will lie at the heart of the gospel message, if for no other reason than the fact that persuasion itself is always a form of power.

Preaching is hardly a nonviolent act. To argue otherwise is to accept the Enlightenment's goal of evacuating words of their transformative power. The Enlightenment's instrumentalization of language cleared Western culture of many superstitions concerning the magic of words, but it also left language a lifeless tool in the service of our attempts to manage each other and manipulate the world. Sound, however, cannot be so easily controlled. Words are proclaimed to others from the gut, and it does not take much manipulation to turn them into projectiles meant to assault and destroy. When it comes to religion, many Americans live in a liberal media cocoon where religious language has been domesticated and depolemicized. This deafens us to the ways in which religion and polemic are interconnected. The New Testament, for example, is a basically polemical text in its arguments against Jews and Greeks alike. The ancient training in rhetoric was for the purpose of competition. The skills of disputation were meant to be used in pursuit of public victory. The church in developing countries empowers the laity to speak the truth, and the truth is always a scandal to tyrannical political establishments.[68]

Whether the West will have the wisdom to reach deep into its own theological past in order to meet the challenge of Islam is doubtful. Muslims are surely right that pluralism is not a strong enough ideology to compete with either Islam or Christianity for global dominance. The phenomenon of pluralism in the West is a fact, and its accompanying ideology has much to recommend it. Pluralism is the engine of cultural change, which is why it spurs economic growth. Far from destroying the local, globalization makes the local universally available. People far and wide who have the same peculiar tastes can compete for a very particular commodity. People who might never have imagined that they would need to choose from among hundreds of French cheeses, for example, can refine their palates with the click of a mouse. If the rest of the world ends up looking more and more like the United States, it will only be because the United States is more like a mirror rather than a steamroller.

From a theological point of view, however, pluralism falls short of providing a comprehensive framework for the forces of globalization. If the consumer is always right, then no product, from pornography to private islands, is wrong. New York City, where you can buy anything at anytime and thus extend your sense of adolescent wonder at the endless possibilities of desire's countless configurations, is the capital of the world because it is the most advanced outpost in the expansion of globalism. Thus understood, globalization is a threat to particular cultures and traditional societies, and that is true to a degree. If everything can be bought, then everything is placed in the same competitive market and on the same expendable level. Local cultures are not immediately destroyed, but they are uprooted and displaced by the need to stimulate and then more efficiently meet ever more sophisticated economic demands. The goal of globalization is to have open markets for every nation, on the condition that their participation involves them in the political changes that are necessary for free trade and the flow of information, but not all cultures are equally adept at participating in global markets. As the great historian of religions Mircea Eliade has argued, the religions of traditional societies protect them from the terrors of historical change.[69] He spoke from personal experience, having grown up in Romania, a country that often was not able to exercise control over its own political destiny. Traditional religions have remained much the same over the centuries precisely because they were successful in retaining their traditions in spite of the intrusion of Western power, yet their flight from history is no longer possible, because globalization leaves nowhere to hide.

From an economic perspective, traditional societies—what is left of them, anyway—are fighting a losing battle. Their religious beliefs will have to be adjusted to the triumph of capitalism's demand for constant change. This is tragic for members of these societies because social transformation on this level always involves significant human costs. Fortunately, Christianity has played an immeasurable role in softening the blows that come with economic and cultural change. The response of Westerners to this process of assimiliation is often hypocritical. Modern Westerners, who have distanced themselves from their own religious roots, have made a fetish out of all things primordial, as demonstrated not least by collecting relics from these cultures as if they were objects of art. The further we move from our religious pasts, it seems, the more we resent it when other people, often voluntarily, leave their religious roots behind. Critics of the West resent the role the Christian church has played in helping people from traditional societies adjust to political and economic change, because they romanticize isolated natives holding out against impossible odds. Critics of globalization want traditionalists to cling to their ancient pasts, even as those same critics enjoy their multicultural education and their ethnic restaurants while nurturing warm feelings for lost causes and dying ways of life.

From a theological perspective, traditional societies should embrace Christianity, for both the sake of their salvation but also as a prelude to their entry into world markets. This, in fact, is what the Christian West long struggled to accomplish through the work of thousands of missionaries. Commerce and Christianity, at least since the days of David Livingstone, have gone hand-in-hand.[70] Saying that Christian missions imposed an external culture on other countries does not mean that all missionaries, as in the stereotypes of popular fiction and movies, were mere stooges for Western imperialism. Recent studies of mission work demonstrate a complex variety of relationships between missionaries and their home countries. Some were rabidly anticolonialist, supporting indigenous political movements and empowering locals with the resources to resist the worst aspects of Western capitalism.[71] The important point that needs to be made is that Western Christian missions were stunningly successful for reasons similar to the factors that made possible the triumph of American globalization. Christianity, like Western culture, has universal ambitions, is highly adaptable, and is capable of high degrees of self-criticism. Academics are so used to setting every religious movement in its particular social circumstances—emphasizing the local at the expense of the global—that the truly radical character of Christianity is often missed.[72] Christianity gave rise to the Reformation, the greatest self-transformation of any religion in history, just as Christianity gave rise to Marxism, an ideology made possible by the very freedoms it sought to destroy. Just as capitalism works not by selling what it thinks people should buy but by exploring and expanding their needs, Christianity works not by telling people what to believe but by cultivating, as well as questioning, their religious needs.

The decisive question confronting America today is whether it will distance itself from Christianity in order to exercise the authority of global management or whether it will find a way of synthesizing its dual commitment to exporting Christianity and democracy. If higher education is any indication, America will not be able to accomplish this holy task, or, put in other words, America has already done as much as it can to make the world safe for Christianity. I have already argued that America serves as the measure of global pluralism, absorbing other cultures in a process that meshes them together in a unique, worldwide product. The same can be said about America's role in the creation of religious pluralism. If a pluralism of religions is to be the ruling theology of the global future, then Religious Studies departments in American colleges and universities will play the crucial role of figuring out how that pluralism is to be achieved. Religious Studies is, in a crucial way, the barometer of globalization. How religions interact in America will determine, ultimately, their interaction abroad. Just as America provides the testing ground for new products, pushing economic development to the cutting edge, so does America provide the cultural space wherein religions can work out their differences, if that is possible. Like globalism itself, the clash of religions is in need of theoretical management. People cannot be expected to live together peacefully without some understanding of how their religious beliefs harmonize with the beliefs of their neighbors. American intellectuals have long been working out the details of a theory of religious pluralism. If pluralism has any hope of success, credit must be given to the academic discipline of Religious Studies. Religious Studies is where religious excess is disciplined.

It is worth pausing to reflect on how Religious Studies is at the center of ideological defenses of globalization. The Religious Studies classroom is a laboratory for defusing religious differences by defining religion as one species with distinct but not separate variations. This puts Religious Studies at the vanguard of post-Christian humanism. Consequently, Religious Studies programs tend to marginalize prehumanistic Christian theology in order to promote the ideal of universal harmony, tolerance, and understanding. The very project of studying religion tends toward a bias against Christianity, because it assumes a definition of religion that can contain all religions, which means that no religion is unique.

My experience in leading and participating in teaching workshops, as well as lecturing on the topic of the role of theology and religious conviction in the Religious Studies classroom, confirms these points. To make a broad generalization, professors who teach religion are frequently drawn to this topic because they have spent so much psychic energy in trying to extricate themselves from its grasp. That they have failed to do this is proven by the fact that they have devoted their lives to studying religion. In other words, Religious Studies professors have deeply ambivalent feelings about Christianity and they have learned to make their anxiety productive by exorcising it in the classroom. It thus makes sense that people of strong faith are not typically drawn to making a career studying religion in the academy. It takes a certain degree of alienation from faith to turn it into an object of reflection.

If one has wrestled with overcoming and thus mastering a devout religious upbringing, for example, one already possesses some of the skills required to teach Religious Studies. Teaching religion is a way of re-creating this background of having obtained mastery over it. Conversely, teaching religion can be a way of dramatizing one's ambivalence about faith. Or it can be a way of passing on one's unbelief in an acceptable manner, since few other outlets in our culture exist for skeptics to be in a position of power and control over the faithful. Whatever the case, I think it should not be surprising that the pious and the devout are not ordinarily found in Religious Studies departments. The more important point is that teachers of religion are typically the last to know just how conflicted they are about the topic, precisely because they have so much invested in maintaining the alienation, tension, or outright disbelief they bring to the Religious Studies classroom. Religious Studies professors are thus the guardians of modernity's most cherished myths, the idea that religion can be subjected to critical intellectual scrutiny, that it can be treated as a dead object of analysis, and that the university can replace the church.[73]

I am not suggesting that globalization and modernization are identical; they are not. But the modern study of religion paves the way for the triumph of a post-Christian secular humanism as the ideological framework for globalization. No recent scholar has done more to demonstrate the connection between the study of religion and the secularistic impulse of modernity than Hans G. Kippenberg.[74] Kippenberg begins by demonstrating how modernization uproots religious traditions from their own place and time. Whereas religions once saturated every aspect of social organization, the modern period saw the differentiation of social systems and consequently their autonomous claims to manage their own spheres without religious aid. Market forces, legal systems, and the scientific organization of knowledge marginalized religious traditions by leaving them with little work to do, other than supplying the emotional support made necessary by the rapid changes and social dislocations brought on by modernity itself.

At the heart of modernity, then, is a troubled relationship to religious tradition. For modern people to know their own hearts, they must reflect on this relationship. We moderns can have a romantic or nostalgic view of religion, or we can take pride in our critical distance from the traditions of our ancestors; we can claim religion in defiance of modern trends, or we can deconstruct religion in order to guarantee the purity of our modern condition. Whatever we do, we cannot understand the nature of modernity, and thus we cannot understand ourselves, without understanding that we are committed to the project of understanding religion. Notice that I am not saying that in order to be modern people we must have religion completely figured out. There is no single understanding of religion. That is just the point. The understanding of religion is both necessary and impossible precisely because modernity is the attempt to be both outside and inside of the religious past. Conversely, to be modern is to be part of an unfinished project. It is to be anxious, restless, uncertain, and unsettled, precisely because modernity can never be completely done with its own religious past.

Protestantism, in its American form, is torn between its Evangelical and modern wings. If Protestantism is to provide leadership for the processes of globalization, it will have to look less modern and more traditional. Whether it can do this is an open question. There are some indications that Christianity in America is in decline. Recent religious trends include what can only be called an Easternization of the West. According to an International Social Survey Program, one-fourth of Europeans and Americans believe in reincarnation.[75] America, like the rest of the developed world, is destined to become increasingly dependent on the South for theological instruction and inspiration.

What I have tried to tell, then, is a story of two globalisms. One is economic, led by multinational corporations and closely connected to American interests. The other is a global explosion of various forms of Evangelical and Pentecostal churches, many of which originated in or were crucially shaped by American Christianity. The one globalism—American economic power—is, in crucial respects, a necessary prerequisite for the other globalism—American-style Christianity. American commerce is serving God's purposes today just as Roman roads were providential for the expansion of Christianity many centuries ago. The destiny of Christianity, however, is much greater than the destiny of America. There is no immediate need to choose between these two globalisms, though ultimately it is possible that their trajectories will diverge if they begin competing with each other. Christians believe only one globalism will triumph in the end—and that it will be a globalism of the one true God—but that does not commit Christians to a wholesale rejection of American-led economic globalism. Christians need an ironic imagination when it comes to interpreting providence, because God's ways are not our own. American Christians need to be clear that, while they support America's investment in democracy and freedom, their loyalties extend beyond American economic expansion and toward a global Christianity that is America's true significance for world history—even if that global Christianity were to result, in the long run, in the decline of American strength and power. For better or worse, American-style Christianity is the future of the global church. Whether it represents the future of America is another question altogether.

A providential interpretation of world history offers no divine guarantee that the American governance of global capitalism will remain within the sphere of Christian influence. Indeed, John of Patmos, in the last book of the

Bible, warns us that the nearness of the kingdom of God will call forth a false double—a parasitical distortion of God's universal rule. That false claim might be already on the horizon. A secular society is not necessarily anti-Christian, as long as it admits that it is unfinished and makes room for a completion of meaning that transcends it. America can be secular in this sense, but it also has helped forge a secularism that seeks to undermine Christianity. America is such a religious nation that an anti-Christian secularism could be widely promulgated only if it is perversely cloaked in the Christian virtues of tolerance and compassion. Anti-Christian secularism accomplishes its distortion of Christian morality by means of a transformation of the human sensorium, which is the way cultures organize, employ, and value the senses. The anti-Christian secular sensorium consists of a pervasive proliferation of entertaining images that relativizes all moral judgments, in opposition to the Christian maxim that faith comes through hearing. A society saturated in images encourages an anxious worship of idols rather than a patient listening to the Word of God.

The question of the cultural ordering of the senses is important because all communities are defined by their privileged modes of communication. By transporting us out of particular relationships and into a world of boundless images, a visual culture erodes the possibility of a providential understanding of history. In a recent book, Oliver O'Donovan demonstrates this point by linking the modern rebellion against providence to a distinctively modern form of representation that he calls "publicity." The obsession with the news is, for O'Donovan, a product of a profoundly anti-providential imagination. Furthermore, as O'Donovan himself argues, we are obsessed not only with the news but also with the newest media that can most quickly get us the news. I have argued elsewhere that the centrality of the cinema for modern society is evidence that the eye has eclipsed the ear as our ruling mode of perception.[76] Consequently, life becomes a screen for the projection, inspection, manipulation, and consumption of otherwise pointless representations. The elevation of sight to the highest of the senses provokes great anxiety. We can never see enough, even when we are able to survey the goods, via the Internet, of the entire world. The global economy can thus signify the open borders and free flow of information that will enable Christianity's ultimate triumph, but it also functions to satisfy the insatiable demands of an organ that needs the whole word in order to stave off boredom. A globalism justified by pluralism and conveyed through images will not be without its small pleasures, but it is hard to see how it could provide the resources for a great and lasting civilization, let alone the framework for a thriving and faithful church.

There is nothing wrong with images in themselves, because God redeemed our desire to see the truth by becoming human. After his ascent to heaven, however, Jesus left us with the church as the means of representing his body. In the church, we experience language as it was meant to be as we hear words that have the power to give us the presence of Christ. All of our senses will one day find their consummation in heaven. In the meantime, we must be wary of the promise of human stars and instead content to listen to the feint echo of God's Word in preaching that is all-too-human. Without the discipline of the ear, we risk losing what it means to be part of a particular time and place. "To have a political identity," O'Donovan writes, "means accepting the contingent determination of one's society by the decrees of God's historical providence, which allows no justification or criticism."[77] We can always imagine that life is elsewhere, or that our society is other than it is, or that a perfect world exists "out there" for the taking, but such exercises of the visual imagination are politically dangerous and morally dubious unless they are disciplined by the humble and patient hearing of the Word, which takes place in the one truly universal society of the church.

NOTES

1. Jack S. Levy, *War in the Modern Great Power System, 1495–1975* (Lexington: University Press of Kentucky, 1983), 97.

2. Joseph S. Nye Jr., *The Paradox of American Power* (New York: Oxford University Press, 2002), 15.

3. Jean Bethke Elshtain, *Just War against Terror: The Burden of American Power in a Violent World* (New York: Basic Books, 2003), 147.

4. Jean-Francois Revel, *Anti-Americanism*, trans. Diarmid Cammell (San Francisco: Encounter Books, 2003).

5. Michael Hardt and Antonio Negri, *Empire* (Cambridge, MA: Harvard University Press, 2000), xiii.

6. Ibid., 21.

7. Charles A. Kupchan, *The End of the American Era: U.S. Foreign Policy and the Geopolitics of the 21st Century* (New York: Alfred A. Knopf, 2002).

8. George Soros, *The Bubble of American Supremacy: Correcting the Misuse of American Power* (New York: Public Affairs, 2003); Robert Jay Lifton, *Supreme Syndrome: America's Apocalyptic Confrontation with the World* (New York: Nation Books, 2003); Emmanuel Todd, *After the Empire: The Breakdown of American Order*, trans. C. Jon Delogu (New York: Columbia University Press, 2004).

9. Note, however, that Nye himself is very careful about drawing the limits to international cooperation. See *The Paradox of American Power*, 163–68.

10. For the best of this kind of analysis, see Teresa Brennan, *Globalization and Its Terrors* (New York: Routledge, 2003). She defines globalization in terms of an acceleration of time that is extended across geographical boundaries and advocates a return to slower, more local economies based on the rhythms of nature. Her hope for building a new earth (163) is dependent on the Christian providential narrative that she utterly rejects.

11. Niall Ferguson, *Empire* (New York: Basic Books, 2002), 360.

12. Ibid., xxiii.

13. Kevin Phillips, *The Cousins' Wars: Religion, Politics, and the Triumph of Anglo-America* (New York: Basic Books, 1999), xiv.

14. Ibid., xv.
15. Theo Hobson, *Against Establishment: An Anglican Polemic* (London: Darton, Longman and Todd, 2003), 47.
16. Quoted in Ernest Lee Tuveson, *Redeemer Nation: The Idea of America's Millennial Role* (Chicago: University of Chicago Press, 1968), 127.
17. John Spurr, "Virtue, Religion and Government: The Anglican Uses of Providence," in *The Politics of Religion in Restoration England*, ed. Tim Harris, Paul Seaward, and Mark Goldie (Oxford: Basil Blackwell, 1990), 30.
18. Hobson, *Against Establishment*, 37.
19. See Stephen H. Webb, *The Divine Voice: Christian Proclamation and the Theology of Sound* (Grand Rapids: Brazos Press, 2003).
20. Hobson, *Against Establishment*, 124–25.
21. Philip Jenkins, *The Next Christendom: The Coming of Global Christianity* (New York: Oxford University Press, 2002).
22. See David Aikman, *Jesus in Beijing: How Christianity Is Transforming China and Changing the Balance of Power* (New York: Regnery Publishing, 2003).
23. Bernice Martin, "From Pre- to Postmodernity in Latin America: The Cast of Pentecostalism," in *Religion, Modernity, and Postmodernity*, ed. Paul Heelas (Oxford: Blackwell Publishers, 1998), 123. My reading of Pentecostalism is also shaped by David Martin, *Tongues of Fire: The Explosion of Protestantism in Latin America* (Oxford: Blackwell, 1990).
24. Martin, "From Pre- to Postmodernity in Latin America," 126.
25. Murray W. Dempster, Byron D. Klaus, and Douglas Petersen, *The Globalization of Pentecostalism: A Religion Made to Travel* (Oxford: Regnum, 1999).
26. Karla Poewe, *The Charismatic Movement as a Global Culture* (Columbia: University of South Carolina Press, 1994).
27. Lamin Sanneh, *Whose Religion Is Christianity? The Gospel beyond the West* (Grand Rapids: Eerdmans, 2003), 113.
28. David F. Wright, "The Charismatic Movement: The Laicizing of Christianity?" in *The Rise of the Laity in Evangelical Protestantism*, ed. Deryck W. Lovegrove (New York: Routledge, 2002), 253–63.
29. Ibid., 259.
30. See D. W. Bebbington, *Evangelicalism in Modern Britain: A History from the 1730s to the 1980s* (London: Unwin Hyman, 1989).
31. Stanley Johannesen, "The Holy Ghost and the Ordering of the World," in *Religion and Global Order*, ed. Roland Robertson and William R. Garrett (New York: Paragon House Publishers, 1991), 127, 129.
32. I am grateful for conversations with Father Richard John Neuhaus, as I was revising this book, for leading to me to a deeper appreciation of how Catholicism continues to maintain the principle of unity for the benefit of all Christians. For an informative history of the relationship between Catholicism and democracy, see John T. McGreevy, *Catholicism and American Freedom: A History* (New York: W. W. Norton, 2003).
33. Nicholas Boyle, *Who Are We? Christian Humanism and the Global Market from Hegel to Heaney* (Notre Dame, IN: University of Notre Dame Press, 1998), 93.
34. Alexis de Tocqueville, *Democracy in America*, trans. George Lawrence (New York: Anchor Books, 1969), 450–51.
35. Nathan O. Hatch, *The Democratization of American Christianity* (New Haven, Conn.: Yale University Press, 1989).
36. Arnold Toynbee, *Christianity among the Religions of the World* (New York: Charles Scribner's Sons, 1957).
37. Arnold Toynbee, "What Should Be the Christian Approach to the Contemporary Non-Christian Faiths?" in *Attitudes Toward Other Religions*, ed. Owen C. Thomas (London: SCM, 1969), 170–71.

38. Arnold J. Toynbee, *A Study of History*, abridgement of vols. 7–10 (New York: Oxford University Press, 1957), 109ff.

39. Stephen R. L. Clark, "World Religions and World Orders," *Religious Studies* 26 (March 1990): 46.

40. Ibid., 49.

41. Ibid., 57.

42. Samuel P. Huntington, *The Clash of Civilizations and the Remaking of World Order* (New York: Touchstone, 1996), 212, 217–18. Huntington has been criticized for equating Islam with a civilization. He knows that there have been several different Islamic civilizations. He is thus using "civilization" in a loose sense in order to stress the unity of much Islamic culture.

43. Kate Zebiri, *Muslims and Christians Face to Face* (Oxford: Oneworld Publications, 1997), 146.

44. See the selection from Sayyid Qutb in *Christianity Through Non-Christian Eyes*, ed. Paul J. Griffiths (Maryknoll, NY: Orbis Books, 1999), chap. 5.

45. Ibid., chap. 8.

46. Oriana Fallaci, *The Rage and the Pride* (New York: Rizzoli, 2002).

47. President Bush's speech can be found at www.whitehouse.gov/news/releases/2003/02/20030226-11.html.

48. This tendency to group all terrorists together and attribute their motivation to the fears and anxieties of religious fundamentalism is exemplified by Jessica Stern, *Terror in the Name of God: Why Religious Militants Kill* (San Francisco: HarperCollins, 2003).

49. Serge Trifkovic, *The Sword of the Prophet* (Boston: Regina Orthodox Press, 2002).

50. Quoted in Bernard Lewis, *The Crisis of Islam: Holy War and Unholy Terror* (New York: The Modern Library, 2003), 32.

51. See Geoffrey Parrinder, *Jesus in the Qur'an* (Oxford: Oneworld, 1995), for an honest examination of the inconsistencies, and Tarif Khalidi, *The Muslim Jesus: Sayings and Stories in Islamic Literature* (Cambridge, MA: Harvard University Press, 2001), for evidence of Muslim fascination with the apocryphal Jesus.

52. Lewis, *The Crisis of Islam*, 31.

53. Bernard Lewis, *What Went Wrong? Western Impact and Middle Eastern Response* (New York: Oxford University Press, 2002), 96.

54. Ibid., 98.

55. For the argument that Islamic equality provides the best possible foundation for an Islamic version of democracy, see Noah Feldman, *After Jihad: America and the Struggle for Islamic Democracy* (New York: Farrar, Straus and Giroux, 2003). For a discussion of the most progressive Islamic intellectuals, see Raymond William Baker, *Islam without Fear: Egypt and the New Islamists* (Cambridge, MA: Harvard University Press, 2003).

56. Bat Ye'or, *The Decline of Eastern Christianity under Islam: From Jihad to Dhimmitude* (London: Associated University Presses, 1996).

57. For two of the best books on this topic, see William Dalrymple, *From the Holy Mountain* (San Francisco: HarperCollins, 1997), and Charles M. Sennott, *The Body and the Blood: The Middle East's Vanishing Christians and the Possibility for Peace* (New York: PublicAffairs, 2003).

58. Bat Ye'or, *Islam and Dhimmitude: Where Civilizations Collide* (Cranbury, NJ: Associated University Presses, 2002), 239.

59. See Nina Shea, *In the Lion's Den: Persecuted Christians and What the Church Can Do About It* (New York: Broadman & Holman, 1997), and Paul Marshall and Lele Gilbert, *Their Blood Cries Out: The Untold Story of Persecution against Christians in the Modern World* (Nashville: Thomas Nelson, 1997). The Christian solidarity movement has stirred a lively debate among Evangelicals. Some see it as a thin cover for promoting the secular, human rights agenda of the United Nations. Liberal or leftist critics see it as supporting American imperialism.

60. Jedediah Purdy, *Being American: Liberty, Commerce, and Violence in an American World* (New York: Alfred A. Knopf, 2003), 118.

61. *Middle East Quarterly* (Summer 2001), available at http://www.meforum.org/article/104.

62. One can acknowledge how American covert operations in Afghanistan had unintended effects without blaming America for terrorism. See George Crile, *Charlie Wilson's War: The Extraordinary Story of the Largest Covert Operation in History* (New York: Atlantic Monthly Press, 2003).

63. Serge Trifkovic, *The Sword of the Prophet*, 299.

64. Ibid.

65. David Frum and Richard Perle, *An End to Evil: How to Win the War on Terrorism* (New York: Random House, 2004).

66. Lamin Sanneh, *Whose Religion is Christianity?* 20.

67. The best book on the theology of power, which also provides an insightful commentary on the Eucharist as the site of Luther's theory of power, is Kyle A. Pasewark, *A Theology of Power: Being beyond Domination* (Minneapolis: Fortress Press, 1993). For an analysis of power and the Eucharist in Calvin, see Christopher Elwood, *The Broken Body: The Calvinist Doctrine of Eucharist and the Symbolization of Power in Sixteenth-Century France* (New York: Oxford University Press, 1999).

68. Just as there is a politics of free speech, so there is a theology of the conditions that make possible the announcement and reception of the Word. The politics of free speech analyzes the conditions that are necessary for open and pluralistic political spaces. Voices do not just happen; they must be trained, exercised, and encouraged. They also must be given the spaces that will do them justice. Without a concert hall, singers cannot achieve their perfect pitch. Without the proper political institutions, democracy sounds like the rumble of anarchy, not the attempt to harmonize the countless demands of the voiceless. Political institutions serve the purpose of teaching us to distinguish between demagoguery and statesmanship, ideology and politics-as-usual, but the skills of hearing have to begin in the family, where we learn to make that most fundamental distinction between sincerity and deception. The theology of free speech analyzes the ecclesial conditions that make possible the proclamation of the gospel. Without the church, God's voice can sound like the musings of romantics in search of meaning in nature. It will have all the authority that we give to ourselves. Protestantism still functions today much like the American Constitution does, by guaranteeing the conditions that make proclamation possible. If Christianity in America has not declined in any way like the churches in Europe, it is because America has been truer to the rhetorical thrust of the Reformation.

69. Mircea Eliade, *The Myth of the Eternal Return: Or, Cosmos and History*, trans. Willard R. Trask (Princeton, NJ: Princeton University Press, 1954).

70. See Brian Stanley, "Commerce and Christianity: Providence Theory, the Missionary Movement, and the Imperialism of Free Trade, 1842–1860," *The Historical Journal* 26, no. 1 (1983): 71–94. The result of this fusion could be the rationalization of all modes of commerce, but the intent was the peaceful spread of Christianity, as Livingstone explained: "When a tribe begins to trade with another it feels a sense of mutual dependence; and this is a most important aid in diffusing the blessings of Christianity, because one tribe never goes to another without telling the news, and the Gospel comes in to be part of their news, and the knowledge of Christianity is thus spread by means of commerce" (quoted by Stanley, 75).

71. See Christopher Hodgkins, *Reforming Empire: Protestant Colonialism and Conscience in British Literature* (Columbia: University of Missouri Press, 2002), as well as the very informative and entertaining book by Tom Hiney, *On the Missionary Trail* (New York: Atlantic Monthly Press, 2000).

72. Paul F. M. Zahl, *The First Christians: Universal Truth in the Teachings of Jesus* (Grand Rapids: Eerdmans, 2003).

73. I recently had a conversation with a friend who teaches in a large Religion department in a university that has retained, albeit minimally, its relationship to the church of its founding. This Religion department was endowed by a pious woman of long ago with a large sum of money with the stipulation that several courses in Bible be required for all students. My friend told me that his colleagues detest the initial intention of this requirement, which was that students become literate in the biblical story and immersed in biblical theology. Because there is a very active chapter of Campus Crusade for Christ at this university, the Religion faculty go overboard in defining themselves as the opposite of anything that smacks of piety. They take their task to be one of shaking the intellectual foundations of their students by demolishing their religious naivete. The students of this university, who are overwhelmingly Christian, would be better off, my friend told me, if there were no Religion requirement. As it is, they are subjected to a very powerful and well-organized assault on their faith, all because a devout woman many years ago thought everyone should know something about the Bible.

74. Hans G. Kippenberg, *Discovering Religious History in the Modern Age* (Princeton, NJ: Princeton University Press, 2001).

75. Bryan Wilson and Jamie Cresswell, eds., *New Religious Movements: Challenge and Response* (New York: Routledge, 1999).

76. Stephen H. Webb, *The Divine Voice: Christian Proclamation and the Theology of Sound* (Grand Rapids: Brazos Press, 2004).

77. Oliver O'Donovan, *Common Objects of Love: Moral Reflection and the Shaping of Community* (Grand Rapids: Eerdmans, 2002), 43.

CHAPTER SEVEN

Carl Schmitt and the Limits of Democracy

Lest I be accused of turning market-based democracy into an idol, and in order to lay my political cards on the table, I want to reflect on the political theologian who has most shaped my thinking about the nature, limits, and future of democracy. Carl Schmitt might seem like an odd choice of a political theorist for a book about God's providential relationship to America. Schmitt (1888–1985) was one of the sharpest critics of modern democracy. Moreover, all of his thought is tainted by his impoverished political decision to join the Nazi Party in 1933, in the same month, May, as did Martin Heidegger. Like many German intellectuals, he was at first enthusiastic about the new regime. By 1936, he came under Nazi Party criticism, but he remained in his position at the University of Berlin. After the war, he was detained by the Allies but never charged with war crimes, although he was not permitted to resume his university teaching. What makes Schmitt even more problematic for some scholars is that he is often taken to be the "godfather" of American neoconservativism, since Leo Strauss, a conservative political theorist who spent most of his career at the University of Chicago, knew Schmitt and wrote an early essay on his work.

Scholarship on Schmitt used to draw a straight line connecting his early work, which launched a devastating critique of the weaknesses of parliamentary government in general and the Weimar Republic in particular, with Schmitt's later support of Hitler. More recent scholarship has shown how Schmitt sought to salvage Weimar by his insistence that democracies need an external principle of authority that can bring public debate to an end.[1] Schmitt called this principle of authority "sovereignty," an outdated term that he used in a provocative way to make an important point. Schmitt was raised in a conservative Catholic family, and he never abandoned his loyalty to the Catholic Church.[2] Throughout his life he was mistrustful of the idea that a rationalistic system of thought can explain everything in a self-contained manner. Translated into political terms, Schmitt argues that no political system, no matter how comprehensive its judiciary, can guard against every challenge to the state. Just as no logical system is ever complete, because it is always dependent on unproven premises, no nation-state can anticipate every hypothetical challenge to its authority. Schmitt calls such challenges "the exception," and the consequence of the exception is the need for someone to take charge. In normal circumstances, authority can be impersonal, embedded in the procedures laid out by a constitution. In principle, however, there will always be exceptional situations that mandate a personal exercise of authority. Legal systems can operate only under normal conditions, but the obligation of the sovereign is to determine what those normal conditions are by deciding how to deal with the exception.

At one point in his development of this theory, Schmitt draws support from Søren Kierkegaard.[3] It should not be surprising that Schmitt found an ally in this nineteenth-century theologian. By embracing the paradox of the individual who stands above the universal demands of morality, Kierkegaard developed one of the most radical critiques of modern liberalism. He held in disdain the confidence of Hegelians in an endless elaboration of the ideal. Hegelian theologians took a kind of procedural approach to faith that privileged thinking over acting. Kierkegaard posed an alternative to this ethical rationalism in the starkest of terms. For Kierkegaard, Christ is the exception to all human ideals, and thus Christ demands a decision. Each of us, in other words, must act as a sovereign when it comes to determining our own spiritual fate. The universal realm of the ethical insists that universal rules exist for every situation. Kierkegaard suspected that, shy of a leap of faith, the spiritual life is bound to be swept up in the mind's fixation on the procedural order of universal ethical claims. Likewise, Schmitt thought that parliamentary systems of government, under the pressure of the possibility of war, showed themselves in dire need of a fundamental decision that represents a break from the democratic examination of every political option. Schmitt and Kierkegaard both defined the exception as that which cannot be subsumed by a general rule. In practical terms, Schmitt wanted Hindenberg to invoke Article 48 of the Weimar constitution—the famous emergency provision—in order to save Weimar against its enemies on both the extreme right and left.

As this brief discussion of Schmitt's relationship to Weimar shows, Schmitt was just as aware as the liberation theologians that all political theory is concrete and of the moment. He was forced to make difficult decisions in his political life and resented the fact that others thought he should have stayed above the fray. One of his last theological arguments, as Michael Hollerich has shown, was over the doctrine of providence.[4] The Catholic theologian Erik Peterson, reacting in part to Schmitt's troubled career, rejected the possibility of any Christian political theology by siding with Augustine's skepticism about the Roman Empire rather than the more optimistic view of Eusebius of Caesarea. Schmitt thought this denied Christians the right to see God's hand at work in their political lives. Peterson had noted Augustine's scorn for Cicero's tragic alliance with Octavian. Schmitt wondered in response what choice Cicero had. Schmitt was obviously trying to rationalize his own decision to join forces with Hitler, but his pitiable self-defense in this debate does not necessarily render his argument without any merit. Like the liberationist unitary view of history, Schmitt knew that without a strong doctrine of providence there can be no political theology.

He shared with the liberationists not only their ambivalence about democracy but also their criticisms of modern individualism. In a book published in 1919 entitled *Politische Romantik* (*Political Romanticism*), Schmitt derided the tendency of modern political theorists to put the individual above the state, which leaves the actual practice of politics adrift. Political romanticism inevitably results in an apolitical cynicism. Individualism sets the state adrift, leaving it prey to every voracious ideology. When nations no longer recognize that they are under judgment to a higher power, the state becomes an individual writ large, with all the danger that entails. Rather than freeing the individual from the state, romanticism ends up making the state the only true individual. It is better to recognize the state one has—and demand of it peace, protection, and order—than to live in a dreamworld of pretend statelessness. The twentieth century was full of history's most tumultuous political events precisely because political leaders tried to create the state anew, granting it enormous power on the basis of godless ideologies. Schmitt's principle of sovereignty was an attempt to preserve the state by acknowledging its limitations and thus its subordination to a higher power. Tragically, he was so insistent on the need for a transcendent power in politics that he did not adequately distinguish between political power that is consonant with the divine and that which is demonic.

Nevertheless, Schmitt's political theory of the Weimar period, which was concerned to salvage order and stability in the midst of a constitutional crisis, should not be read through the lens of his later involvement with the Nazis. Now that we have some distance from that period, we can treat Schmitt's work more carefully. Even if his acceptance of modern constitutionalism was begrudging—he thought that political liberalism could be defined by the unfortunate effort at eliminating the need for sovereignty— he was sincere in his attempts to save it by a recovery of the personal element involved in making a sovereign decision. Indeed, his Weimar writings were

relentless in their pursuit of a comprehensive political theory that would
ensure public order. His most important work during this period is an objec-
tive investigation into the foundation of the autonomy of the political realm.[5]
His basic premise is that people are dangerous. Whether this is a theological judgment—it seems obviously grounded in the doctrine of original sin—
is ambiguous in Schmitt's thought. While he argues that all political ideas are
translations from a theological script, he also wants to circumscribe the
political as a realm independent of all others. The political has to do with a
basic distinction between friends and enemies. Only the state can determine
who is the enemy, and only the state can decide to fight the enemy. Outside
of the political sphere, there is no way to justify whether an enemy is actually
a threat to a nation's way of life. The friend-enemy distinction is what gives
meaning to national politics.

The contrast with contemporary political theology could hardly be more
striking. Nearly the whole of political theology today is in denial of the
friend-enemy distinction as Schmitt understands it. In Schmitt's terms, the
church is fundamentally liberal in that it wants to usurp the personal authority of the sovereign for the formal rule of law. The problem is not that the
church embraces peace but that the church wants to displace the political
sphere with its legitimate determination of who is to count as the enemy.
This point needs to be made very carefully and deliberately, because it could
be easily misunderstood. Christianity teaches us to forgive our enemies, but
the church has also long recognized the need for political authority and the
demand for justice. Forgiveness can be applied to the political realm in
provocative and transformative ways—and there has been significant recent
scholarship on the role of religion in statecraft[6]—but the friend-enemy distinction can be completely dismissed only at the cost of neglecting the doctrine of providence. God works through history, which means that God
defeats obstacles to the divine plan. God's enemies are not necessarily our
own, of course, but to be a friend of God is to seek out God's purposes in history, and those purposes are not unrelated to the struggle for freedom, a
struggle that involves the tragic necessity of war.

John Milbank, a prominent socialist theologian, is a good example of the
problems that arise when the friend-enemy distinction is neglected or
rejected outright. The leader of a theological movement known as Radical
Orthodoxy, Milbank argues that Christianity presupposes an ontological
peace that sets Christian politics apart from all philosophical disputes.
Milbank does not just place this ontology of peace at the beginning of time.
He argues that the Christian liturgy, every time it is performed, makes this
peace available for our ongoing participation. He blames modernity for
turning God into an object separable from the world and thus subjecting
God to the kind of intellectual analysis that leads, inevitably, to a skeptical

conclusion. By contrast, Milbank's philosophical instincts are platonic in that he endeavors to provide theology with a metaphysical foundation. The mind knows only what it loves, and every act of knowledge is but a partial realization of the desire for God. All forms of knowledge should thus acknowledge God as the source of all truth, an ambitious claim that demands the complete reconstruction of modern society.

Milbank admires the medieval milieu of an organic society wherein the church saturates every aspect of life. The rule of the church provides the necessary condition for the Thomistic synthesis of Greek and Christian thought that guides Milbank's own metaphysics. As Christopher J. Insole has recently argued, Milbank's critique of liberal democracy involves a "strong form of communitarianism, vastly extended in scope, invoking participatory and transformative communities and structures at every level of a hierarchical, teleological and analogically interrelated cosmos."[7]

Although Milbank is not a pacifist, he does envision the church as providing a counterpolitical sphere that challenges the apparent triumph of democracy and capitalism.[8] As a result, his rhetoric can be extremely radical in its rejection of all things modern. Capitalism for Milbank is incompatible with Christianity because capitalism is nothing more than a Christian heresy. Capitalism assumes an account of human exchange that denies the primacy of gift giving and thus the reality of grace. For this reason, Christians must "strive still to abolish capitalism."[9] Milbank does not think that contracts can protect the freedom to give, nor does he think that possession is an essential moment in the life of the gift. He seeks a community grounded in communion, but he does not want to limit communion to the church. Every human exchange, for Milbank, should be suffused with grace. Although Milbank speaks the language of Christian peace, in practice, it is hard to imagine how his nostalgic longing for a return to a more organically ordered society could be achieved without violence, on the part of God or humanity. Indeed, his radical rejection of democracy makes Schmitt look like a liberal by comparison.

Milbank wants to replace the present political order, a goal that gives his rhetoric an apocalyptic tone that is at odds with the serenity of his platonic metaphysics. For all of his appeal to metaphysics, he also talks about outnarrating, rather than outsmarting, his opponents, so that the friend-enemy distinction survives in his intellectual practices, if not in his political theology.[10] Schmitt, for all of his teutonic bombast, wants to recognize the limits of liberalism from within in order to show how liberal democracies can best survive. Milbank places his hope in global governance through organizations that can supersede the role of nations. Schmitt suspects that such alliances only increase the number of opportunities and causes for war.[11] That people are dangerous means that people will always have enemies as well as friends, and this distinction cannot be obliterated by an international organization dedicated to promoting good will among nations.

When nation-states make decisions about life and death, as in whether to go to war, that power must be located in a sovereign act. In other words, there must be a final authority, something that liberalism cannot acknowledge. Democracies can locate sovereignty in "the people," but a pure democracy would be rule by the mob, a frightening possibility. Democracies can also suspend their own rules and permit rule by a dictator, which is also a frightening possibility. It would be better, Schmitt argues, to prepare for the eventuality of exceptional circumstances by providing clear limits to liberal proceduralism. Authority by definition is a transcendent and not immanent phenomenon. War is what makes this clear. It would be very hard, though perhaps not impossible, for an assembly of citizens, equal in rank, to make a decision about whether to go to war. Without a provision for a mechanism that allows someone to make the final decision, a deliberative body would be left to an interminable debate about whether to go to war.

Schmitt's insistence that the decision to go to war must be made by someone in the position of the political sovereign does not mean that he thinks that all wars are good or that war is something to be celebrated and romanticized. His attitude is just the opposite. There is no acceptable justification for war other than the case when one is threatened by one's enemy. "There exists no rational purpose, no norm no matter how true, no program no matter how exemplary, no social ideal no matter how beautiful, no legitimacy nor legality which could justify men killing each other for this reason. If such physical destruction of human life is not motivated by an existential threat to one's own way of life, then it cannot be justified."[12] This is a sharp departure from the just war tradition, which allows warfare in order to protect the innocent, especially those who cannot protect themselves.[13] Schmitt narrows the justification of warfare to self-defense, because he believes that the friend-enemy distinction is so existentially strong that, in time of war, it will absorb into the political sphere every other criteria or motive. The question he raises is not whether the church should displace the political but whether the church should put itself in a position to transform the political by expanding the range of friends and reducing the number of enemies in the world. Christians, for example, should be friends with other Christians regardless of where they live. Christians can also work with all those who want to support the growth of freedom in the world. Expanding the range of friends in the world, however, does not mean ignoring the reality of enemies. Indeed, the pursuit of justice suggests that wars will need to be fought on behalf of the innocent, something Schmitt does not affirm.

Stanley Hauerwas, a pacifist theologian, often laments the fact that American Christians no longer are willing to die for their faith. Christians, when confronted with the choice of death or apostasy by an enemy of the faith, should choose death. American Christians do not have the opportunity to be tested by this dire circumstance, although Christians throughout the world continue to die in significant numbers for their faith. Hauerwas wishes martyrdom could play a more significant role in the church because he wants the church to be more like a political institution. Martyrdom, however, is not a political decision. It exists outside of the friend-enemy distinction. There are cases, as with the heroism of the Jewish fighters at Masada, where groups of people choose to die on their own terms rather than the terms of their enemies. Nation-states, however, cannot be founded on the principle of this willingness to die rather than to fight. Individuals can choose to be martyrs, but nations are nations precisely because they choose to defend themselves when they are attacked. A people becomes a nation when it must deliberate about how to identify and what to do with enemies. If it were not for the necessity of this decision to fight, no matter how occasionally it arises, the political would cease to exist.

Contrary to Hauerwas's position, the sporadic practice of martyrdom, regardless of how important it was for the early church, does not make the church a polis. That is, the church is not a political institution in the sense that Schmitt defines the political, yet it has a stake in the political because of its commitment to peace, its transnational character, and its recognition that the pursuit of justice can involve warfare. As Schmitt puts the matter in *The Concept of the Political*, "A religious community, a church, can exhort a member to die for his belief and become a martyr, but only for the salvation of his own soul, not for the religious community in its quality as an earthly power; otherwise it assumes a political dimension."[14] The church can make the decision to go to war, as the example of the Crusades demonstrates, but when it makes this decision, it ceases to be a religious community and becomes a political community. In order to remain religious, the church should not go to war. The church should instead advise the nation-state on the merits of any particular decision to go to war—and the just war tradition has emerged to guide the advice Christians can offer to their political leaders—but the church is not in the position to become a political body in Schmitt's sense.[15]

Rather than dismissing the church as irrelevant to the political, Schmitt's analysis shows just how important the church can be in times of war. Schmitt believed that the Catholic Church, for example, can accommodate liberalism but can never enter into an alliance with it. The church has its own authority, distinct from the political realm. It is not the role of the church, then, to vilify the enemy or to rationalize the conflict. Neither is it the role of the church to pretend that it can be the site of a politics that—this side of the coming kingdom—transcends the political altogether. Engagement of this kind can only make the church appear all the more imaginary, the more self-righteously it denounces what is a fundamental aspect of humanity's fallen condition. The church has its practice of peace, but given the ever present danger presented by a potential enemy, the church cannot demand the immediate cessation of all warfare. The church can mitigate the need to go to war by asking that certain moral guidelines are followed in the preliminary stages of the conflict, and the church can minimize the damage of the war by asking that the battle be fought according to moral rules. Indeed, some battles are fought in order that moral rules will have a sphere in which to rule. The decision to go to war, however, is out of the church's hands, if the church is to be true to its mission. The church advises, but it does not decide.

Schmitt leaves open the question as to whether universal peace can ever reign on earth.[16] That is, in a way, the most important question for a political theology, but it need not interfere with the philosophical demarcation of the political as such. The political is made necessary by the existence of enemies, no matter how much we would like to think that nation-states can learn always to get along with each other. Even Christian theology has found it tremendously difficult to imagine a faithful humanity united without an enemy, as demonstrated by inconclusive debates among the church fathers concerning whether Satan will be saved at the end of time. The two greatest Christian moralists of the twentieth century, Reinhold Niebuhr and Rene Girard, have both acknowledged the foundational role of conflict and violence in all societies.

Niebuhr, in *Moral Man and Immoral Society*, broke ranks from the social gospel movement of the early part of the twentieth century by rejecting the translation of the doctrine of providence into the celebration of progress.[17] People are always less moral in groups than by themselves, Niebuhr argued. Evil is compounded by the good intentions that lead people to work so hard in constructing viable social and political institutions. Niebuhr locates this evil in the heart of the individual, but his social psychology shows how groups are more limited than individuals in their capacity to transcend themselves and thus see their own motives as mixed with pride and ambition. For Niebuhr, the political always results in a moral dilemma: We need to act as groups in order to achieve the common good, but groups have the capacity to do much more harm in the world than individuals. Niebuhr's only solution to this dilemma is the balance of powers. If a government has no soul that grants it the ability for self-transcendence and thus moral reflection, at least the government's power can be divided and dispersed. Political transcendence in a democracy becomes horizontal, not vertical; that is, the branches of the government serve as a conscience for each other, checking the pride of ambition by keeping the branches in good order. Like Schmitt, Niebuhr was pessimistic not about God's ability to achieve a new kingdom but rather any human government's ability to achieve it. Democracies are hardly perfect; they do not erase social conflict. Instead, they postpone conflict by dispersing political antagonism among a variety of branches. Niebuhr sidesteps the problem of the emergency associated with the exception, which haunted Schmitt all his life, and thus he remains more optimistic than Schmitt about the ability of democracies to perpetuate themselves in an impersonal division of powers. Nevertheless, both thinkers recognize that the inevitability of conflict makes for the necessity of the state.

Rene Girard's treatment of the political is more profound than Niebuhr's because he does not rely on a social psychology of group dynamics.[18] Instead, he anthropologically discloses a hidden logic in the formation of communities that is always distorted by religious myth. That logic is what Girard calls the phenomenon of the scapegoat. Communities, simply put, are made possible only by labeling one of their own as an internal enemy. Schmitt also applied his concept of the enemy to the domestic enemy, the enemy that can lead to civil war, but for Girard, the enemy is constitutive of the religious, not the political. For Girard, societies are never united except by the perceived threat of an enemy that always turns out to be nothing more than a scapegoat. Girard shows that the political is constituted by the religious inasmuch as national myths are needed to explain the existence of the enemy.

Schmitt understood that nations make themselves sacred by demonizing their enemies, and he had very little sympathy for the myriad ways people have invented to rationalize scapegoating. The question is whether his concept of the political can contribute anything to Girard's analysis. Girard sees the church, through its eucharistic renunciation of the making of victims, as the reversal of scapegoating. By proclaiming the peace of God, Jesus began the process of unmasking scapegoating practices, and the church, by worshiping Jesus as the divinely innocent victim, shows the way forward to a future without scapegoating. A future without scapegoating would be a future without politics, and Girard is less than clear about what institutional form this social peace should take. For Schmitt, the state cannot simply wither away once people realize how terribly wrong scapegoating is. If the church should try to embody this peace, it would become one institution among many, with its own enemies, and thus the church would become just another state. The church, in other words, even as it preaches peace, is in need of the balance of powers between nation-states in order to protect it and provide the space for its mission. Only God can bring scapegoating to an end; until then, states are necessary to keep enemies in check.

Nevertheless, both Niebuhr and Girard point to the role of theology in limiting the political, something Schmitt did not allow. The political is fundamental, but it is also self-enclosed. That is, the political cannot solve the problem of violence on its own terms. Its autonomy is only provisional, so to speak, given Christianity's eschatology of global peace. As long as there is violence in the world, there will be a need for national politics, but the question still needs to be asked about the possibility of overcoming violence altogether, outside of the political. The political is fundamental, but Christians should have some reservation about Schmitt's claim that the political is total. For Schmitt, the political is the outermost sphere that makes possible all other cultural activities and social relations. Christians believe that there is yet one more sphere outside of and encompassing the political, and that is the kingdom of God. The kingdom of God is not unrelated to the political because God uses nation-states to advance the dual cause of freedom and the gospel.

That Schmitt did not have a well-developed sense of an alternative to the political left him acutely vulnerable to the Nazi ideology, which in some ways imitated his own rhetoric of the fundamental and ultimately extra-rational distinction of the friend and the enemy. Schmitt cannot be criticized for giving up on Weimar when everyone else did, nor can he be faulted for not being a theologian. He was a political theorist. Yet because he refused to acknowledge the possibility and relevance of a theological discourse on violence that can, no matter how far into the future, trump the political, Schmitt was too ready to throw his lot in with the Nazis. No doubt, ambition drove Schmitt to take advantage of his relationship with the Nazis. More fundamentally, he was too quick to see the political as subsuming the theological. He accepted, in other words, the modern world's story about itself as the secularization of the theological, rather than the church's story about modernity as just another heresy. By his own account, the political can also be explained in terms of the theological. For example, he explains his own favorite term, "the exception," in terms of the Christian idea of a miracle.[19] Liberal proceduralism, which denies the significance of the exception, would thus be the political system that has absorbed the miraculous into itself, permitting no intrusion of the supernatural from outside of the drama of the community of citizens.

In the eighteenth century, by contrast, with the rise of deism, the sovereign was portrayed as existing outside of the natural laws. The intervention of the sovereign was a kind of *deus ex machina*. Modernity begins when people start believing that the sovereign is subjected to the same universal rules that govern both the political and the natural. Indeed, just as modern people find it hard to believe that God intervenes into worldly affairs, modern people resist any political system that leaves room for the sovereign. Americans especially resent any political act that appears to be above the law, and this resentment has grown in the wake of Watergate and the Clinton scandals. President Ford's pardon of Nixon, for example, contributed to his subsequent defeat because Ford's decision was widely interpreted as making Nixon's actions an exception to the rule of law.

Schmitt recognizes that people today no longer regard their political systems as reflective of theological beliefs. The political realm has been emptied of any transcendent meaning. This statement is not quite true, however, because God cannot simply disappear. God as a transcendent and supreme being is eclipsed, but God reappears as that which is immanent and natural. Democracy and the rule of law are thought to need no external justification precisely because God is identified with the natural. Thus, the decline in belief in the radical nature of original sin has the utmost political importance. Without the fall, nature can be understood as good. People can be trusted; the political need not be justified in terms of the danger of war. America, for Schmitt, represents the furthest extreme of this collapse of the transcendental: "In America this manifested itself in the reasonable and pragmatic belief that the voice of the people is the voice of God—a belief that is at the foundation of Jefferson's victory of 1801."[20] The people take the place of God, and the state perpetuates itself without any need of external authority. Consequently, according to Schmitt, political battles on behalf of democracy become of necessity theological battles against Christian tradition.

Schmitt was not wrong about democracy in general, but he was wrong about democracy in America. It was an easy mistake to make, because American democracy is unique. For one thing, America's relationship to the emergence of democracy was radically different from Europe's. Without the heavy weight of an established church, Americans felt little need to rebel against the clerical class. Moreover, because democracy did not break the hold of the church on society, there was no backlash based on a Restorationist nostalgia for the reunification of church and state in the person of the sovereign.[21] Americans were never forced into thinking that they had to make a decision for either the state or the church. Schmitt is right that liberalism, through its faith in rational discourse, has a dissolving effect on metaphysics. Nevertheless, American democracy was not stripped bare of all vestiges of the transcendent. Precisely because American democracy was born outside of the context of battles between the political and the ecclesial in Europe, Americans had to tell a new story about their past. They had to put democracy in a new context, and that context was providence.

Schmitt insisted throughout his career that all social and cultural activities are premised upon a decision about their boundaries that must be made by a principle of sovereignty. Politics is a matter of borders, and the authority that determines a border by definition transcends it.[22] Schmitt understood that the modern world had lost the capacity to appreciate transcendence, which is the source of all true authority. Democratic forms of government for Schmitt were nothing more than a prolonged and futile attempt to deny the basic fact of the need for transcendent authority. Schmitt was a powerfully systematic thinker, but America is a stunning exception to his theory of democracy. For one thing, the boundaries that the democratic government established in America were intended to give Christians great freedom to express themselves, even to the point of challenging the government itself.[23] Moreover, Americans are democrats who agree with his argument about authority. The authority that makes American democracy possible, I have argued throughout this book, is the doctrine of providence. In American hands, this doctrine explains the miraculous success of the newborn country, but it is also a forward-looking doctrine, guiding the aspirations of a country that has few traditions to serve as fixed points on the map of history. Providence is far from an idealization of history. The critics of providence caricature it as an elaborate ruse of self-congratulations, but it is better understood as a form of trust and gratitude that frees the individual for confident action in the world. Freedom would have little meaning if it had no purpose or direction, and it would have little chance in the short run if there were no hope for its ultimate fulfillment. Democracy is a gamble on freedom and providence is its surety.

NOTES

1. For a fine summary of the various misreadings of Schmitt, see Joseph W. Bendersky, "The Definite and the Dubious: Carl Schmitt's Influence on Conservative Political and Legal Theory in the US," *Telos* (Winter 2002): 33-47.

2. Heinrich Meier has emphasized the religious dimension of Schmitt's mistrust of democracy and liberalism. See *Carl Schmitt and Leo Strauss: The Hidden Dialogue*, trans. J. Harvey Lomax (Chicago: University of Chicago Press, 1995).

3. Carl Schmitt, *Political Theology: Four Chapters on the Concept of Sovereignty*, trans. George Schwab (Cambridge, MA: MIT Press, 1985). This book was originally published in 1922; the translation is based on the revised edition of 1934. Schmitt was reading the neoorthodox theologians in the 1920s. In the preface to the second edition of *The Concept of the Political* he refers to Friedrich Gogarten and the theology of the "wholly other." He seems to read this theology as an attempt to protect God from the realm of the political. For Schmitt, the modern period is characterized as the dominance of the political over all other forms of thought; theology survives in terms of its being subsumed into the political. In terms of his theory of sovereignty, it could be argued that Karl Barth and company were trying to preserve a decisionist and personalist paradigm of political activity in the guise of a transcendent deity who nonetheless did not transform the political sphere but hovered above it.

4. I draw my account of this debate from Michael Hollerich, "Carl Schmitt," in *The Blackwell Companion to Political Theology*, ed. Peter Scott and William T. Cavanaugh (Oxford: Blackwell Publishing, 2004), 120.

5. Carl Schmitt, *The Concept of the Political*, trans. and intro. George Schwab (Chicago: University of Chicago Press, 1996). The original edition of *Der Begriff des Politischen* was published in 1927; the translation is taken from the expanded version published in 1932.

6. Douglas Johnston and Cynthia Sampson, eds., *Religion, the Missing Dimension of Statecraft* (New York: Oxford University Press, 1994). Also see the very important book by Jeffrie G. Murphy, *Getting Even: Forgiveness and Its Limits* (New York: Oxford University Press, 2003).

7. Christopher J. Insole, "Against Radical Orthodoxy: The Dangers of Overcoming Political Liberalism," *Modern Theology* 20, no. 2 (April 2004): 213.

8. For Milbank's criticisms of pacifism, see the interviews with him included in *Must Christianity Be Violent? Reflections on History, Practice, and Theology*, ed. Kenneth R. Chase and Alan Jacobs (Grand Rapids: Brazos Press, 2003), chaps. 12, 13.

9. John Milbank, "Socialism of the Gift, Socialism by Grace," *New Blackfriars* 77 (December 1996): 544. For an alternative account of gift giving—one that preserves the distinct moment of possession from collectivization and emphasizes the freedom necessary for true charity, thus demonstrating the limits of a welfare state that transfers giving out of the hand of individuals and asks nothing of recipients in return for their gifts; replacing, in a word, giving with entitlement—see Stephen H. Webb, *The Gifting God: A Trinitarian Ethics of Excess* (Oxford: Oxford University Press, 1996).

10. R. R. Reno points out how Milbank is guilty of a certain kind of intellectualism: The Radical Orthodox are "driven by ambition: if the actual practice of the churches in our time fails to make the truth of the gospel potent and clear, then theologians, theoretical shepherds of the speculative grasp, shall" (*The Ruins of the Church* [Grand Rapids: Brazos Press, 2002], 77).

11. Schmitt, *Concept of the Political*, 56.

12. Ibid., 49.

13. For reflection on the presumption of justice in the just war tradition, as well as a reevaluation of the role of the sovereign in making the decision to go to war, see the work of James Turner Johnson, *Morality and Contemporary Warfare* (New Haven, CT: Yale University Press, 1999).

14. Schmitt, *Concept of the Political*, 48.

15. Even the state, which can draft individuals into the army, is limited in its ability to call upon its citizens to become martyrs, which is to be distinguished from becoming soldiers. The state owes the citizen protection, and only on this basis can the state ask the citizen to die on its behalf. Schmitt himself was not willing to be a martyr during the 1930s. As he wrote after the war, "If the situation becomes so completely abnormal, and no one from the outside protects an individual from the terror from within, then he must determine for himself the limits of his loyalty, especially when the situation becomes so abnormal that one no longer knows the real position of his closest friend. The obligation to unleash a civil war, to engage in sabotage and to become a martyr has its limits." Quoted in Joseph W. Bendersky, *Carl Schmitt: Theorist for the Reich* (Princeton, NJ: Princeton University Press, 1983), 267. Schmitt did not even know that his closest friend at the time, Johannes Popitz, was involved in the aborted plot to assassinate Hitler until after Popitz was arrested and executed.

16. The controversial passage, which appears to lament the possibility of a world without war, is as follows: "A world in which the possibility of war is utterly eliminated, a completely pacified globe, would be a world without the distinction between a friend and enemy and hence a world without politics. It is conceivable that such a world might contain many very interesting antitheses and contrasts, competitions and intrigues of every kind, but there would not be a meaningful antithesis whereby men could be required to sacrifice life, authorized to shed blood, and kill human beings. For the definition of the political, it is here even irrelevant whether such a world without politics is desirable as an ideal situation" (Schmitt, *Concept of the Political*, 35).

17. Reinhold Niebuhr, *Moral Man and Immoral Society* (New York: Charles Scribner's Sons, 1932). It is important to note, however, how much the social gospel movement was indebted to the language of providence. For an informative survey, see Peter J. Frederick, *Knights of the Golden Rule: The Intellectual as Christian Social Reformer in the 1890s* (Louisville: University Press of Kentucky, 1976).

18. See René Girard, *The Scapegoat*, trans. Yvonne Freccero (Baltimore: Johns Hopkins University Press, 1986).

19. Schmitt, *Political Theology*, 36.
20. Ibid., 49.
21. Although I disagree with his reading of the role of religion in the American Enlightenment, Henry Steele Commager's book is helpful on these points. See *The Empire of Reason: How Europe Imagined and America Realized the Enlightenment* (London: Phoenix Press, 1978).
22. For an incisive examination of Schmitt on the nature of limits, see Andrew Norris, "Carl Schmitt's Political Metaphysics: On the secularization of the Outermost Sphere," *Theory and Event* 4, no. 1 (Summer 2000). http://muse.jhu.edu/journals/tae. Norris draws drastically different political conclusions from Schmitt. See Norris, "'Us' and 'Them': The Politics of Self-Assertion after 9/11," *Metaphilosophy* 35, no. 3 (April 2004): 249–72.
23. Many leftist critics of American democracy simply ignore this point. The idea that democratic nation-states like America substitute the state for the church—something which actually happened in totalitarian states—is hard to square with American history or politics. Leftists, however, continue to misread American patriotism as a form of idolatry rather than providence: "The longing for genuine communion that Christians recognize at the heart of any truly common life is transferred onto the nation-state." William T. Cavanaugh, "Killing for the Telephone Company: Why the Nation-State Is Not the Keeper of the Common Good," *Modern Theology* 20, no. 2 (April 2004): 266.

Conclusion
American Democracy as the Dream of the Church

—ɯɯ—

Carl Schmitt asked the deepest political questions about the nature of authority. His work also sheds considerable light on the most immediate of current events. President Bush, who had suggested his disdain for nation building and unnecessary foreign expeditions while on the campaign trail, acted decisively after 9/11. Bush exercised the authority of a sovereign. America was not prepared for this kind of attack. It was so exceptional that it was not anticipated. An attack of this nature did not call for discussion, although much occurred. Instead, the attack called for action. Liberals did not like the way Bush acted—the way he took the authority upon himself to act, without much public deliberation and without much international approval. But such cries of dismay from liberals would be exactly what Schmitt would lead us to expect and thus one reason that Schmitt is such a helpful political theorist in the current tumultuous climate.

Schmitt argued that the political is always a translation of the theological, an observation that is especially true of American presidential politics. Boyd Hilton, in a discussion about the correlation between providence and politics in nineteenth-century English evangelical social thought, says something that is doubtless applicable to Bush today: "Those who held an intervention-ist view of Providence, who saw God as constantly directing earthly affairs by special warnings and judgments, also believed that governments on earth should take a similarly interventionist approach to social and economic problems. Moderate Evangelicals, on the other hand, matched their *laissez-faire* or neutral conception of Providence with a similar approach to the condition of England."[1] Substitute "foreign policy" for "social and economic problems," and you have a sense of how providential theology can shape an interventionist program of international problem-solving. Schmitt too was attracted to certain aspects of Evangelical theology. He appealed to Kierkegaard for support in his development of the concept of the sovereign, and his emphasis on a decision is easily translated into the culture of Evangelical Christianity. Being a Christian, like being a political ruler, is about taking a decisive act.

For President Bush, our friends are not necessarily our allies. Countries like France constrain us as much or more than countries that are more open about their animosity toward us. Much has been made of the Bush doctrine of preemptive war and regime change, but the goal of global stability has long been a fundamental American interest. Indeed, it is the inescapable interest of any empire worthy of the name.[2] Just as it is the duty of the state to monopolize the use of violence and thus to establish the order citizens require to pursue the goods that they choose, the duty of an empire is to establish international order so that nations can pursue the trade that is necessary for economic growth. The difference between an empire and the world government that cosmopolitan liberals hope for is that the former recognizes the need for one nation to make the final decisions that cannot come about through the interminable discussions of a league of nations. Schmitt's analysis of the limitations of democracy thus applies just as well to the limitations of a democratic organization of nations. Just as liberals shy away from the fact that democracies need an external source of authorization and that procedural rules are not sufficient to guarantee a decision in times of crisis, liberals resist recognizing the need for a single nation to ensure what chance there is for global order. In times of crisis, only a strong decision can create the conditions that make consensus possible, which is exactly what the Bush administration chose to do. The new world order is the declaration by America that it will monopolize the use of international force for the good of all nations.

Of course, other nations will resent this state of affairs, but they will be most likely to resist it actively only if America forgets that it stands under the judgment of God. American providence is an interpretation of American history set in a global, indeed a cosmic, context. In the end, American providence is not really about America. America's heart is so often in the right place because the American government was designed as a safe harbor for the Christian faith. If America were to stop providing that safe harbor, then providence would cease being, in any sense of the term, American.

The significance of America has to do with what it believes in, not what it is. America is the dream that faith and freedom can be mutually reinforcing within a given social order. The church holds faith and freedom together, but the church is not a social order in the strictly political sense. By expecting the return of Jesus Christ, the church keeps alive the dream of a kingdom under divine rule. The church dreams of America, but when the faithful awake into the kingdom of God, America will seem like just a dream.

The church, as a sacramental reality of God's presence in the world, symbolizes the future unity of humankind. The unity of humankind, however, must be achieved on a political basis. Any discourse on the meaning of the church or the history of nation-states will be incomplete and distorted unless it acknowledges their ultimate convergence in the kingdom of God. To talk about the church outside of this horizon risks a romantic view of Christianity that runs aground in abstraction and irrelevance. Likewise, to talk about politics without attending to the church risks a reduction of freedom to mere consumerism. True freedom must ultimately be found in full obedience, wherein our fulfillment will coincide with a divinely orchestrated harmony of the wills. America is often criticized for representing a crass kind of spiritual impoverishment, with shopping malls replacing churches, but closer to the heart of America is a different story. America is the experiment of maximizing faith and freedom simultaneously. Putting faith and freedom to work for each other is America's contribution to the coming of the kingdom of God.

In sum, there is overlap, continuity, and complementarity between God's salvific and God's providential action in the world. How God will save us in the end is not separate from how God is moving through history in the meantime. God brings direction and purpose to history by authorizing political authority, which not only protects and promotes the common goods not destroyed by sinful humanity but also permits us to read history as the desire for faithful freedom in God. America stands as the gateway of that desire. For decades now, America's power in the world has been checked first by the external threat of the Soviet Union and second by the internal crisis of confidence brought about by the Vietnam War. The war against Iraq is a world historical gamble, with unknown repercussions for politics at home and abroad, but it represents a new era in international relations. America is ready to resume its providential role in the world. The risk is great, and the outcome is known only to God.

NOTES

1. Boyd Hilton, "The Role of Providence in Evangelical Social Thought," in *History, Society and the Churches*, ed. Derek Beales and Geoffrey Best (Cambridge: Cambridge University Press, 1985), 224. Updating Hilton, it could be argued that, today, Evangelicals believe in special providence and thus preach the importance of personal acts of holiness and charity, while liberals tend to believe in general providence and thus want the government to regularize and systematize support for the poor.

2. For a careful analysis of how America is a liberal, reluctant, and peculiar empire that should be more forthright in accepting its responsibility to provide the necessary coherence for globalism, see Niall Ferguson, *Colossus: The Price of America's Empireu* (New York: Penguin Press, 2004).

Appendix
Providence and Progress

—m—

The relationship between providence and progress is complex. Ironically, the doctrine of providence gave rise to the ideology of progress, which in turn announced the irrelevance of all theological doctrines. Indeed, one of the most characteristic features of modernity is the expectation that progress will inevitably erase religion from the modern world. Some scholars, following the work of Hans Blumenberg, *The Legitimacy of the Modern Age*,[1] have argued that the modern notion of progress has its roots in the irreversible accumulation of knowledge in the natural sciences, not in a secularization of the Hebraic interpretation of time as linear and the Christian expectation of the coming kingdom of God. Blumenberg's work is an attempt to save modernity from the clutches of religious history. For Blumenberg, modernity springs fully formed and motherless, independent of the religious traditions that precede it. That makes modernity truly exceptional to the point of being miraculous, because the discipline of history is predicated upon the assumption that every social movement must be understood in the context of what comes before it. Even if the purity of modernity's genealogy is preserved by tracing it solely to the natural sciences, the question remains as to the origin of the natural sciences. In *The Religion of Technology*, David Noble has demonstrated how science emerged in the Middle Ages through a revolutionary change in how people understood the technological arts.[2] When Christians began hoping for the new millennium, the recovery of humankind's original likeness to the divine seemed to be within sight. Technology became a concrete way of anticipating eschatology. The useful arts could be usefully employed in the restoration of paradise. Human progress was the means of divine providence.

Whatever its origins, modernity is imbued with the confidence that secularization is inevitable and will become, some day, total. This belief, which scholars call the secularization thesis, once governed much of modern sociology but is now in a state of serious disrepair. The secularization thesis claims that people are less religious today than they used to be and that pluralistic societies inevitably render religious commitments looser than they would be in more traditional societies. Steve Bruce, a professor of sociology at the University of Aberdeen, is the most persistent defender of the secularization thesis today. Most of his research, as in *God Is Dead: Secularization in the West*, concerns England and Europe.[3] Bruce, like most sociologists, considers America an exception to the secularization thesis. When global history is taken into account, however, Europe, not America, looks religiously out of place. One need only look at the controversy generated by whether the pan-European constitution should mention God to understand how difficult it is for Europeans to acknowledge their own history and traditions. Thus it is no coincidence that an American sociologist, Rodney Stark, a professor at Baylor University, has been the most strident critic of the secularization thesis. Stark, in a book co-authored with Roger Finke, *Acts of Faith: Explaining the Human Side of Religion*, relies on a model of rational choice that was first developed in economics in order to argue that the variety of religious options in the modern world can increase rather than decrease religious commitment.[4] For Stark, the demand for religion remains basically the same throughout history. What changes is the marketplace of supply. A free market for religious goods forces consumers to be more careful about what they choose and to claim their choices as their own. Stark seems to have history on his side: the disestablishment of religion in America created an atmosphere of vigorous and popular religious growth.

Secularization theorists begin with the premise that faith and freedom are, on some deep level, incompatible. Ernst Troeltsch, in his book, *Protestantism and Progress*, first put forth the thesis that religious toleration was forced upon the West as a virtue of necessity after the sixteenth century, when Catholics and Protestants begrudgingly had to learn to accept one another.[5] Troeltsch was revising the then-conventional thesis that Luther introduced true freedom to Europe. Troeltsch's revisionism became common wisdom in the academy. Perez Zagorin, a distinguished professor of history, represents a new wave of revising the revisionists. In *How the Idea of Religious Toleration Came to the West*, Zagorin demonstrates that tolerance, far from being a product of political expediency, has its roots in Western theological concerns for the spiritual welfare of religion itself.[6] French philosopher Marcel

Gauchet pushes the origins of tolerance even further back in Christian history. In *The Disenchantment of the World: A Political History of Religion*, Gauchet argues that the message of Jesus was responsible for Western society's exit from the domination of the sacred.[7] By eradicating the pagan gods, Christianity freed the West not only from a variety of corrosive superstitions but also from the association of every natural occurrence with the power of fate.

If secularization has roots in the Christian critique of paganism, then secularism is not quite so secular after all. Indeed, far from triumphing, secularists today are on the defensive, guarding their social gains and lamenting their loss of influence. Alan Wolfe, a cultural critic who is himself an agnostic when it comes to religious faith, has made the starling claim that not only has Evangelical Christianity become mainstream but that the mainstream in America has become Evangelical. Wolfe agrees with Stark: "American religion survives and flourishes not so much because it instructs people in the right ways to honor God but because people have taken so many aspects of religion into their own hands."[8] Throughout the nineteenth century, capitalism, democracy, and Christianity established themselves together, as a unifying force in American history.

NOTES

1. Hans Blumenberg, *The Legitimacy of the Modern Age*, trans. Robert M. Wallace (Boston: MIT Press, 1983).

2. David Noble, *The Religion of Technology* (New York: Penguin Books, 1999).

3. Steve Bruce, *God Is Dead: Secularization in the West* (Oxford: Blackwell, 2002).

4. Rodney Stark and Roger Finke, *Acts of Faith: Explaining the Human Side of Religion* (Berkeley: University of California Press, 2000).

5. Ernst Troeltsch, *Protestantism and Progress* (Eugene, OR: Wipf & Stock Publishers, 1999).

6. Perez Zagonn, *How the Idea of Religious Toleration Came to the West* (Princeton, NJ: Princeton University Press, 2003).

7. Marcel Gauchet, *The Disenchantment of the World: A Political History of Religion*, trans. Oscar Burge (Princeton, NJ: Princeton University Press, 1997).

8. Alan Wolfer, *The Transformation of American Religion* (New York: Free Press, 2003), 36.

Index

—ᴟᴟ—

Nye, Russell B., 9, 10, 30

Ochs, Peter, 81
O'Donovan, Oliver, 104–7, 146, 147
open theism, 102, 103
Origen, 92
Orosius, Paulus, 93, 94
Owen, Robert, 37

paranoia
as modern, degenerate form of American providence, 85, 86
Parrinder, Geoffrey, 149n51
Pentecostalism, 25, 120–25, 138, 145
Perle, Richard, 139
Peterson, Erik, 155
Phillips, Kevin, 116, 117
Pilgrim, Walter, 58
Pinnock, Clark H., 102
Placher, William C., 22
pluralism
America as uniquely, 13, 143
critique of, 141
dependence on providence, 13, 39, 45
ideology of America, 15, 19, 46, 141
ideology of globalism, 146
and Islam, 140
and missionary work, 45
religious, 18, 138, 143
and Tower of Babel, 103
Poland,
providential view of, 60, 61
political dualism, 105
political theology,
American need for, 35
and Carl Schmitt, 155

connection between providence and progress in, 43
contemporary, 156
and friend-enemy distinction, 157
and General Boykin, 20
and question of universal peace, 160
relation to providence, 9
and Stanley Hauerwas, 70, 74
postmillennialism, 36, 91
postmodernism
irrelevance after 9/11, 83
poverty and terrorism
critique of the relationship between, 86n7
preaching
and rhetorical violence, 140
premillennialism, 24, 91
process philosophy/theology, 22, 53, 54
Protestant Reformation, 31, 62, 125, 132, 140, 142
Proverbs, book of
19:21   4
21:1   97
Psalms, book of
47:8   6
68:31   40
Purdy, Jedediah, 150n60
Puritans, 2, 3, 30–34, 38, 39, 46, 84, 117, 118

Qutb, Sayyid, 131

racism, 25, 45, 80
Rawls, John, 53
Reagan, President Ronald, 26, 114
reincarnation
as example of Easternization of the West, 145

Religious Studies, 128, 143, 144,
  151n73
Reno, R. R., 21, 73, 165n10
Revel, Jean-Francois, 110
Revelation, book of
  7:9–12   104
Rhode Island, 32
Richey, Russell E., 41
Rieger, Joerg, 65, 66
Roman Catholicism, 2, 33, 36, 39,
  60, 118, 119, 121–26, 148n32,
  154, 155, 159, 172
Roman Empire, 31, 38, 92–94, 104,
  112, 114, 127, 154
  as compared to America, 8,
    39, 77, 87n14
Romans, book of
  8:28   4
Roosevelt, President Franklin, 43,
  115, 116
Russia, 26, 60, 101, 110, 111, 139

Sanders, John, 102
Sanneh, Lamin, 122, 139
Saum, Lewis O., 40
Schmitt, Carl, 15, 114, 153–66, 167,
  168
Schneider, John R., 58
secularization thesis, 172
Shea, Nina, 138
sixties, 25, 26, 128
Smith, Adam, 90
Social Gospel, 3, 165n17
Socrates, 45
Soros, George, 113
Soto, Hernando de, 63
South Korea, 10
Soviet Union, 15, 26, 101, 110, 169
special providence
  Barth's view of, 101
  and Bismarck's remark, 20

defined, 13
and evangelicals, 169fn1
and God's action, 103
and Israel, 105
Milbank undercuts, 79
mistaken rejection of, 1021
relation to general providence,
  14, 98
Stanley, Brian, 150n70
Stark, Rodney, 172
Stepanson, Anders, 30
Stern, Jessica, 149n48
Stout, Jeffrey, 74, 75
supersessionism, 23, 79

Tanner, Kathryn, 101, 102
theodicy, 8, 15fn6, 26, 42, 100
Tocqueville, Alexis de, 126
Todd, Emmanuel, 113
Tower of Babel, 37, 103
Toynbee, Arnold, 127–29
traditional societies, 142
Transcendentalists, 30
Trifkovic, Serge, 134, 138, 139
Troeltsch, Ernst, 172
Turkey, 137
Tuveson, Ernest Lee, 37

unitary view of history, 60, 61, 99,
  155
utopia
  collusion with terror, 8
  and Pentecostals, 123
  and the promotion of
    democracy, 139
  and Puritans, 46
  and the sixties, 26
  and views of history, 8

Veith, Gene Edward, 83
Vietnam, 3, 5, 25, 26, 43, 76, 169